Studies in Jewish and Christian Literature

Messiah and the Throne, Timo Eskola

Defilement and Purgation in the Book of Hebrews, William G. Johnsson

Father, Son, and Spirit in Romans 8, Ron C. Fay

Within the Veil, Félix H. Cortez

Jude's Apocalyptic Eschatology as Theological Exclusivism, William Renay Wilson II

Jude's Apocalyptic Eschatology as Theological Exclusivism

Jude's Apocalyptic Eschatology as Theological Exclusivism

William Renay Wilson II

Fontes

CONTENTS

Abbreviations

Ancient Texts

Apoc. Ab.	Apocalypse of Abraham
Bar	Baruch
2 Bar.	2 Baruch
3 Bar.	3 Baruch
Did.	Didache
Jub.	Jubilees
1–4 Kgdms	1 Kingdoms
1-2-3-4 Macc	1 Maccabees, etc.
Pss. Sol.	Psalms of Solomon
Sib. Or.	Sibylline Oracles
Sir	Sirach
T. Ab.	Testament of Abraham
T. Ash.	Testament of Asher
T. Benj.	Testament of Benjamin
T. Dan	Testament of Dan
T. Gad	Testament of Gad
T. Iss.	Testament of Issachar
T. Jos.	Testament of Joseph
T. Jud.	Testament of Judah
T. Levi	Testament of Levi
T. Mos.	Testament of Moses
T. Naph.	Testament of Naphtali
T. Reu.	Testament of Reuben

| T. Zeb. | Testament of Zebulun |
| Wis | Wisdom of Solomon |

General Abbreviations

AB	Anchor Bible
ABD	Anchor Bible Dictionary
ABRL	Anchor Bible Reference Library
AGJU	Arbeiten zur Geschichte des antiken Judentums und des Urchristentums
AMWNE	Apocalypticism in the Mediterranean World and the Near East: Proceedings of the International Colloquium on Apocalypticism
ANRW	Aufstieg und Niedergang der römischen Welt
Arch	Archaeology
AUSS	Andrews University Seminary Studies
BA	Biblical Archaeologist
BAGD	Bauer, Walter, William F. Arndt, F. Wilbur Gingrich, and Frederick W. Danker. *Greek-English Lexicon of the New Testament and Other Early Christian Literature.* 3rd ed. Rev. and ed. Frederick W. Danker. University of Chicago Press, 2000 (Bauer-Arndt-Gingrich-Danker)
BASOR	Bulletin of the American Schools of Oriental Research
BBR	Bulletin for Biblical Research
BECNT	Baker Exegetical Commentary on the New Testament
BEMCT	Blackwell Encyclopedia of Modern Christian Thought
Bib	Biblica
BibInt	Biblical Interpretation Series
BibS(F)	Biblische Studien (Freiburg, 1895–)
BJRL	*Bulletin of the John Rylands University Library*
BSac	*Bibliotheca Sacra*
BZ	Biblische Zeitschrift
CBC	Cambridge Bible Commentary
CBQ	*Catholic Biblical Quarterly*
CEB	Commentaire évangélique de la Bible
Chm	Churchman
ChrT	Christianity Today
CNT	Commentaire du Nouveau Testament
ConBNT	Coniectanea Biblica: New Testament Series

CTJ	Calvin Theological Journal
CurBS	Currents in Research: Biblical Studies
CurTM	Currents in Theology and Mission
DLNT	Dictionary of the Later New Testament and Its Developments
DPL	Dictionary of Paul and His Letters
DTC	Dictionnaire de théologie catholique
EBC	Expositor's Bible Commentary
EDNT	Exegetical Dictionary of the New Testament
EEC	Evangelical Exegetical Commentary
EKKNT	Evangelisch-katholischer Kommentar zum Neuen Testament
EncJud	Encyclopaedia Judaica
ExpTim	Expository Times
FBBS	Facet Books, Biblical Series
FF	Foundations and Facets
FilNeot	Filologia Neotestamentaria
HNT	Handbuch zum Neuen Testament
HNTC	Harper's New Testament Commentaries
HThKNT	Herders theologischer Kommentar zum Neuen Testament
HTR	Harvard Theological Review
HvTSt	Hervormde teologiese studies
IBC	Interpretation: A Bible Commentary for Teaching and Preaching
IBJ	Irish Biblical Studies
ICC	International Critical Commentary
IDBSup	Interpreter's Dictionary of the Bible: Supplementary Volume
IEJ	Israel Exploration Journal
Int	Interpretation
IRT	Issues in Religion and Theology
ISBE	International Standard Bible Encyclopedia
ITL	International Theological Library
JBL	Journal of Biblical Literature
JETS	*Journal of the Evangelical Theological Society*
JJS	*Journal of Jewish Studies*
JNES	Journal of Near Eastern Studies
JSJ	Journal for the Study of Judaism
JSNT	Journal for the Study of the New Testament
JSNTSup	Journal for the Study of the New Testament Supplement Series

JSOT	Journal for the Study of the Old Testament
JSOTSup	Journal for the Study of the Old Testament Supplement Series
JSPSup	Journal for the Study of the Pseudepigrapha Supplement Series
JSSR	Journal for the Scientific Study of Religion
JTS	Journal of Theological Studies
KEK	Kritisch-exegetischer Kommentar über das Neue Testament
KNT	Kommentar zum Neuen Testament
LB	Linguistica Biblica
LCL	Loeb Classical Library
L&N	Louw, Johannes P., and Eugene A. Nida, eds. *Greek-English Lexicon of the New Testament: Based on Semantic Domains.* 2nd ed. United Bible Societies, 1989.
LSJ	Liddell, Henry George, Robert Scott, Henry Stuart Jones. *A Greek-English Lexicon.* 9th ed. with revised supplement. Clarendon, 1996.
MQR	Michigan Quarterly Review
Mus	Le Muséon
NA$^{27/28}$	*Novum Testamentum Graece,* Nestle-Aland, 27th/28th ed.
NAC	New American Commentary
NCBC	New Century Bible Commentary
Neot	Neotestamentica
NICNT	New International Commentary on the New Testament
NICOT	New International Commentary on the Old Testament
NIDNTT	New International Dictionary of New Testament Theology
NEchtB	Neue Echter Bibel
NHS	Nag Hammadi Studies
NIB	The New Interpreter's Bible
NIGTC	New International Greek Testament Commentary
NPNF	The Nicene and and Post-Nicene Fathers
NovT	Novum Testamentum
NovTSup	Supplements to Novum Testamentum
NTAbh	Neutestamentliche Abhandlungen
NTD	Das Neue Testament Deutsch
NTS	New Testament Studies
OEANE	Oxford Encyclopedia of Archaeology in the Near East
OTL	Old Testament Library
PVTG	Pseudepigrapha Veteris Testamenti Graece
RB	Revue biblique

RefR	Reformed Review
RelSRev	Religious Studies Review
RevExp	Review and Expositor
RNT	Regensburger Neues Testament
SB	Sources Bibliques
SBLDS	Society of Biblical Literature Dissertation Series
SBLMS	Society of Biblical Literature Monograph Series
SBLSCS	Society of Biblical Literature Septuagint and Cognate Studies
SBT	Studies in Biblical Theology
ScrHier	Scripta Hierosolymitana
SKKNT	Stuttgarter kleiner Kommentar, Neues Testament
SNTSMS	Society for New Testament Studies Monograph Series
SR	Studies in Religion
STDJ	Studies on the Texts of the Desert of Judah
SUNT	Studien zur Umwelt des Neuen Testaments
SVTP	Studia in Veteris Testamenti Pseudepigraphica
SJSJ	Supplements to the Journal for the Study of Judaism
TDNT	Theological Dictionary of the New Testament
Them	Themelios
THKNT	Theologischer Handkommentar zum Neuen Testament
TimesLitSupp	Times Literary Supplement
TLNT	Theological Lexicon of the New Testament
TNTC	Tyndale New Testament Commentaries
TOTC	Tyndale Old Testament Commentaries
TRE	Theologische Realenzyklopädie
TRu	Theologische Rundschau
TynBul	*Tyndale Bulletin*
TZ	Theologische Zeitschrift
UBS[4/5]	*The Greek New Testament*, United Bible Societies, 4th/5th ed.
VT	Vetus Testamentum
VTSup	Supplements to Vetus Testamentum
WBC	Word Biblical Commentary
WC	Westminster Commentaries
WMANT	Wissenschaftliche Monographien zum Alten und Neuen Testament
WUNT	Wissenschaftliche Untersuchungen zum Neuen Testament
ZAW	Zeitschrift für die alttestamentliche Wissenschaft
ZNW	Zeitschrift für die neutestamentliche Wissenschaft
ZRGG	Die Zeitschrift für Religions- und Geistesgeschichte
ZTK	Zeitschrift für Theologie und Kirche

PREFACE

MY INTEREST IN JUDE began with a personal burden for the contemporary church's theological integrity. It seemed to me that many professing Christians uncritically adopt a postmodern passion for tolerance and autonomy that refuses to tolerate specific New Testament teaching. Concepts such as doctrine, sin, heresy, and even truth have become new profanities, divisive and brutish ideas best abandoned in the race toward enlightenment. What I found in Jude was a self-contained and neglected textual unit that addresses my concerns with stunning, though controversial, clarity. It is my hope that this study of God's Word will encourage those who love the truth and embolden them to lovingly guard and proclaim it regardless of the consequences.

My thanks are due to Todd Scacewater at Fontes Press for agreeing to publish such a narrowly focused study and to Craig V. Mitchell for introducing us. I am deeply grateful for my parents, Charles and Jackie Shore, who took a risk in the Winter of 1987 by welcoming home a troubled prodigal. Their faith, forgiveness, and self-sacrifice led me to the Savior, sheltered me from the storm, and continue to model love. I could not have completed this study without the faithful friendship of the late Dr. Raymond Bernard Spencer, my true brother. To my excellent wife, Lori, I dedicate this monograph. The teaching of kindness is always on her lips, and her husband trusts in her.

Above all, I wish to thank the Lord Jesus Christ, my Hope. To him belong all glory, majesty, dominion, and authority forever. Amen.

William Renay Wilson II

INTRODUCTION

HE EPISTLE OF JUDE has suffered a general neglect since the formative stages of New Testament canon related debate.[1] Influential voices belittled Jude's significance, propagating during the Reformation[2] and into the modern period what would become a near consensus of scholarly disdain.[3] According to its critics, Jude's epistle, the "least creative in the New Testament,"[4] demonstrates "more zeal than ability"[5] and provides only post-apostolic inflammatory rhetoric[6] penned by an

---

1 Eusebius (ca. A.D. 260–339), in a statement relating to the canonical status of James reports some difficulties with Jude: "It should be noted that [the Epistle according to James] is in fact rejected, since not many of the ancient ones mention it. The same is true for that which is called Jude, itself one among the seven so called catholic epistles" (*The Ecclesiastical History* 2.23.25 [Lake, LCL]). Jerome (ca. A.D. 346–420), in *Lives of Illustrious Men* 4, discloses the specific issue that prompted doubt and discussion surrounding Jude's canonicity: "Jude the brother of James, left a short epistle ... and because in it he quotes from the apocryphal book Enoch it is rejected by many" (*NPNF*2 3:362).

2 Martin Luther concluded that the letter "does not contain anything special beyond pointing" to 2 Peter (*The Catholic Epistles*, Luther's Works, ed. Jaroslav Pelikan and Walter A. Hansen, vol. 30 [Concordia Publishing House, 1967], 203). See the synopsis of Luther's position in the German summary of C. A. Albin's Swedish work *Judasbrevet: Traditionen Texten Tolkningen* (Natur och Kultur, 1962), 713–4.

3 Richard Bauckham, "The Letter of Jude: A Survey of Research," in *Jude and the Relatives of Jesus in the Early Church* (T&T Clark, 1990), 134–5; Douglas J. Rowston, "The Most Neglected Book in the New Testament," *NTS* 21, no. 4 (1975): 554–63; Birger A. Pearson, "James, 1–2 Peter, Jude," in *The New Testament and Its Modern Interpreters*, ed. Eldon Jay Epp and George W. MacRae (Fortress Press, 1989), 385–8. "With regard to content, [Jude and 2 Peter] are not very important ... " and are valuable only as "exercises for literary-critical observations" (Hans Conzelmann, *Interpreting the New Testament: An Introduction to the Principles and Methods of N. T. Exegesis*, trans. Siegfried S. Schatzmann [Hendrickson, 1988], 274).

4 R. H. Fuller, *A Critical Introduction to the New Testament* (Duckworth, 1966), 161.

5 Adolf Jülicher, *An Introduction to the New Testament*, trans. Janet Penrose Ward (Smith, Elder, 1904), 230.

6 Frederick Wisse, "The Epistle of Jude in the History of Heresiology," in *Essays on the Nag Hammadi Texts in Honour of Alexander Böhlig*, NHS 3 (E. J. Brill, 1972), 134; Werner Georg

ecclesiastical[7] zealot.

At the heart of historical critical contempt for Jude lies the charge of its "early Catholicism."[8] Jude's unflagging commitment to an objective "faith once for all delivered to the saints" (v. 3) and to the "words spoken in advance by the apostles" (v. 17) supposedly presents clear evidence of a post-apostolic concern for formulaic doctrinal precision.[9] Once European, primarily German, exegetes concluded the "Catholic" epistles had corrupted pristine Pauline theology,[10] Jude and the others were effectively excluded from the "canon within the canon."[11] As academic interest gradually increases however,[12] more accurate and comprehensive exegetical understandings of Jude's provenance and theology reveal its profound relevance for the twenty-first-century church.[13]

Kümmel, *Introduction to the New Testament*, rev. ed., trans. Howard Clark Kee (Abingdon Press, 1973), 426–7.

7 Norman Perrin and Dennis C. Duling, for example, assigns Jude to an emergent "institutional Christianity" (*The New Testament - An Introduction: Proclamation and Paraenesis, Myth and History*, 2nd ed. [Harcourt Brace Jovanovich, 1982], 379).

8 For general definitions of "early Catholicism" emphasizing the "de-eschatologizing" of apostolic Christianity see Martin Werner, *The Formation of Christian Dogma: An Historical Study of Its Problem*, trans. S. G. F. Brandon (Adam and Charles Black, 1957), 297.

9 K. H. Schelkle, "Spätapostolische Briefe als frühkatholisches Zeugnis," in *Neutestamentliche Aufsätze: Festschrift für Professor Josef Schmid*, ed. J. Blinzler, O. Kuss, and F. Mußner (Verlag Friedrich Pustet, 1963), 225–6; W. Schrage, *Der Judasbrief*, NTD 10, *Die "Katholischen" Briefe: Die Briefe des Jakobus, Petrus, Johannes und Judas* (Vandenhoeck and Ruprecht, 1980), 228; Daniel J. Harrington, "The 'Early Catholic' Writings of the New Testament: The Church Adjusting to World-History," in *The Word in the World: Essays in Honor of Frederick L. Moriarty*, ed. Richard J. Clifford and George W. MacRae (Weston College Press, 1973), 107; James Dunn, *Unity and Diversity in the New Testament: An Inquiry into the Character of Earliest Christianity*, 2nd ed. (Trinity Press International, 1990), 341, 345, 361–2.

10 Ernst Käsemann, "The New Testament Canon and the Unity of the Church," in *Essays on New Testament Themes*, trans. W. J. Montague (SCM Press, 1964), 102–3; Günther Bornkamm, *The New Testament: A Guide to Its Writings*, trans. Reginald H. Fuller and Ilse Fuller (Fortress Press, 1973), 127. According to Vincent Taylor, Jude's "mere denunciation" of opponents can be contrasted negatively with Paul's "noteworthy" methodology ("The Message of the Epistles: Second Peter and Jude," *ExpTim* 45 no. 10 (1934): 439.

11 Because, in Kurt Aland's opinion, the NT canon is *"in practice* undergoing a narrowing and a shortening," the Church and the academy should endeavor to discover the "correct principles of selection from the formal Canon and of its interpretation with the purpose of achieving a common, actual Canon" (*The Problem of the New Testament Canon* [A. R. Mowbray, 1962], 28, 30). The title of Werner Georg Kümmel's work is particularly suggestive: *The Theology of the New Testament according to Its Major Witnesses: Jesus – Paul – John*, trans. John E. Steely (Abingdon Press, 1973). Cf. the rebuttals in Bruce Metzger, *The Canon of the New Testament: Its Origin, Development, and Significance* (Clarendon Press, 1987), 275–82, and F. F. Bruce, *The Canon of Scripture* (InterVarsity Press, 1988), 270–83.

12 See Peter Müller, "Der Judasbrief," *TRu* 63, no. 3 (1998): 267: "In den letzten Jahren ... die Forschung ist intensiv weitergeführt worden" ("In recent years ... the research has continued with intensity," my translation).

13 See especially Herbert W. Bateman IV's "Application and Devotional Implications" sections in *Jude*, ECC (Lexham Press, 2015).

The contemporary church faces a cultural climate that aggressively pre-
scribes pluralism as the only legitimate worldview.[14] Such pluralism contends
that all theological perspectives "are in contact with the same ultimate religious reality, and all of them offer paths to salvation or liberation that are, as
far as anyone can tell, equally effective in producing transformations from
self-centeredness to reality-centeredness."[15] Notions of truth, error, authority,
and the distinctiveness of Christian doctrine are therefore automatically suspect[16]—abrasive specters of defunct modern theologizing and incompatible
with the emergent postmodern spirit of freedom and tolerance.[17] Elements
within the church itself have embraced a pluralistic bias, demanding that the
"fictive" elements of Scripture be "responded to with an immediacy and freedom often denied to 'sacred texts,' weighed down by theological preconcep-
tion or prejudice."[18] An interpretive syncretism now lauds every point of view
as equally acceptable: "None privileged and all equally valid ... [The future of
biblical interpretation] will be a veritable paradise of (non)aggressive differ-
ing-but-equal biblical readings in which every man and every woman will sit
under their own vine and fig tree undisturbed by any point of view alien to
themselves."[19] Such "radical hospitality" or "radical inclusiveness" is quickly
disintegrating into an "ideal" gospel that openly accommodates immorality.[20]

Jude and his audience faced comparable invasive pluralism from professing
Christians willing to declare their Christian identity (vv. 4, 12–13) while simultaneously fusing it with theological and ethical antinomianism.[21] Rather than
capitulate to dissidents who from their positions of leadership[22] undoubtedly

---

14 Allan Bloom, *The Closing of the American Mind* (Simon and Schuster, 1987), 25–6; D. A.
Carson, *The Gagging of God: Christianity Confronts Pluralism* (Zondervan, 1996), 19.

15 Kevin Meeker and Philip L. Quinn, "Introduction: The Philosophical Challenge of Religious Diversity," in *The Philosophical Challenge of Religious Diversity* (Oxford University Press,
2000), 3.

16 Alister McGrath, *A Passion for Truth: The Intellectual Coherence of Evangelicalism* (InterVarsity Press, 1996), 228.

17 Brian Ingraffia, *Postmodern Theory and Biblical Theology: Vanquishing God's Shadow*
(Cambridge University Press, 1995), 6.

18 David Jasper, "Literary Readings of the Bible," in *The Cambridge Companion to Biblical
Interpretation*, ed. John Barton (Cambridge University Press, 1998), 26.

19 Robert Carroll, "Poststructuralist Approaches: New Historicism and Postmodernism,"
in *The Cambridge Companion to Biblical Interpretation*, ed. John Barton (Cambridge University Press, 1998), 62. Cf. Grant R. Osborne's critique of reader-oriented hermeneutics (*The Hermeneutical Spiral: A Comprehensive Introduction to Biblical Interpretation* [InterVarsity Press,
1991], 366–415).

20 Carolyn Riehl, "Pulpit Fiction: Lives and Perspectives of Gay and Lesbian Persons Serving in the ELCA's Ordained Ministry," *CurTM* 27, no. 1 (2000): 28.

21 Cf. their licentiousness, anti-authoritarian biases, and general self-indulgence (vv. 4,
8, 10, 12).

22 Cf. v. 12 and the pastoral "shepherding" motif.

campaigned for tolerance, Jude condemned those who violated the received worldview,[23] "the faith once for all delivered to the saints" (v. 3). This theologically exclusive reaction is multi-dimensional, operating on the macro and micro levels to affirm the legitimacy of only one religion and its specific doctrinal formulations.[24] In order to advance his polemic Jude employed the key presuppositions of a Judeo-Christian apocalyptic eschatology[25] that is itself an exclusionary correction of aggressive theological pluralism. The following study will attempt, therefore, to examine Jude in terms of its worldview, endeavoring to identify within the epistle any major themes that accurately reflect both Jewish and Christian historical and theological contexts. This process of contextual comparison and thematic distillation will reveal a cluster of worldview non-negotiables that directly addresses parallel challenges faced by Jude's ancient readers and the contemporary church.

Chapter 1 will attempt to summarize and evaluate recent progress in research relevant to Jude. Chapter 2 serves as a foundational effort at exploring and clarifying a categorical framework for interpreting the apocalyptic eschatology in Jude. Chapter 3 will endeavor to interpret Jude in terms of its pronounced apocalyptic eschatological worldview. Chapter 4 will investigate the implications of Jude's worldview for the church confronted by a similar influx of theological pluralism. Finally, the conclusion will synthesize insights from the study and assess their contribution to the understanding of Jude.

---

23 Cf. vv. 4, 8, 10, 16, 19.

24 Kevin Meeker and Philip L. Quinn, "Philosophical Challenge of Religious Diversity," 3.

25 Richard J. Bauckham, *Jude, 2 Peter*, WBC 50 (Word Books, 1983), 8–11.

CHAPTER 1

JUDE: SURVEY OF RESEARCH

TEXTUAL CRITICISM

ESPITE JUDE'S BREVITY and its notorious textual difficulties,[1] the volume of text-critical research dedicated to Jude is steadily increasing. Charles Landon's doctoral dissertation at the University of Stellenbosch, *A Text-Critical Study of the Epistle of Jude*, provides the first available systematic study of every variant issue in Jude.[2] Methodologically, Landon's "thoroughgoing eclecticism" concentrates almost exclusively on internal evidence and generally disregards any particular reading's antiquity or text-familial relationships.[3] After a detailed analysis of 95 variation units, Landon selected 21 readings against the printed UBS[4] text. His unique and detailed work includes in appendices a summary of variants accepted, an internal evaluation of manuscripts cited consistently, and his "eclectic" Greek text of Jude.

The publication of the third-century manuscript $\mathfrak{P}^{72}$ in 1959[4] continues to generate discussion of the "baffling"[5] problems with Jude 22–23a.[6] The text as

---

1 Joseph B. Mayor, *The Epistle of St. Jude and the Second Epistle of St. Peter* (Macmillan, 1907), clxxxi; Bauckham, "Survey of Research," 135.

2 Charles Landon, *A Text-Critical Study of the Epistle of Jude*, JSNTSup 135 (Sheffield Academic Press, 1996), 13.

3 Ibid., 14–8.

4 For the text and descriptions of $\mathfrak{P}^{72}$ see Michel Testuz, *Papyrus Bodmer VII-IX* (Bibliothèque Bodmer, 1959), 19–25; Winfried Grunewald and K. Junack, *Die katholischen Briefe*, Das Neue Testament auf Papyrus 1 (Walter de Gruyter, 1986), 16–25, 159–71. Cf. also the four volume work by Kurt Aland, Annette Benduhn-Mertz, and Gerd Mink, eds., *Die katholischen Briefe*, Text und Textwert der griechischen Handschriften des Neuen Testaments 1 (Walter de Gruyter, 1987). The editors of this series collated 600 manuscripts at 98 sample points throughout the General Epistle corpus and assembled the statistical results.

5 Bauckham, *Jude, 2 Peter*, 108.

6 Manuscript abbreviations conform to those provided by NA[28], 54–76, 684–718.

attested by א and printed in NA²⁸ and UBS⁵ suggests a three-clause admonition involving three distinct groups of people:

(1) οὓς μὲν ἐλεᾶτε διακρινομένους
    ("have mercy on those who doubt"),
(2) οὓς δὲ σῴζετε ἐκ πυρὸς ἁρπάζοντες
    ("and save others, snatching them from the fire"),
(3) οὓς δὲ ἐλεᾶτε ἐν φόβῳ μισοῦντες καὶ τὸν ἀπὸ τῆς σαρκὸς ἐσπιλωμένον χιτῶνα
    ("and on others have mercy with fear, hating even the garment stained by the flesh").

The more ancient reading of 𝔓⁷², however, provides only a two-clause format:

(1) οὓς μὲν ἐκ πυρὸς ἁρπάσατε
    ("snatch some from the fire")
(2) διακρινομένους δὲ ἐλεεῖτε ἐν φόβῳ
    ("and have mercy with fear on those who doubt").

Numerous ancient variations of these two basic traditions further complicate the issues⁷ and impede scholarly consensus.

Because of 𝔓72's antiquity and the manuscript distribution of its supporting texts,⁸ S. C. Winter favors the two-clause format defended by earlier studies.⁹ Though the two-clause traditions often place their clauses in different order, the fact that Jude introduces only two groups in the epistle (the audience and the false teachers) appears to substantiate the shorter reading. According to Winter, the three-clause printed reading suffers minimal manuscript attestation¹⁰ and does not adequately separate the clauses with the necessary particles. After adopting the two clause variant, Winter provides a unique translation for

---

7 See especially Sakae Kubo, "Jude 22–23: Two-division Form or Three?" in *New Testament Textual Criticism: Its Significance for Exegesis*, ed. Eldon Jay Epp and Gordon D. Fee (Clarendon Press, 1981), 239–41, for a summary of the complicated evidence. Cf. Aland, Benduhn-Mertz, and Mink, eds., *Die katholischen Briefe*, 215–20.

8 Cf. the readings of t, sa, and sy^ph.

9 S. C. Winter, "Jude 22–23: A Note on the Text and Translation," *HTR* 87, no. 2 (1994): 215–22. For earlier arguments in favor of 𝔓⁷², see J. Neville Birdsall, "The Text of Jude in P⁷²," *JTS* 14, no. 2 (1963): 396–9; Carroll D. Osburn, "The Text of Jude 22–23," *ZNW* 63 (1972): 139–44; Sakae Kubo, *P⁷² and the Codex Vaticanus*, Studies and Documents 27, ed. Jacob Geerlings (University of Utah Press, 1965), 89–92; Bauckham, *Jude, 2 Peter*, 108–11.

10 Winter erroneously asserts, "Only A and Sinaiticus have the three clauses" ("Jude 22–23," 216), when in fact Ψ and several other minuscules and versions also support the printed text reading (see Kubo, "Jude 22–3," 240–1).

the concluding participial phrase καὶ τὸν ἀπὸ τῆς σαρκὸς ἐσπιλωμένον χιτῶνα. The "flesh," typically understood metaphorically, and the "garment," generally interpreted literally, should both be translated metaphorically. The preposition ἀπό then signifies source, rendering the translation "hating the defiled garment made of flesh."[11] On the basis of this translation, Winter identifies a sexual ascetic theme in Jude and attempts to connect the epistle with the Nag Hammadi tractate Book of Thomas.[12]

Richard Bauckham developed part of his influential defense of the 𝔓72 two-clause reading by translating διακρίνω in both v. 9 and v. 22 uniformly. In v. 9 two parties, Michael and the Devil, "disputed" (διακρινόμενος) over Moses' body. According to 𝔓72, in v. 23 Jude commands, "On those who dispute [or doubt] (διακρινομένους) have mercy with fear." It seems reasonable, therefore, that Jude has only two parties in mind in both contexts where the same terminology is used.[13] Anton Vögtle's limited rebuttal does, however, weaken the case for 𝔓72 and a synonymous translation of διακρίνω. While in v. 9 the disputing parties (Michael and the Devil) and the object of contention (Moses' body) are specified, "those who dispute [or doubt]" (διακρινομένους) in v. 23, regardless of their identity, are in need of mercy. This ambiguity would then imply a blanket rebuke of both the false teachers and the orthodox who contend or dispute with them. The middle voice translation of διακρίνω as "doubting" better suits the context of v. 23 and eliminates a direct correspondence to v. 9's two-class distinction.[14]

Translation difficulties related to the three-clause reading of ℵ inspired Joel Allen's simplified proposal.[15] While clause one specifies a target group (οὓς ... διακρινομένους, "those ... who doubt"), clauses two and three do not provide descriptions of those who should be saved and those who should be pitied with fear. By compiling evidence from Jude 10 and classical Greek literature, Allen argues that the μέν ... δέ construct can signify a series of emphases with one referent. In this case, "the descriptive force of the participle διακρινομένους is thus carried through the whole sentence so that the three clauses do not indicate distinct groups of persons, but amplification of the same group, i.e., those who doubt."[16]

---

11 Winter, "Jude 22–23," 219.

12 Ibid., 220–2.

13 Bauckham, *Jude, 2 Peter*, 108, 110.

14 Anton Vögtle, *Der Judasbrief/Der 2. Petrusbrief*, EKKNT 22 (Benziger Verlag, 1994), 103. Cf. also Henning Paulsen, *Der Zweite Petrusbrief und der Judasbrief*, KEK 12/1 (Vandenhoeck and Ruprecht, 1992), 82–3.

15 Joel S. Allen, "A New Possibility for the Three-Clause Format of Jude 22–3," *NTS* 44, no. 1 (1998): 133–43.

16 Ibid., 143.

Charles Landon introduces the first detailed study of a single variant in Jude 4.[17] Relying solely on internal evidence supported by an "etymological narrative," Landon has attempted to establish the reading δεσπότην θεόν ("Master God," P, Ψ, n, vgms, sy) against the printed UBS4 (= UBS5) and NA27 (= NA28) shorter reading δεσπότην (𝔓72, P78, ℵ, A, etc.). According to Landon, the Attic and Judeo-Hellenic etymological background of δεσπότην clearly identifies the term as a metaphorical description of God. Scribal pressures to economize eventually led to the deletion of the tautological qualifier θεόν, resulting in a blurred distinction between God and Jesus in v. 4. Jude's effort to preserve this distinction in other contexts (vv. 1, 21, 25) seems therefore to argue for including θεόν and against interpreting δεσπότην as a modifier for Ἰησοῦν Χριστόν ("Jesus Christ").[18]

The most dramatic development in recent text-critical research on Jude concerns the variants in verse 5. When the unbelieving Israelites were destroyed during the exodus, who was the executioner, Ἰησοῦς ("Jesus," NA28 = UBS5) or [ὁ] κύριος ("[the] Lord," NA27 = UBS4)? By reading Ἰησοῦς instead of [ὁ] κύριος, one impressive strand of manuscript tradition adopted by the NA28/UBS5 interpreted the Judge in vv. 5–7 as the preincarnate Jesus (A, B, 33, 81, 1241, 1739, 1881, 2344, *pc*, vg, co, Or1739mg, et al. [θεός Χριστός, 𝔓72c]).[19] The evidence for [ὁ] κύριος (with or without the article), is however, equally weighty (ℵ, Ψ, K, L, 049, 1175, syh, et al.). By assigning a grade C to the newly printed reading Ἰησοῦς in the UBS5, the editorial committee reveals a telling level of indecision. Although the external evidence seems evenly matched between the arlternate readings, the internal evidence may be decisive for reverting back to the NA27/UBS4 [ὁ] κύριος. Herbert Bateman provides several convincing reasons why [ὁ] κύριος should be retained: (1) nowhere else does Jude mention Ἰησοῦς without Χριστός; (2) nowhere else in the NT is Jesus explicitly identified as exodus savior or judge; (3) according to v. 1, θεός does the salvific "keeping" of saints for Jesus (Ἰησοῦ Χριστῷ τετηρημένοις, "kept for Jesus Christ"). It stands to reason θεός would also be the subject of the judgmental "keeping" activity in vv. 5 and 6 (ἀγγέλους... εἰς κρίσιν... τετήρηκεν, "he

---

17 Landon, "The Text of Jude 4," *HvTSt* 49, no. 4 (1993): 823–43.

18 Ibid., 828–33.

19 Cf. F. F. Bruce, *The New Testament Development of Old Testament Themes* (Eerdmans, 1968), 35-6; Allen Wikgren, "Some Problems in Jude 5," in *Studies in the History and Text of the New Testament in Honor of Kenneth Willis Clark*, ed. Boyd L. Daniels and M. Jack Suggs (University of Utah Press, 1967), 148–9. For arguments in favor of Ἰησοῦς see Carroll D. Osburn, "The Text of Jude 5," *Bib* 62, no. 1 (1981): 107–15; Jarl Fossum, "Kyrios Jesus as the Angel of the Lord in Jude 5–7," *NTS* 33, no. 2 (1987): 226–43; Gene L. Green, *Jude and 2 Peter*, BECNT (Baker Academic, 2008), 65

has kept angels for judgment"); (4) finally, κύριος is divine judge in both vv. 9 and 14.[20]

TRADITION/SOURCE/LITERARY CRITICISM

The density and complexity of Jude's dependence on traditions, sources, and literary links reveals the author's indebtedness to ancient apocalyptic Judaism.[21]

OLD TESTAMENT

Though older works consistently proposed a dependence on the LXX,[22] contemporary studies are pointing to Hebrew as the source of Jude's frequent OT allusions. According to Bauckham, "In two of these cases [Jude] must depend on the Hebrew text because the Septuagint does not give even the meaning he adopts (v. 12: Prov 25:14; v. 13: Isa 57:20), while in three other cases his vocabulary notably fails to correspond to that of the LXX (v. 11: Num 26:9; v. 12: Ezek 24:2; v. 23: Amos 4:11; Zech 3:3)."[23]

1 ENOCH

The explicit quotation of 1 Enoch 1:9 in Jude 14–15 and various other possible allusions[24] to the apocryphal work have been both recognized and problematic since the early Fathers.[25] Since publication of the Aramaic Qumran fragment 4QEn^c 1.1.15–17,[26] scholarly confidence that Jude employed a Greek

---

20 Bateman, *Jude*, 160–162. See also Bauckham, *Jude, 2 Peter*, 43; Thomas R. Schreiner, *1, 2 Peter, Jude*, NAC 37 (B&H Publishing Group, 2003), 397–98.

21 Udo Schnelle, *The History and Theology of the New Testament Writings*, trans. M. Eugene Boring (Fortress Press, 1998), 421; Thomas Wolthuis, "Jude and Jewish Traditions," *CTJ* 22, no. 1 (1987): 21–41.

22 F. H. Chase, "Jude, Epistle of," in *A Dictionary of the Bible*, ed. James Hastings, vol. 2 (Charles Scribner's Sons, 1900), 800; J. W. C. Wand, *The General Epistles of St. Peter and St. Jude*, WC (Methuen, 1934), 192; J. N. D. Kelly, *A Commentary on the Epistles of Peter and Jude*, HNTC (Hendrickson, 1969), 272.

23 Bauckham, *Jude, 2 Peter*, 7, 87–8. Cf. also Otto Knoch, *Der Erste und Zweite Petrusbrief, Der Judasbrief*, RNT (Verlag Friedrich Pustet, 1990), 153; Raymond E. Brown, *An Introduction to the New Testament*, ABRL (Doubleday, 1997), 757.

24 See Theodor Zahn, *Introduction to the New Testament*, trans. John Moore Trout et al., vol. 2 (1909; repr., Klock and Klock, 1977), 288; Bauckham, "Survey of Research," 139–40.

25 Jerome *Lives of Illustrious Men* 4 (*NPNF*² 3:362).

26 J. T. Milik, *The Books of Enoch: Aramaic Fragments of Qumrân Cave 4* (Clarendon, 1976), 184–5.

version of 1 Enoch[27] has been challenged by the possibility that Jude made his own translation from an Aramaic original.[28] If so, Jude likely derives from early Palestinian Jewish Christianity where such apocalyptic literature was widely disseminated.[29] Scholars are increasingly asserting Jude's fundamental dependence on 1 Enoch, declaring for example that the "whole of Jude's exegetical work [vv. 4–19] has 1 Enoch 1–5 as its base, and all other texts to which he alludes can be seen to be reached by association with 1 Enoch 1–5."[30]

According to Roman Heiligenthal, Jude should be interpreted primarily in terms of these connections. In his opinion, the influence of 1 Enoch is so profound, Jude "als ein christianisierter Teil der Henochüberlieferung aufgefaßt werden könnte."[31] Because both documents display a dependence on Jewish apocalyptic motifs,[32] Jude can be characterized as "Christian" in only a very discreet sense ("sehr vorischtigen Maß").[33] Their shared esteem for faithfulness versus apostasy and ethical purity against antinomianism, combined with a centralized contempt for blasphemers, cements their *theologiegeschichtliche* ("theological-historical") continuity in response to pagan Hellenism.[34]

Rather than overemphasize Jude's deference to assimilated Jewish apocalyptic material, J. D. Charles outlines the relationship in terms of literary strategy. Jude incorporated eclectic selections that "were conventions of his day, in order to address specific needs of his audience."[35] Jude's appropriation of themes and language from 1 Enoch and the Assumption of Moses, describing disenfranchised angels (v. 6), Michael's dispute with the devil (v. 9), and the

---

27 Jean Cantinat, "L'épître de Jude," in *Les épîtres apostoliques*, Introduction critique au Nouveau Testament, ed. Augustin George and Piere Grelot, vol. 3 (Desclée, 1977), 277; Kümmel, *Introduction*, 428; Michael Green, *The Second Epistle General of Peter and the General Epistle of Jude: An Introduction and Commentary*, TNTC (Eerdmans, 1987), 192.

28 Carroll D. Osburn, "The Christological Use of 1 Enoch 1:9 in Jude 14, 15," *NTS* 23, no. 3 (1977): 335–8; Bauckham, *Jude, 2 Peter*, 94–6.

29 Bauckham, "Survey of Research," 140–1.

30 Richard J. Bauckham, "Jude's Exegesis," in *Jude and the Relatives of Jesus in the Early Church* (T&T Clark, 1990), 211; Stephan J. Joubert, "Facing the Past: Transtextual Relationships and Historical Understanding in the Letter of Jude," *BZ* 42, no. 1 (1998): 63; Osburn, "The Christological Use of 1 Enoch 1:9," 340–1; Wolthuis, "Jude and Jewish Traditions," 37–8; Vögtle, *Judasbrief*, 83–6.

31 Roman Heiligenthal, *Zwischen Henoch und Paulus: Studien zum theologiegeschichtlichen Ort des Judasbriefes*, Texte und Arbeiten zum neutestamentlichen Zeitalter 6 (Francke Verlag, 1992), 9 (Jude "could be understood as a Christianized part of the Enoch tradition," my translation).

32 Ibid., 32–6, 64–70, 73–5, 94.

33 Ibid., 26.

34 Ibid., 32–6, 94.

35 J. D. Charles, "Jude's Use of Pseudepigraphal Source-Material as Part of a Literary Strategy," *NTS* 37, no. 1 (1991): 130. Cf. also Robert L. Webb, "The Eschatology of the Epistle of Jude and Its Rhetorical and Social Functions," *BBR* 6 (1996): 139–51; Joubert, "Facing the Past," 60; idem, "Language, Ideology and the Social Context of the Letter of Jude," *Neot* 24, no. 2 (1990): 340.

judgment of the ungodly (vv. 14–15), serves primarily as illustrative support for key issues of concern.[36] The focal errors and examples provided by such contexts parallel realities in the audience's immediate circumstance, providing allusions adaptable to a specific theological and literary purpose.[37] For example, Jude's antithesis of the ungodly (vv. 8, 10, 11, 12, 14, 16, 19) and the faithful (vv. 5, 17, 18, 20) is resolved by God's impending appearance for judgment (vv. 14–15). In vv. 14–15 Jude's appeal to an Enochic prophecy (1 Enoch 1:9) closely follows plentiful and recognizable OT theophany patterns,[38] thus raising the salient questions:

> Would a theophany-statement direct from the OT not have generated as full a force with the audience? Were the readers – or opponents – devotees of Enoch literature? Rather than merely ascribe to Jude "respect" for 1 Enoch as a prominent first-century work circulating among certain sectarian Jewish or Jewish-Christian circles (the approach most commentators would assume), we would suggest that the writer is exploiting, if not the *readers'* devotion to Enoch literature, then that of his *opponents* ... without necessarily implying that the *entirety* of the works being cited ... is historical, edifying or authoritative.[39]

By drawing from material revered by his audience, or perhaps his opponents, Jude strategically recruits their Jewish-Christian preferences and presuppositions[40] to empower his pastoral exhortations. By so doing Jude accomplishes both "faithfulness to the OT tradition of theophany-statements ('"Behold the Lord comes"') and exploitation of a literary work of sectarian Judaism to which his audience possibly may have been devoted."[41] It appears therefore, that Jude's "allusions to extra-canonical source material are appropriate inasmuch as they amplify particular OT notions."[42] First Enoch and the Assumption of Moses serve to subsidize Jude's *pesharim* commentaries[43] on OT types

---

36 Charles, "Jude's Use of Pseudepigraphal Source-Material," 131.

37 Ibid., 144.

38 J. D. Charles, "The Use of Tradition-Material in the Epistle of Jude," *BBR* 4 (1994): 4–5. Cf. Deut 33:2–3; Ps 68:17; Isa 33:5; Jer 25:31; Mal 3:3–5.

39 J. D. Charles, "'Those' and 'These:' The Use of the Old Testament in the Epistle of Jude," *JSNT* 38 (1990): 119, n. 4.

40 Charles, "Jude's Use of Pseudepigraphal Source-Material," 144. Cf. Joubert's "interpretive framework" ("Facing the Past," 63).

41 Charles, "The Use of Tradition-Material," 5.

42 Charles, "'Those' and 'These,'" 109; Walter M. Dunnett, "The Hermeneutics of Jude and 2 Peter: The Use of Ancient Jewish Traditions," *JETS* 31, no. 3 (1988): 287–91.

43 E. Earle Ellis, "Prophecy and Hermeneutic in Jude," in *Prophecy and Hermeneutic in Early Christianity* (Eerdmans, 1978; repr., Baker, 1993), 226.

by linking past judgment with the present circumstances.[44]

Testament of Moses

Bauckham's re-collation of the fragmentary evidence for the source of Jude's obscure angelic dispute over Moses' body (v. 9) challenges an ancient interpretive tradition. Early Church Fathers commenting on Jude 9 attribute the narrative to the Assumption of Moses.[45] The work itself is no longer extant, but various similar accounts are often combined into a composite under the same title.[46] Bauckham, however, noting what he considers incompatible variations within the sources, proposes the possibility of a dual tradition.[47] Segments of the tradition detailing the angelic dispute, including Jude 9, best correspond stylistically and thematically to a fragmentary Latin Testament of Moses.[48] The second version of the story was a later anti-Gnostic revision of the first and became known as the Assumption of Moses among the Alexandrian Fathers.[49] If Bauckham's thesis is correct, Jude employed a very ancient Jewish source (The Testament of Moses) virtually unknown to other early Christian writers, mentioned by name only in lists of apocrypha. Jude's knowledge of such a work could imply a very specific Palestinian Jewish Christian milieu consistent with the "circles from which an authentic letter of Jude the Lord's brother would come."[50]

Christian Tradition

Scholarly fascination with Jude's OT and extra-biblical connections can obscure the prevalence of genuine Christian confessional traditions.[51] Appeals

44 Charles, "'Those' and 'These,'" 109.

45 Clement, *Fragments: Comments on the Epistle of Jude;* Didymus the Blind *In epistola Judae catholica* (see Friedrich Zoepfl, ed. *Didymi Alexandrini in Epistolas Canonicas Brevis Enarratio*, NTAbh 4/1 [Aschendorffsche Verlagsbuchhandlung, 1914], 92); Origen, *De Principiis* 3.2.1; Eusebius, *Ecclesiastical History* 2.17.17.

46 Montague Rhodes James, *The Lost Apocrypha of the Old Testament: Their Titles and Fragments* (MacMillan, 1920), 43–51; Samuel E. Loewenstamm, "The Death of Moses," in *Studies on the Testament of Abraham*, ed. George W. E. Nickelsburg, Jr., SBLSCS 6 (Scholars Press, 1976), 209–10.

47 Bauckham, "Survey of Research," 141–4.

48 Bauckham, "Jude and the Testament of Moses," in *Jude and the Relatives of Jesus in the Early Church* (T&T Clark, 1990), 235–58. See the critical edition in R. H. Charles' *The Assumption of Moses* (Adam and Charles Black, 1897). Though Charles entitles his book *The Assumption of Moses*, he describes the manuscript at the center of his study as the Testament of Moses: "The original Assumption preserved only in a few quotations" (xlv).

49 Bauckham, "Jude and the Testament of Moses," 259–70.

50 Ibid., 278–80.

51 Peter Müller, "Der Judasbrief," 281.

to a fixed body of Christian truth (v. 3), apostolic prophecy (v. 17), and the "most holy faith" (v. 20), combined with Christological affirmations connecting Jesus with God (vv. 1, 4, 21, 24), all assert Jude's thoroughly Christian character. The author in fact takes over 1 Enoch's apocalyptic vision of the "Day of the Lord" (v. 14) and recasts the episode in terms of the Christian parousia (v. 21).[52] Jewish liturgical practices, such as prayer (v. 20), the sacred meal (v. 12), and the prophetic word (v. 17), are translated into Christian conventions.[53]

2 PETER

The unmistakable literary relationship between Jude and 2 Peter[54] has spawned several competing arguments for the priority of 2 Peter, the priority of Jude, or mutual dependence on a common source. Older discussions favoring the priority of 2 Peter[55] have been abandoned in recent scholarship. The most enduring interpretation concludes that 2 Peter's rough style and longer more generalized readings are likely deliberate redactions[56] of Jude's stylistic precision and shorter more specific readings.[57]

The possibility that Jude and 2 Peter shared a common "sermon pattern formulated to resist the seducers of the church"[58] has recently been supported by George Barr's work with literary "scale." By measuring sentence length Barr isolates a text's detail "scale" in order to identify the subconscious "shape" or rhythmic patterns contained in an author's work.[59] Barr's analysis of unique "prime patterns" found in 2 Peter and Jude provides no evidence of a literary

---

52 Ibid.

53 Knoch, *Judasbrief*, 165.

54 Cf. Jude 4–18; 2 Pet 2:1–3:3.

55 Friedrich Spitta, *Der zweite Brief des Petrus und der Brief des Judas* (Verlag der Buchhandlung des Waisenhauses, 1885), 381–470; Zahn, *Introduction*, 250–1, 265–7, 285; Charles Bigg, *A Critical and Exegetical Commentary on the Epistles of St. Peter and St. Jude*, ICC (T&T Clark, 1978), 216–24.

56 Bauckham, *Jude, 2 Peter*, 141–3; idem, "2 Peter: An Account of Research," *ANRW* 25.5:3714–16.

57 Friedrich Maier, *Der Judasbrief: Seine Echtheit, Abfassungszeit und Leser: Ein Beitrag zur Einleitung in die katholischen Briefe*, BibS(F) 11/1–2 (Herdersche Verlagshandlung, 1906), 105–8; James Moffat, *An Introduction to the Literature of the New Testament*, 2nd rev. ed., ITL (T&T Clark, 1912), 350–2; Walter Grundmann, *Der Brief des Judas und der zweite Brief des Petrus*, 3. Auflage, THKNT 15 (Evangelische Verlagsanstalt, 1986), 102–7; Paula-Angelika Seethaler, *1. und 2. Petrusbrief, Judasbrief*, 2. Auflage, Stuttgarter Kleiner Kommentar: Neues Testament 16 (Verlag Katholisches Bibelwerk, 1986), 70; Knoch, *Judasbrief*, 205–6; Paulsen, *Judasbrief*, 97–100; Vögtle, *Judasbrief*, 122–3; Pheme Perkins, *First and Second Peter, James, and Jude*, IBC (John Knox Press, 1995), 178; Brown, *Introduction*, 761; Schnelle, *New Testament Writings*, 429.

58 Bo Reicke, *The Epistles of James, Peter, and Jude*, AB 37 (Doubleday and Company, 1964), 190.

59 George K. Barr, "Scale and the Pauline Epistles," *IBS* 17 (1995): 22–41.

dependence in the sense of one author copying or incorporating the text of another. At every point of correspondence each author "has expressed himself in his own way and there is a substantial proportion of synonyms and alternative terms."[60] The answer to these similarities lies in a shared preaching campaign developed jointly by the earliest church leaders designed to combat widespread antinomian tendencies. The authors of Jude and 2 Peter "then wrote it up each in his own way, maintaining the general order, preserving the illustrations and vocabulary, but showing great individuality in their perceptions and in their expression."[61]

RHETORICAL CRITICISM

Analysis of Jude in terms of its rhetorical form, structure, and style has stimulated a growing interest and appreciation for this short document and its artistry.[62]

Form

Jude's rhetorical form has been described as a pseudo-letter[63] disguising a Jewish *haggada* or homily,[64] a polemical diatribe,[65] or an anti-heretical tract.[66] Jude's unity[67] and epistolary character should not, however, be questioned simply because the document contains a sharp tone and diverse literary

---

60 Barr, "Literary Dependence in the New Testament Epistles," *IBS* 19 (1997): 158.

61 Ibid., 160.

62 For surveys of rhetorical criticism's development and its specific application to Jude see E. R. Wendland, "A Comparative Study of 'Rhetorical Criticism,' Ancient and Modern - with Special Reference to the Larger Structure and Function of the Epistle of Jude," *Neot* 28, no. 1 (1994): 193–228; Duane Frederick Watson, *Invention, Arrangement, and Style: Rhetorical Criticism of Jude and 2 Peter* (Scholars Press, 1988).

63 Jülicher, *Introduction*, 229: "The epistolary form here is purely artificial"; Kümmel, *Introduction*, 427.

64 Jean Cantinat, "The Catholic Epistles," in *Introduction to the New Testament*, ed. A. Robert and A. Feuillet (Desclee, 1965), 594; idem, *Les Épitres de Saint Jacques et de Saint Jude*, SB (J. Gabalda, 1973), 270; James I. H. McDonald, *Kerygma and Didache: The Articulation and Structure of the Earliest Christian Message*, SNTSMS 37 (Cambridge University Press, 1980), 61. Cf. Moshe David Herr, "*Aggadah*," in *EncJud*, ed. Cecil Roth (Macmillan, 1971), 2:354–6.

65 Alfred Loisy, *The Origins of the New Testament*, trans. L. P. Jacks (George Allen and Unwin, 1950), 279–81; Hubert Frankemölle, *1. und 2. Petrusbrief, Judasbrief*, NEchtB 18/20 (Echter Verlag, 1987), 127: "Polemischen Kampfbrief."

66 Philipp Vielhauer, *Geschichte der urchristlichen Literatur: Einleitung in das Neue Testament, die Apokryphen und die Apostolischen Väter* (Water de Gruyter, 1975), 590; Vögtle, *Judasbrief*, 4; Ferdinand Hahn, "Randbemerkungen zum Judasbrief," *TZ* 37, no. 4 (1981): 214–5; Stephen L. Harris, *The New Testament: A Student's Introduction*, 2d. ed. (Mayfield Publishing Company, 1995), 310.

67 Watson, *Invention, Arrangement, and Style*, 29.

forms.[68] According to Bauckham, the only determinative feature for an ancient letter's authenticity was an epistolary opening specifying the author and intended recipients.[69] Jude includes this specification (vv. 1–2) and also provides an introductory statement of occasion (vv. 3–4) typical of ancient letter forms.[70] The letter's homiletic qualities including an extensive midrash (vv. 5–19), paraenesis (vv. 20–23), and a doxology (vv. 24–25) reveal a hybrid "epistolary sermon"[71] form.

Structure

Despite Norman Perrin's contention that Jude "defies structural analysis,"[72] numerous recent efforts have produced valuable results. Jude's conspicuous introductory address (vv. 1–2), purpose statement (vv. 3–4), and concluding doxology (vv. 24–25)[73] have produced little structural debate.[74] The body of the document (vv. 5–23), however, continues to solicit commentary.

Identification of several transitional elements[75] throughout vv. 5–23 has provided an influential method for outlining the text. Jean Cantinat's juxtaposition of pronominal signals, οὗτοι ("these," vv. 8, 10, 12, 16, 19), οὓς μὲν ... οὓς δὲ ("some ... and others," vv. 22–23), and ὑμεῖς δέ ("but you," vv. 17, 20), produced an eight-fold division,[76] but E. Earle Ellis' recognition and interpretation of such details has resulted in "perhaps the most important advance in recent studies on Jude."[77] By analyzing the placement of formulaic

---

68 Paulsen, *Judasbrief*, 41; Cf. Georg Strecker, *Literaturgeschichte des Neuen Testaments* (Vandenhoeck und Ruprecht, 1992), 66–73, who identifies three sub-forms within the ancient letter's "literarische Gattung:" (1) "Homilie," 1 John, Hebrews, 1 Peter; (2) "Traktat," Ephesians, James, Jude; and (3) "Testament," 2 Peter.

69 Richard J. Bauckham, "Pseudo-Apostolic Letters," *JBL* 107, no. 3 (1988): 473.

70 William G. Doty, *Letters in Primitive Christianity* (Fortress Press, 1973), 14, 34–5.

71 Bauckham, *Jude, 2 Peter*, 3; James I. H. McDonald, *Kerygma and Didache*, 60–1.

72 Perrin and Duling, *Introduction*, 380.

73 For a discussion of the doxological structure in vv. 24–25 compared to other early Christian hymns and "praise speeches" ("Lobsprüche") see Reinhard Deichgräber, *Gotteshymnus und Christushymnus in der frühen Christenheit: Untersuchungen zu Form, Sprache und Stil der frühchristlichen Hymen*, SUNT 5 (Vanderhoeck and Ruprecht, 1967), 27–9, 100–4.

74 Peter Müller, "Judasbrief," 273; Eric Fuchs and Pierre Reymond, *La Deuxième Épitre de Saint Pierre l'*Épitre de Saint Jude, CNT 13b (Delachaux and Niestlé, 1980), 140–1; Vögtle, *Judasbrief*, ix; Heiligenthal, *Zwischen Henoch und Paulus*, 21; Cf. however, Watson, *Invention, Arrangement, and Style*, 77, and Albin, *Judasbrevet*, 741–2, who unnecessarily separate vv. 3–4 and their unified statement of Jude's dual exhortation to (1) contend for the faith and (2) beware of the ungodly.

75 Cf. Jeffrey T. Reed and Ruth A. Reese's analysis of shifts in verb tense which theoretically identify the author's subjective understanding of an event's thematic importance ("Verbal Aspect, Discourse Prominence, and the Letter of Jude," *FilNeot* 9, no. 18 [1996]: 181–99).

76 Cantinat, *Jude*, 267–8.

77 Bauckham, "Survey of Research," 152.

expressions and catchword connections, Ellis uncovered in vv. 5–19 a consistent "commentary" or "midrash" pattern common in first-century Jewish exegesis, the Qumran *pesharim*, and early Christian literature.[78] Δέ ("but," v. 9), ὅτι ("that," vv. 5, 11), and λέγω ("say," vv. 14, 17) introduce "texts" for consideration. These "quotations" are then followed by commentary/application signaled by a shift in verb tense and the appearance of οὗτοι ("these," vv. 8, 10) or οὗτός ἐστιν ("these are," vv. 12, 16, 19). The inclusion of multiple "catchwords" unifies the composition by connecting the "texts" with every element of the letter from the introduction through the final application.[79] Ellis concludes that the "whole piece (vv. 5–19) is a carefully worked-out commentary that Jude has then introduced (vv. 1–4) and supplied with a concluding exhortation (vv. 20–23)."[80]

Basing his conclusions on Ellis's work, Bauckham has determined that Jude's primary emphasis has been generally misunderstood. The large midrash section (vv. 5–19) is not the center of Jude's concern but serves as critical background to the overall appeal in vv. 20–23.[81] Bauckham's outline integrates the midrash/commentary and the paraenesis into a convincing whole:

Address and Greeting (vv. 1–2)
Occasion and Theme of the Letter (vv. 3–4)
    A. The Appeal (v. 3)
    B. The Background to the Appeal (v. 4)
B. The Background to the Appeal: A Midrash on the Prophecies of the Doom of the Ungodly (vv. 5–19)
    (1) Three OT Types (vv. 5–7)
       plus interpretation (vv. 8–10)
       (1a) Michael and the Devil (v. 9)
    (2) Three More OT Types (v. 11)
       plus interpretation (vv. 12–13)
    (3) The Prophecy of Enoch (vv. 14–15)

---

78 Ellis, "Prophecy and Hermeneutic in Jude," 224. Cf. M. P. Miller, "Targum, Midrash and the Use of the Old Testament in the New Testament," *JSJ* 2 (1970): 29–82; James L. Bailey and Lyle D. Vander Broek, *Literary Forms in the New Testament: A Handbook* (Westminster/John Knox, 1992), 157–8.

79 Ellis, "Prophecy and Hermeneutic in Jude," 224–5.

80 Ibid., 225. Subsequent descriptions of Jude's structure in one way or another make use of this method and generally divide the text body by the recurrence of οὗτοι. Cf. Heiligenthal, *Zwischen Henoch und Paulus*, 21; Fuchs and Reymond, *Jude*, 140–1; Paulsen, *Judasbrief*, 58–9; Jerome H. Neyrey, *2 Peter, Jude: A New Translation with Introduction and Commentary*, AB 37c (Doubleday, 1993), 23–5; Peter Müller, "Judasbrief," 273.

81 Bauckham, *Jude, 2 Peter*, 4; Vögtle, *Judasbrief*, 111.

       plus interpretation (v. 16)

    (4) The Prophecy of the Apostles (vv. 17–18)

       plus interpretation (v. 19)

A. The Appeal (vv. 20–23)

Closing Doxology (vv. 24–25)[82]

Duane Watson's experimental application of classical categories (*Exordium, Narratio, Probatio,* etc.) supplies evidence of Jude's literary skill commensurate with the Greco-Roman rhetoricians.[83] Watson's methodological inflexibility, however, distorts his interpretation and forces categorical conformity.[84] E. R. Wendland's "rhetorical-critical corrective" to Watson's excesses builds on the observations recorded by Ellis and Bauckham and proposes a secondary "affective" climax at the center of an "extended chiasm."[85] With the "woe" statement in v. 11, "Jude for the only time other than in his opening words interjects himself overtly and personally into the discourse."[86] This prophetic denunciation heightens the connection between Jude's opponents and the three examples of archetypal Jewish apostasy, resulting in a "classic case of *vituperatio*: 'Would anyone dare to identify with people who will be damned by God? Certainly not.'"[87]

Style

Jude's Greek style and vocabulary have been impugned by less detailed studies,[88] but focused exegesis has disclosed the author's remarkable verbal and stylistic skill.[89] The author's use of catchword connections,[90] synonymous[91]

---

82 Bauckham, *Jude, 2 Peter,* 5–6.

83 Watson, *Invention, Arrangement, and Style,* 29–79; Neyrey, *2 Peter, Jude,* 23–7; Thomas Wolthuis' article "Jude and the Rhetorician: A Dialogue on the Rhetorical Nature of the Epistle of Jude," *CTJ* 24, no. 1 (1989): 126–34, is actually a fictional dialogue between Cicero and Jude describing the letter's accidental classical rhetorical design.

84 Peter Müller, "Judasbrief," 272. See for example Watson's description of the epistolary prescript as "Quasi-*Exordium*" (Watson, *Invention, Arrangement, and Style,* 40–3).

85 Wendland, "Comparative Study of 'Rhetorical Criticism,'" 210.

86 Ibid., 213.

87 Ibid., 213.

88 See for example Donald Guthrie, *New Testament Introduction* (InterVarsity Press, 1970), 927.

89 H. J. Cladder, "Strophical Structure in St Jude's Epistle," *JTS* 5 (1904): 601; J. D. Charles, "Literary Artifice in the Epistle of Jude," *ZNW* 82 (1991): 106–24; Bauckham, *Jude, 2 Peter,* 6–7.

90 See, for examples, ἀσεβεῖς/ἀσέβεια ("ungodly/ungodliness," vv. 4, 15[3x], 18); ὑμεῖς/ὑμᾶς/ὑμῖν ("you," vv. 3[3x], 5[2x], 12, 17, 18, 20[2x], 24); τηρέω/φυλάσσω ("keep/guard," vv. 1, 6[2x], 13, 21, 24); οὗτοι ("these," vv. 4[τινές ("certain ones")], 8, 10, 11[αὐτοῖς ("them")], 12, 14, 16, 19; etc.

91 Cf. σπουδὴν ποιούμενος = ἀνάγκην ἔσχον ("although I was eager = I felt the need," v. 3); δεσπότην = κύριον ("Master =Lord," v. 4); ὑπομνῆσαι = εἰδότας ("remind = know," v. 5); etc.

and antithetical[92] parallelism, paronomasia (sound resemblances),[93] and "triadic illustrations"[94] displays his rhetorical skill in communicating a message forceful in both form and content.[95] Jude's stylistic penchant for triplets adds rhetorical reinforcement for his basic dichotomy between the ungodly and the faithful. With two specific sets of three,[96] each depicting archetypal examples of ungodliness, Jude validates his condemnation of intruders by providing the "evidence of two witnesses or three witnesses" (Deut 17:6).[97] The author's poetic command of literary and idiomatic Greek,[98] combined with a "terse, picturesque, and impassioned style … make Jude distinct among the writings of the NT."[99]

Stephan J. Joubert's "sociolinguistic" study examines stylistic conventions such as vocabulary and syntax in an effort to reveal the normative ideology embraced by Jude and his community. Jude's "textual strategy" employs a multi-step linguistic progression that accomplishes his dual purposes of (1) encouraging the faithful and (2) condemning the deviants.[100] By appealing to the OT, apocryphal literature, nature (vv. 12–13), and apostolic teaching, Jude indirectly demands conformity to his authoritative ideological viewpoint. Rich negative metaphors and condemning vocabulary applied to the intruders compels the audience to reject a "fallacious interpretation of reality." Jude's "apocalyptic eschatological ideology" promises divine judgment for any belief system in conflict with that "most holy faith" once for all revealed to the community. Jude's presupposed authority leaves the readers with "no other choice, apart from completely rejecting the ideology he represented, than to acknowledge his right to exercise control over their behavior." His language is therefore a "language of social and religious control." The letter does not, however, "merely reflect certain beliefs and social processes"; it also "actively

---

92 Cf. such obvious examples as οὗτοι ("these," vv. 4, 8, 10, 11, 12, 16, 19) versus ὑμεῖς ("you," vv. 3, 5, 12, 17, 18, 20, 24); ἀσεβεῖς ("ungodly," vv. 4, 15, 18) versus ἅγιος ("holy," vv. 3, 14, 20, 24); ἔλεος ("mercy," vv. 2, 21, 22, 23) versus κρίσις/κρίμα ("judgment/condemnation," vv. 4, 6, 19, 15); etc.

93 Cf. v. 3, (alliteration) Ἀγαπητοί, πᾶσαν σπουδὴν ποιούμενος … περὶ … γράψαι … παρακαλῶν ἐπαγωνίζεσθαι … ἅπαξ παραδοθείσῃ … πίστει; v. 7, (homoioteleuton) ἐκπορνεύσασαι … ἀπελθοῦσαι … πρόκεινται … ὑπέχουσαι; v. 8, (assonance) μιαίνουσιν … ἀθετοῦσιν … βλασφημοῦσιν.

94 Cf. v. 1, Ἰούδας, δοῦλος, ἀδελφός ("Jude, slave, brother" = author); ἠγαπημένοις, τετηρημένοις, κλητοῖς ("loved, kept, called" = audience); v. 2 ἔλεος, εἰρήνη, ἀγάπη ("mercy, peace, love" in greetings); etc.; Charles, "'Those' and 'These,'" 124, n. 60, lists a total of twenty triplets.

95 Charles, "Literary Artifice," 110–23; idem, "'Those' and 'These,'" 110; Paulsen, Judasbrief, 41.

96 Unbelieving Israel, the rebellious angels, and Sodom and Gomorrah (vv. 5–7); Cain, Balaam, and Korah (v. 11).

97 Charles, "'Those' and 'These,'" 110–1, 117–8.

98 Bauckham, Jude, 2 Peter, 6.

99 Charles, "Literary Artifice," 111.

100 Joubert, "Language, Ideology, and the Social Context," 342–3.

establishes and maintains" them.[101]

AUTHOR, DATE, DESTINATION

Conclusions concerning Jude's authorship, date, and destination depend on a complex matrix of interwoven exegetical decisions. Ernst Käsemann, observing Jude's keen interest in the "faith once for all delivered to the saints" (v. 3) and the "words spoken in advance by the apostles" (v. 17), categorized the letter in terms of an early Catholic polemic armed with tradition rather than the Spirit.[102] By interpreting Jude's ἡ πίστις ("the faith," v. 3) in terms of post-apostolic ecclesiastical tradition, Käsemann created a pervasive exegetical template[103] that presupposes Jude's pseudepigraphy and late date.[104] According to James Dunn, for example, "centered on the 'trajectory' of emerging Catholic orthodoxy," Jude's theological disposition is a "second generation development at best and cannot be traced back to the beginning of Christianity."[105]

There is little doubt that the author described as Ἰούδας Ἰησοῦ Χριστοῦ δοῦλος, ἀδελφὸς δὲ Ἰακώβου ("Jude, a slave of Jesus Christ and brother of James," v. 1) refers to the younger half brother of Jesus (Matt 13:55; Mark 6:3).[106] The modifier ἀδελφὸς Ἰακώβου ties Jude to the only "man in the primitive church who could be called simply 'James' without risk of ambiguity."[107] Recent commentators often simply refute Jude's authenticity by restating arguments describing the letter as pseudepigraphal:[108] A normative faith (v. 3) set in opposition to early Gnosticism[109] transcends even the "post-apostolic" foundation of "apostles and prophets" (Eph 2:20) by establishing an immutable

---

101 Ibid., 343–4, 347.

102 Ernst Käsemann, "Eine Apologie der urchristlichen Eschatologie," *ZTK* 49 (1952): 272–96.

103 See, however, rebuttals in Cantinat, "L'épitre de Jude," 281–3; idem, *Jude*, 285–7; Fuchs and Reymond, *Jude*, 157–8.

104 Cf. Schelkle, "Spätapostolische Briefe als frühkatholisches Zeugnis," 225–6; Harrington, "The 'Early Catholic' Writings of the New Testament", 107; Schrage, *Judas Brief*, 228.

105 James D. G. Dunn, *Unity and Diversity*, 341, 345, 361–2.

106 Kümmel, *Introduction*, 427; Fuchs and Reymond, *Jude*, 144–8; Brown, *Introduction*, 750; Paulsen, *Judasbrief*, 44; Vögtle, *Judasbrief*, 5; Peter Müller, "Judasbrief," 285. Cf. however, John Calvin, *The Epistles of James and Jude*, trans. A. W. Morrison (Eerdmans, 1972), 322; Helmut Koester, "ΓΝΩΜΑΙ ΔΙΑΦΟΡΟΙ: The Origin and Nature of Diversification in the History of Early Christianity," *HTR* 58, no. 3 (1965): 297; Ellis, "Prophecy and Hermeneutic," 226–9.

107 Bauckham, "Survey of Research," 172.

108 Cf. Jülicher, *Introduction*, 231–2; Karl Hermann Schelkle, *Die Petrusbriefe - Der Judasbrief*, HThKNT 13/2 (Herder, 1964), 142–3; Reicke, *Jude*, 191; Grundmann, *Brief des Judas*, 13–5. As early as 1909 Zahn noted that credibility for an epistolary forgery comes from a kind of name recognition that "Jude the brother of James" cannot provide; the identifier's obscurity itself defeats a pseudepigrapher's goal (Zahn, *Introduction*, 268–70).

109 John J. Gunther, "The Alexandrian Epistle of Jude," *NTS* 30, no 4 (1984): 549–62.

church tradition.[110] The appeal to apostolic teaching (v. 17) supposedly betrays a second or third generation tendency to view the apostles as an authoritative closed community,[111] and the possibility that the Galilean half brother of Jesus could write a letter with such rhetorical and linguistic skill is rejected outright.[112] As an early Catholic pseudepigraphal text penned in opposition to intrusive Gnostic influences, it is necessarily dated later, sometime between A.D. 80 and 120.[113]

Despite the dogmatic confidence with which some hold to the pseudepigraphal view,[114] compelling arguments for Jude's authenticity contradict the "scholarly doubt"[115] presupposed by many. The theological framework of early Catholicism as a legitimate NT interpretive tool has nearly collapsed,[116] and its application to Jude has been severely tested. Second-century early Catholic writing purportedly displays an increased emphasis on ecclesiastical structure and a decreased emphasis on apocalyptic imagery including the parousia.[117] Jude, however, provides no discussion of church structure and focuses almost entirely on apocalyptic imagery including the parousia (cf. vv. 14, 21, 24).[118]

Though often identified as later Catholic traditionalism, Jude's ἅπαξ παραδοθείσῃ τοῖς ἁγίοις πίστις ("faith once for all delivered to the saints," v. 3)

---

110 Vögtle, *Judasbrief*, 8.

111 Seethaler, *Judasbrief*, 125–6; Frankemölle, *Judasbrief*, 129; Paulsen, *Judasbrief*, 79; Schnelle, *New Testament Writings*, 417.

112 Neyrey, *2 Peter, Jude*, 31; Vögtle, *Judasbrief*, 9; Frankemölle, *Judasbrief*, 130; Russell Pregeant, *Engaging the New Testament: An Interdisciplinary Introduction* (Fortress Press, 1995), 489; Schnelle, *New Testament Writings*, 417; Perkins, *Jude*, 142; Peter Müller, "Judasbrief," 286; Bart D. Ehrman, *The New Testament: A Historical Introduction to the Early Christian Writings*, 2d. ed. (Oxford University Press, 2000), 420.

113 Gunther, "Alexandrian Epistle of Jude," 558 (A. D. 120–131); Grundmann, *Brief des Judas*, 16; Vögtle, *Judasbrief*, 11–2; Harris, *Introduction*, 310; Peter Müller, "Judasbrief," 287.

114 Roman Heiligenthal erroneously asserts, "Der pseudepigraphe Charakter des Jud wird nicht mehr bestritten" ("The pseudepigraphical character of Jude is no longer disputed," my translation) ("Der Judasbrief: Aspekte der Forschung in den letzten Jahrzehnten," *TRu* 51, no. 2 [1986]: 120). Cf. also, Bart Ehrman, *The New Testament: A Historical Introduction to the Early Christian Writings*, 2d. ed. (Oxford University Press, 2000), 393.

115 According to Hans Conzelmann, "The general starting point for the contemporary exegetical work in the NT is the scholarly doubt by which historical investigation questions the ancient ecclesiastical tradition regarding the Bible" (*Interpreting the New Testament*, 32).

116 The terminology itself is passé, results in "distorted judgments," and characterizes phenomena "almost entirely a legacy of Judaism" (Martin Hengel, *Acts and the History of Earliest Christianity*, trans. John Bowden [SCM Press, 1979], 121–2); see also Stephen Neill, *The Interpretation of the New Testament: 1861–1961* (Oxford University Press, 1964), 186–90; Ralph P. Martin, *The Acts, the Letters*, vol. 2 of *The Apocalypse New Testament Foundations: A Guide for Christian Students*, rev. ed. (Eerdmans, 1986), 382–3; Schreiner, *1, 2 Peter, Jude*, 365.

117 Dunn, *Unity and Diversity*, 341–66.

118 Brown, *Introduction*, 757.

and his appeal to the words of the apostles (v. 17) mirror emphases on "delivered" (παραδίδοσθαι) authoritative tradition (2 Thess 2:15; 3:6; 1 Cor 15:3), ἡ πίστις ("the faith") as a body of teaching (Gal 1:23), and appeals to apostolic authority (1 Cor 9:1; 2 Cor 11:13) found in the early Pauline material (ca. A.D. 50–56).[119] As part of his ongoing statistical study of "scale" in New Testament literature,[120] Barr identifies unique literary patterns that intimately connect the Pauline corpus and Jude. Shared detail patterns are distinctive enough to rule out literary dependence (copying) while their similarities "reflect a common store of preaching material used by the apostles repeatedly."[121] According to Barr's calculations, scalometric consistency could only occur subconsciously as each author recorded in his own way the common material "prepared by the apostles to meet a threat posed by false teaching." The Pauline corpus and Jude may in fact be products of a cooperative missionary effort, written within the timeframe of Paul's journeys, between A.D. 56 and 60.[122]

Evidence pointing to Jude's Palestinian provenance[123] further validates the epistle's implicit claim to authenticity. The letter's exegetical method directly parallels distinctive first-century Jewish *pesher* forms common throughout the Qumran material,[124] and Jude's extensive allusions to OT and pseudepigraphal materials are probably derived from Hebrew and Aramaic, not the LXX or other Greek documents.[125] Jude's apocalyptic eschatology comes not from static Greek Catholicism but the Palestinian Judeo-Christian "worldview within which he naturally thinks."[126]

---

119 Bauckham, *Jude, 2 Peter*, 32–3; idem, "Survey of Research," 159; Brown, *Introduction*, 758; Ellis, "Prophecy and Hermeneutic in Jude," 233–4. For dating the Pauline material cited see Kümmel, *Introduction*, 269, 279, 293, 304.

120 Barr, "Scale and the Pauline Epistles," 22–41; idem, "The Structure of Hebrews and of 1ˢᵗ and 2ⁿᵈ Peter," *IBS* 19 (1997): 17–31; idem, "Literary Dependence in the New Testament Epistles," 148–60; idem, "Scaleometry and the Dating of the New Testament Epistles," *IBS* 22 (2000): 71–90.

121 Barr, "Scaleometry," 80.

122 Ibid., 81, 89; Walter A. Elwell and Robert W. Yarbrough, *Encountering the New Testament: A Historical and Theological Survey* (Baker, 1998), 371 (A.D. 60–80); Duane Frederick Watson, *The Letter of Jude*, NIB 12 (Abingdon Press, 1998), 474 (ca. A.D. 50–60); Knoch, *Judasbrief*, 158, considers between A.D. 70 and 90 a possibility. Lee Martin McDonald and Stanley E. Porter are undecided but appear to favor authenticity and a date between A.D. 50 and 80 (*Early Christianity and Its Sacred Literature* [Hendrickson, 2000], 542).

123 Bateman, *Jude*, 19-26.

124 Bauckham, "Jude's Exegesis," 179–234; Ellis, "Prophecy and Hermeneutic in Jude," 221–6; Green, *Jude and 2 Peter*, 13.

125 Bauckham, *Jude, 2 Peter*, 7, 87, 116; idem, "Survey of Research," 136–7; Brown, *Introduction*, 753, 757.

126 Bauckham, "Survey of Research," 161–2; Brown, *Introduction*, 757; Paul J. Achtemeier, Joel B. Green, and Marianne Meyer Thompson, *Introducing the New Testament: Its Literature and Theology* (Eerdmans, 2001), 533.

Finally, the assumption that first-century Galilean Jews were incapable of writing Greek with rhetorical skill neglects the dissenting body of evidence growing out of Galilean archaeology. Herod Antipas' first-century urbaniza-tion campaigns at Tiberias and Sepphoris in Lower Galilee may have suc-ceeded in subtly injecting Hellenistic culture into otherwise intolerant Jewish circles.[127] The overtly Greek cities Tiberias and Sepphoris do not necessari-ly represent Hellenism superimposed on a Jewish heartland; both locations may have grown partly out of the changing complexion of Judaism itself, re-flecting emergent cultural and political changes within the nation.[128] Statis-tical surveys of epigraphic remains found at sights along the western shore of the Sea of Galilee and into the heart of Lower Galilee reveal that "Greek inscriptions are virtually all Jewish" in content, indicating that Jews in Low-er Galilee were likely trilingual in Hebrew, Aramaic, and Greek.[129] Within an hour's walk of Nazareth stood Sepphoris, a Hellenistic administrative center settled by the Seleucids, occupied by Rome,[130] and rebuilt by Antipas in A.D. 4 to serve as the hub for central Galilean Hellenistic urbanization.[131] Situated between a pivotal trade route (*Via Maris*)[132] and Sepphoris, the most promi-nent *polis* apart from Tiberias, Nazareth would have certainly fallen under the jurisdiction and social influence of Antipas' first capital city.[133] The cumulative evidence reveals that rural Galilean villages such as Nazareth were profound-ly affected by these two powerful centers of Roman urbanization. It is unlike-ly that anyone living in Lower Galilee could have escaped the cultural influ-ence of Sepphoris or Tiberias.[134] The simple implication is that the ignorance

127 Michael Avi-Yonah, "The Foundation of Tiberias," *IEJ* 1, no. 3 (1950–1951): 161.

128 Martin Hengel, *Judaism and Hellenism*, trans. John Bowden (Fortress Press, 1974), 103–6.

129 Eric M. Meyers, "Galilean Regionalism as a Factor in Historical Reconstruction," *BA-SOR* 221 (1976): 97. Cf. Hengel, *Judaism and Hellenism*, 58–65; Stanley E. Porter, "Jesus and the Use of Greek in Galilee," in *Studying the Historical Jesus: Evaluations of the State of Current Re-search*, ed. Bruce Chilton and Craig A. Evans (E. J. Brill, 1994), 137–47.

130 In 57 B.C. Pompey's Syrian legate Gabinius divided Palestine into five districts gov-erned by five councils (συνέδρια). Among the five, Sepphoris was designated the Galilean cap-ital. See Josephus, *Jewish Antiquities* 14.91; Carol Meyers and Eric Meyers, "Sepphoris," *OEANE* 4:529–30.

131 Richard A. Horsley, *Archaeology, History, and Society in Galilee: The Social Context of Je-sus and the Rabbis* (Trinity Press International, 1996), 47–52; Neil Asher Silberman, "Searching for Jesus: The Politics of First-Century Judea," *Arch* 47, no. 6 (1994): 37; Richard A. Batey, *Jesus and the Forgotten City: New Light on Sepphoris and the Urban World of Jesus* (Baker, 1991), 11–4. Note in particular the dramatic aerial view of Sepphoris from modern Nazareth on pages 15–6.

132 Yohanan Aharoni, *The Land of the Bible: A Historical Geography* (Westminster Press, 1979), 52–3; Eric Meyers and James Strange, *Archaeology, the Rabbis, and Early Christianity* (Abingdon Press, 1981), 43.

133 James Strange, "Nazareth," *OEANE* 4:113.

134 Seán Freyne, "The Geography, Politics, and Economics of Galilee and the Quest for the Historical Jesus," in *Studying the Historical Jesus: Evaluations of the State of Current Research*,

and "isolation that one often associates with the Galilean personality, then, can hardly be supported by the evidence."[135] As Watson has noted, "Having an elementary education (which included rhetorical training), hearing weekly exposition of the Old Testament in the synagogue, living in Galilee (an area dotted with Greek-speaking cities), and needing to increase proficiency in Greek to effectively preach to Greek audiences would have gone a long way toward explaining how Jesus' brother could come to possess competency" in rhetorical Greek.[136]

According to Bauckham, Jude is not only the genuine work of the Lord's brother and "among the earliest of the New Testament documents,"[137] but the missionary efforts of Jesus' relatives (1 Cor 9:5) can also "be given a considerable amount of theological content from careful study of the letter."[138] Traditions found in the NT, the early Fathers, and Rabbinic literature combine to depict the relatives of Jesus, including Jude, as the most venerated patriarchs of early Palestinian Jewish Christianity.[139] According to a letter from Julius Africanus (ca. A.D. 160–240) preserved by Eusebius (ca. 260–339), Jesus' missionary relatives traveled throughout Palestine expounding the Messianic implications of Jesus' genealogy.[140] Precise parallel allusions to 1 Enoch's apocalyptic sabbatical structure found in both Jude and the Lukan genealogy reveal that both come from the first generation of Jesus' relatives.[141] Jude is not, therefore, merely an authentic letter from the brother of Jesus, but documentary evidence of the earliest pristine "theological foundations on which all subsequent Christianity was built."[142]

The ambiguity of Jude's address, τοῖς ... κλητοῖς ("to ... the called"), leaves the letter's destination up to educated guesswork.[143] That Clement (ca. A.D. 215) cited Jude as Scripture[144] and may have composed a commentary on the

---

ed. Bruce Chilton and Craig A. Evans (E. J. Brill, 1994), 84.

135 Meyers, "Galilean Regionalism," 95.

136 Watson, *Letter of Jude*, 474; Knoch, *Judasbrief*, 161; Green, *Jude and 2 Peter*, 8.

137 Bauckham, "Survey of Research," 178.

138 Richard J. Bauckham, "Introduction," in *Jude and the Relatives of Jesus in the Early Church* (T&T Clark, 1990), 3.

139 Richard J. Bauckham, "The Relatives of Jesus in the Early Church," in *Jude and the Relatives of Jesus in the Early Church* (T&T Clark, 1990), 45–133.

140 Eusebius, *Ecclesiastical History* 1.7.14.

141 Richard J. Bauckham, "The Lukan Genealogy of Jesus," in *Jude and the Relatives of Jesus in the Early Church* (T&T Clark, 1990), 313–63. Cf. Jude 6 and 1 Enoch 10:12.

142 Richard J. Bauckham, "Conclusion," in *Jude and the Relatives of Jesus in the Early Church* (T&T Clark, 1990), 376.

143 Bauckham, *Jude, 2 Peter*, 16; Knoch, for example, only admits that Jude was intended for Hellenized Jewish Christians anywhere in Palestine, Syria, Egypt, or Asia Minor who revered the authority of Jesus' brothers (*Judasbrief*, 158).

144 Clement, *Paedagogus* 3.8.44: Εἰδέναι γὰρ ὑμᾶς›, φησὶν ὁ Ἰούδας, ‹‹ βούλομαι, ὅτι ὁ θεὸς ἅπαξ ἐκ γῆς Αἰγύπτου λαὸν σώσας τὸ δεύτερον τοὺς μὴ πιστεύσαντας ἀπώλεσεν ("For I want you

letter[145] has led some to assert an Alexandrian provenance.[146] Internal evidence such as Jewish tradition material, exegetical method, apocalyptic imagery, and the prominence of Jesus' brothers favors a Jewish Christian audience in Palestine. The antinomian and angeology problems, however, sound related to issues confronted by Paul in Hellenistic Colossae. The combined evidence suggests a "Jewish Christian community in a Gentile society"[147] or a heterogeneous congregation somewhere between Jerusalem and Asia Minor.[148]

Opponents

The majority opinion in the history of research describes Jude's adversaries as proponents of specific Gnostic sects[149] or libertine Gnosticism in general.[150] Their denial of Christ (v. 4), rebellion against authority (v. 8), and contempt for angels (v. 8), could be easily interpreted to reflect docetic Christology,[151] rebellion against the subordinate Demiurge,[152] and disdain for evil archons.[153] This majority interpretation continues in recent works where it is all but assumed from the outset that Jude represents an early Catholic response to

---

to know,' says Jude, 'that God, having once saved the people from Egypt, later destroyed those who did not believe' " (my translation). The Greek text for Clement comes from *Le Pédagogue*, Sources Chrétiennes, ed. Claude Mondésert, Chantal Matray, and Henri-Irénéne Marrou, no. 158, Livre 3 (Les Éditions du Cerf, 1970).

145 Eusebius, *Ecclesiastical History* 6.14.1: Clement "has given abridged narrations of all the canonical writings, not even neglecting the disputed books, including Jude and the rest of the catholic epistles" (Oulton and Lawlor, LCL). See James A. Brooks, "Clement of Alexandria as a Witness to the Development of the New Testament Canon," *SecCent* 9, no. 1 (1992): 44.

146 Paulsen, *Judasbrief*, 45; Neyrey, 2 *Peter, Jude*, 30. Gunther assumes from the outset that Jude attacked a mature libertine Gnosticism identified as the Alexandrian Carpocratian heresy. Justus, Bishop of Alexandria (ca. A.D. 125), therefore penned the letter pseudonomously to combat a distinct Egyptian error ("Alexandrian Epistle of Jude," 549–58).

147 Bauckham, *Jude, 2 Peter*, 16; Vögtle, *Judasbrief*, 12; Schnelle, *New Testament Writings*, 419. Cf. Hahn, "Randbemerkungen zum Judasbrief," 216; Schelkle, *Judasbrief*, 137.

148 Grundmann, *Brief des Judas*, 17–9; Brown, *Introduction*, 756; Seethaler, *Judasbrief*, 126–7; Heiligenthal describes them as "Jewish Christian Pharisees" (*Zwischen Henoch und Paulus*, 89–94).

149 Cf. for examples James Vernon Bartlet, *The Apostolic Age: Its Life, Doctrine, Worship and Polity* (Charles Scribner's Sons, 1899), 346–7 (Nicolaitans); Thomas Barns, "The Epistle of St Jude: A Study in the Marcosian Heresy," *JTS* 6, no. 23 (1905): 391–411.

150 Jülicher, *Introduction*, 230–1; Taylor, "The Message of the Epistles: Second Peter and Jude," 438–9; Schrage, *Judas Brief*, 223–5; Helmut Koester, *History and Literature of Early Christianity*, vol. 2 of *Introduction to the New Testament* (Walter de Gruyter, 1982), 246–7; Kümmel, *Introduction*, 426; Grundmann, *Brief des Judas*, 18; Vielhauer, *Geschichte*, 590–1; Schelkle, *Judasbrief*, 230–4; Kelly, *Jude*, 284–5; Hahn, "Randbemerkungen zum Judasbrief," 213.

151 Green, *Jude*, 162.

152 Otto Pfleiderer, *Primitive Christianity: Its Writings and Teachings in Their Historical Connections*, trans. W. Montgomery (G. P. Putman, 1911), 4:251; Grundmann, *Brief des Judas*, 30.

153 Frederic W. Farrar, *The Early Days of Christianity*, 3rd ed. (Cassell, Petter, Galpin, 1882), 1:242–3.

developed Gnosticism.[154] Paula-Angelika Seethaler, for example, finds Gnostic technical terminology in Jude's distinction between his faithful audience and the intruding ψυχικοί ("worldly") who do not have the πνεῦμα ("Spirit," v. 19). Such language in Gnostic parlance described those who had acquired an enlightened spirituality (πνεῦμα) that elevated them above mundane Christians (ψυχικοί) and freed them from the "worldly-minded" constraints suffered by the less astute.[155]

The charismatic and antinomian characteristics of Jude's opponents have also been viewed as aberrations of Pauline theology.[156] Paul himself confronted abuses of Christian freedom,[157] and charismatic pride flared up in both Corinth and Colossae.[158] A flawed application of Christ's preeminence over angelic power[159] could have inspired contempt for celestial authority of the type opposed by Jude. Such possible connections have led to descriptions of Jude's opponents in terms of post-Pauline libertines,[160] the "same deviant Hebraists who have disturbed Paul's churches,"[161] or "antinomian proto-gnostics" who arrived at their beliefs "through a distortion of the Pauline understanding of salvation."[162]

Certain exegetes unwilling to identify the opponent's with Gnosticism, Paulinism, or a combination of the two have developed speculative new proposals. According to Frederick Wisse, Jude has no specific audience in view and "there are no historical references in the description of the opponents."[163] Jude only intends to encourage vigilance against general representations of eschatological false teaching.[164] To suggest, however, that Jude warned against the threat of future deception without reference to error in his audience's

---

154 Paula-Angelika Seethaler, "Kleine Bemerkungen zum Judasbrief," *BZ* 31, no. 2 (1987): 262; idem, *Judasbrief*, 127; Frankemölle, *Judasbrief*, 125; Gunther, "Alexandrian Epistle of Jude," 549–58.

155 Seethaler, "Kleine Bemerkungen," 262. Cf. Kelly, *Jude*, 284–5.

156 Zahn, *Introduction*, 279–83; Heiligenthal, *Zwischen Henoch und Paulus*, 10, 140–50; Cantinat, "L'épître de Jude," 281; Fuchs and Reymond, *Jude*, 143; Bauckham, *Jude, 2 Peter*, 12; Peter Müller, "Judasbrief," 283–5; cf. Gerhard Sellin, "Die Häretiker des Judasbriefes," *ZNW* 77 (1986): 224–5, who identifies the theology and practice of Jude's opponents with the theology defended by Paul in Colossians.

157 Cf. Rom 3:8; 6:1, 15; Gal 5:13.

158 Cf. 1 Cor 2:13–16; 2 Cor 12:1–3; Col 2:18.

159 Cf. Rom 8:38; Col 1:16; 2:16–18.

160 Ulrich B. Müller, *Zur frühchristlichen Theologiegeschichte* (Gütersloher Verlagshaus Mohn, 1976), 24.

161 Ellis, "Prophecy and Hermeneutic in Jude," 235; Fuchs and Reymond, *Jude*, 143.

162 Douglas James Rowston, "The Setting of the Letter of Jude" (Th.D. diss., Southern Baptist Theological Seminary, 1971), 34.

163 Wisse, "The Epistle of Jude in the History of Heresiology," 134–5, 142.

164 Ibid., 142.

present circumstance is to miss the point of the epistle entirely.[165] Michel Desjardins' study reverses the roles completely, depicting Jude as an "Orwellian" isolationist confronted by progressive Christian realists. According to Desjardins, the author of Jude was in fact an ascetic autocrat guilty of condemning a dissident leadership whose only real error was the attempt to "domesticate" the faith. Jude merely exaggerated accusations against those who, embarrassed by the delay of the parousia, were in the "process of setting their faith in a *domus* larger than their community, a process which in many respects must have been as painful for them" as it was for Jude.[166]

More cautious recent studies essentially abandon the effort to equate Jude's opponents with a specific sect from theological history,[167] attempting instead to characterize them primarily by the textual indicators. Vögtle concludes that Jude confronted nonconforming elitists who denied Christ's judgmental parousia and who were convinced that charismatic prowess exempted them from moral constraint.[168] Regardless of what specific philosophical or theological category might be advanced to describe Jude's opponents, Ferdinand Hahn determines that their greed and immorality follow a pattern typical of godless intruders throughout sacred history.[169] According to Bauckham, their "antinomianism and rejection of moral constraints" is the key concern against which "all of Jude's argument is directed."[170] Their error is not doctrinal but ethical, a fundamental rejection of all moral authority as represented by the Law of Moses (vv. 8–10), angelic guardians of the moral order (vv. 8–10), and Christ himself (v. 4). As newcomer itinerants (v. 4) possessing charismatic gifts (v. 8), they abuse their apparent leadership roles for personal gain (vv. 11–13, 16). They twisted grace into a "deliverance from all external moral constraint, so that the person who possesses the Spirit ... becomes the only judge of his or her own actions, subject to no other authority." After assembling the evidence, though it does not prove a definitive connection, Bauckham acknowledges the potential parallels between Jude's opponents and distortions of Pauline teaching.[171]

While Bauckham's treatment fairly and accurately addresses the textual specifics without recourse to the old early Catholic template, his rigid

---

165 Bauckham, "Survey of Research," 167.
166 Michel Desjardins, "The Portrayal of the Dissidents in 2 Peter and Jude: Does It Tell Us More about the 'Godly' Than the 'Ungodly?'" *JSNT* 30 (1987): 95–9.
167 See, however, Bateman's lengthy and well documented argument that Jude confronts the Zealot or Sicarri revolutionaries aggitating for war with Rome in the A.D. 60s (*Jude*, 51–80).
168 Vögtle, *Judasbrief,* 3, 95–8.
169 Hahn, "Randbemerkungen zum Judasbrief," 215.
170 Bauckham, "Survey of Research," 166.
171 Ibid., 167–8.

distinction between ethics and doctrine seems unnecessarily reactionary. He asserts that Jude's is a "controversy about antinomian teaching rather than about doctrine,"[172] but repeatedly points to the "message of the false teachers" and their "antinomian doctrine."[173] This confusing dichotomy between the cognitive and behavioral aspects of the faith fails to clarify in what sense antinomians could actually teach and yet avoid doctrine. Doctrine forms the "necessary and essential background for the interpretation and application of Christian ethics."[174] That Jude's opponents could teach a flawed ethic in the name of Christ exposes a fundamental error in their doctrinal[175] understanding of Christianity. By condemning immorality Jude was in fact correcting its interdependent theology.

CONCLUSION

The growing body of research dedicated to Jude promises to correct its lengthy history of neglect and misunderstanding. Daunting problems at certain points in Jude's textual history continue to stir scholarly attention, and it is unlikely that the three clause/two clause debate at vv. 22–23a will ever reach a unilateral consensus. Among rational eclectics, the combined weight of Sinaiticus and Alexandrinus in favor of three clauses will probably continue to dominate printed texts. Careful analyses of Jude's tradition material and rhetorical composition are rightfully discrediting the older skepticism regarding Jude's artistry and authenticity. The technique of employing ancient apocalyptic materials woven together with a characteristically Jewish exegetical method favors a very early Jewish, Christian, Palestinian provenance. Jude's demand for doctrinal and ethical purity reflects a first-century missionary emphasis better attested by Paul than second-century early Catholicism. Insights into the matrix of first-century Galilean Judaism further substantiates the conclusion that Jude the half-brother of Jesus penned this short, brilliantly conceived, epistle in order to combat an influx of itinerant antinomian syncretists.

---

172 Bauckham, "Survey of Research," 177.

173 Bauckham, *Jude, 2 Peter*, 113–5.

174 James Leo Garrett, *Systematic Theology: Biblical, Historical, Evangelical*, 2nd ed., vol. 1 (Bibal Press, 2000), 14; Alister McGrath, *Understanding Doctrine: What It Is, and Why It Matters* (Zondervan, 1990), 90–8. Without its doctrinal foundation "Christian ethics remain hanging in mid-air" (Hendrikus Berkhof, *Christian Faith: An Introduction to the Study of the Faith*, trans. Sierd Woudstra [Eerdmans, 1979], 501).

175 "The error had both a theological and moral component," (Green, *Jude and 2 Peter*, 18).

CHAPTER 2

APOCALYPTIC ESCHATOLOGY IN
JUDAISM AND EARLY CHRISTIANITY

T HE PROBLEM OF TERMINOLOGY in "apocalyptic" studies has been
documented at length.[1] "Apocalyptic" has been used both as a noun
and an adjective, sometimes in the same context,[2] to describe literary and theological phenomena that no two scholars define alike. Within the
scholarly debate "crosswinds" of opinion can be "violent:"

> The degree of conflict is indicative of the chaotic state of historical and
> theological scholarship where apocalyptic is concerned. Premises are
> rarely shared; definitions often diverge; significance is variously assessed.
> Few other themes, perhaps, open the seams in the historical and theolog-
> ical fabric so readily and so completely.[3]

Friedrich Lücke inadvertently precipitated a terminological morass[4] by

1 Margaret Barker, "Slippery Words, III. Apocalyptic, *ExpTim* 89, no. 11 (1978): 324–9; T.
Francis Glasson, "What is Apocalyptic?" *NTS* 27, no. 1 (1980): 98–105; Robert L. Webb, "'Apocalyptic:' Observations on a Slippery Term," *JNES* 49, no. 2 (1990): 115–26; Michael A. Knibb,
"Prophecy and the Emergence of the Jewish Apocalypses," in *Israel's Prophetic Tradition: Es-
says in Honour of Peter R. Ackroyd*, ed. Richard Coggins, Anthony Phillips, and Michael Knibb
(Cambridge University Press, 1982), 155–80; Richard E. Sturm, "Defining the Word 'Apocalyptic:' A Problem in Biblical Criticism," in *Apocalyptic and the New Testament*, ed. Joel Marcus
and Marion L. Soards, JSNTSup 24 (Sheffield Academic Press, 1989), 17–48; Charles D. Myers
Jr., "The Persistence of Apocalyptic Though in New Testament Theology," in *Biblical Theology:
Problems and Perspectives*, ed. Steven J. Kraftchick, Charles D. Myers Jr., and Ben. C. Ollenburger (Abingdon, 1995), 211.
2 See for examples Klaus Koch, *The Rediscovery of Apocalyptic*, trans. Margaret Kohl, SBT,
Second Series, 22 (Alec R. Allenson, 1970), 18; D. S. Russell, *The Method and Message of Jewish
Apocalyptic: 200 BC–AD 100*, OTL (Westminster Press, 1964), 104; Paul D. Hanson, "Prolegomena
to the Study of Jewish Apocalyptic," in *Magnalia Dei: The Mighty Acts of God*, ed. Frank Moore
Cross, Werner E. Lemke, and Patrick D. Miller Jr. (Doubleday and Company, 1976), 389.
3 Robert W. Funk, ed., *Apocalypticism* (Herder and Herder, 1969), 13.
4 According to Walter Schmithals, "We can credit Friedrich Lücke with having established

employing the transliteration of ἀποκάλυψις derivatively to describe a literary genre (*Apokalypse*, "apocalypse"), a theological concept (*Apokalyptik*, "apocalyptic"), and the nature of their relationship (*apokalyptischen*, "apocalyptical").[5] By focusing almost entirely on genre, however, Lücke failed to adequately integrate or differentiate his study of literary character and theological concept.[6] Descriptions of apocalyptic have since ranged from very specific literary definitions[7] to very ambiguous theological "impressions" or "moods."[8]

Ongoing scholarly revisions of the terminology provide a serviceable, though tenuous, heuristic device by distinguishing between apocalypse (genre) and apocalyptic eschatology (worldview).[9]

APOCALYPSE

In Rev 1:1 John described the contents of his book as ἀποκάλυψις, a "revelation" or "uncovering." Though the term never appears again in Revelation, and John himself preferred to describe his work as προφητεία ("prophecy," 1:3; 22:7, 10, 18–19), the title Ἀποκάλυψις Ἰωάννου ("Apocalypse of John") was permanently

---

the independent investigation of apocalyptic" (*The Apocalyptic Movement: Introduction and Interpretation*, trans. John E. Steely [Abingdon Press, 1975], 52). Glasson rejects the term altogether as a "useless word which no one can define and which produces nothing but confusion and acres of verbiage" ("What is Apocalyptic?" 105).

5 Friedrich Lücke, *Versuch einer vollständigen Einleitung in die Offenbarung des Johannes oder allgemeine Untersuchungen über die apokalyptische Literatur überhaupt und die Apokalypse des Johannes insbesondere* (Eduard Weber, 1852), 17–25.

6 Sturm, "Defining the Word 'Apocalyptic,'" 18–9.

7 John J. Collins, "Introduction: Towards the Morphology of a Genre," in *Apocalypse: The Morphology of a Genre*, Semeia 14 (Society of Biblical Literature, 1979), 9.

8 Russell, *Method and Message*, 104–5.

9 For this two pronged categorization see Philipp Vielhauer, "Introduction," in *New Testament Apocrypha*, ed. R. McL. Wilson (Westminster Press, 1964), 2:582; Gerhard Ebeling, "The Ground of Christian Theology," in *Apocalypticism*, ed. Robert W. Funk (Herder and Herder, 1969), 52; Hans Dieter Betz, "On the Problem of the Religio-Historical Understanding of Apocalypticism," Ibid., 135; Michael E. Stone, "Lists of Revealed Things in the Apocalyptic Literature," in *Magnalia Dei, the Mighty Acts of God: Essays on the Bible and Archaeology in Memory of G. Ernest Wright*, ed. Frank Moore Cross, Werner E. Lemke, and Patrick D. Miller Jr. (Doubleday, 1976), 439–44; Myers, "Persistence of Apocalyptic Thought," 210. Cf., however, those who include a third category, "apocalypticism" (socio-ideological movement): Paul D. Hanson, "Apocalypticism," in *IDBSup*, ed. Keith Crim (Abindgon Press, 1984), 29–30; idem, *The Dawn of Apocalyptic: The Historical and Sociological Roots of Jewish Apocalyptic Eschatology*, rev. ed. (Fortress Press, 1979), 429; John J. Collins, *The Apocalyptic Imagination: An Introduction to Jewish Apocalyptic Literature*, 2nd ed. (Eerdmans, 1998), 2–11; idem, "Apocalypses and Apocalypticism: Early Jewish Apocalypticism," *ABD* 1:282–88; David E. Aune, *Prophecy in Early Christianity and the Ancient Mediterranean World* (Eerdmans, 1983), 107; Larry J. Kreitzer, "Apocalyptic, Apocalypticism," in *DLNT*, ed. Ralph P. Martin and Peter H. Davids (InterVarsity Press, 1997), 55–68.

affixed to the document by the second century A.D.[10] Prior to this NT example, no texts describe themselves or their contents as ἀποκάλυψις;[11] afterward the title was applied by Christians to a vast body of Jewish and Christian material that resembled canonical Revelation.[12] Despite the absence of the title ἀποκάλυψις before its appearance in Rev 1:1, the genre designation "apocalypse" is consistently used to describe a corpus of Jewish and Christian literature that adheres loosely to a rather complex formal definition. In 1979 the Apocalypse Group of the Society of Biblical Literature's Genres Project published the results of their three year seminar in *Apocalypse: The Morphology of a Genre*.[13] The group's proposed definition of the apocalypse genre continues to define the basic parameters of discussion[14] by addressing issues of both form and content:

> "Apocalypse" is a genre of revelatory literature with a narrative framework, in which a revelation is mediated by an otherworldly being to a human recipient, disclosing a transcendent reality which is both temporal, insofar as it envisages eschatological salvation, and spatial insofar as it involves another, supernatural world.[15]

In 1986 the SBL published *Early Christian Apocalypticism: Genre and Social Setting*[16] as an extension of the earlier genre seminar and added to the "apocalypse" definition an amendment specifying matters of function. An apocalypse is "intended to interpret present, earthly circumstances in light of the supernatural world and of the future, and to influence both the understanding and the behavior of the audience by means of divine authority."[17] Despite

10 David E. Aune, *Revelation 1–5*, WBC 52 (Word, 1997), 4, 12. See Bruce Metzger's translation of the second-century Muratorian fragment, lines 57–58 and 71 (*Canon of the New Testament*, 307).

11 Morton Smith, "On the history of ΑΠΟΚΑΛΥΠΤΩ and ΑΠΟΚΑΛΥΠΨΙΣ," in *AMWNE*, ed. David Hellholm (J. C. B Mohr [Paul Siebeck] 1983), 14, 18.

12 Vielhauer, "Introduction," 582; Collins, "Early Jewish Apocalypticism," 283.

13 John J. Collins, ed., *Apocalypse: The Morphology of a Genre*, Semeia 14 (Society of Biblical Literature, 1979).

14 Cf. Paul D. Hanson, "Apocalypses and Apocalypticism: The Genre," *ABD* 1:279; David Hellholm, "The Problem of Apocalyptic Genre and the Apocalypse of John," in *Early Christian Apocalypticism: Genre and Social Setting*, ed. Adela Yarbro Collins, Semeia 36 (Scholars Press, 1986), 27; David E. Aune, "The Apocalypse of John and the Problem of Genre," Ibid., 68–70.

15 Collins, "Introduction: Towards the Morphology of a Genre," 9.

16 Adela Yarbro Collins, ed., *Early Christian Apocalypticism: Genre and Social Setting*, Semeia 36 (Scholars Press, 1986).

17 Adela Yarbro Collins, "Introduction: Early Christian Apocalypticism," in *Early Christian Apocalypticism: Genre and Social Setting*, Semeia 36 (Scholars Press, 1986), 7; Hellholm, "The Problem of Apocalyptic Genre," 27; Aune, "The Apocalypse of John and the Problem of Genre," 87.

these advances in formal definition, lists of works that meet these criteria remain fluid and "ill-defined."[18] The bulk of the material is pseudepigraphal, written roughly between the third century B.C. and the second century A.D. In addition to 1 Enoch, 4 Ezra, and 2 Baruch, most lists include a wide range of Jewish and Christian texts.[19] From the biblical material, only Daniel and Revelation are technically categorized as apocalypses.[20]

The SBL's restricted focus on the definable apocalypse genre does not negate the fact that apocalyptic phenomena appear in much broader literary contexts. The adjective "apocalyptic" characterizes themes "typical of apocalypses, even when they occur elsewhere."[21] Though, for example, the Qumran community composed no apocalypses, its literature does reflect a worldview compatible with the genre.[22] Apocalyptic themes also appear in certain OT texts and throughout most of the NT.[23] Isaiah 24–27, 34–35, 56–66, and Zechariah 9–14 are often identified as apocalyptic or proto-apocalyptic literature.[24]

18 Collins, "Introduction: Towards the Morphology of a Genre," 3.

19 Cf. Koch, *Rediscovery*, 23; H. H. Rowley, *The Relevance of Apocalyptic: A Study of Jewish and Christian Apocalypses from Daniel to the Revelation*, rev. ed. (Lutterworth Press, 1963), vi; Christopher Rowland, *The Open Heaven: A Study of Apocalyptic in Judaism and Early Christianity* (Crossroad, 1982), 14–5; Russell, *Method and Message*, 37–8; John J. Collins, "Apocalyptic Literature," in *Early Judaism and Its Modern Interpreters*, ed. Robert A. Kraft and George W. E. Nickelsburg (Scholars Press, 1986), 346; David E. Aune, *The New Testament in Its Literary Environment* (Westminster Press, 1987), 229–31.

20 Paul D. Hanson, "Apocalypse, genre," in *IDBSup*, ed. Keith Crim (Abingdon Press, 1984), 27–8; John J. Collins, "The Jewish Apocalypses," in *Apocalypse: The Morphology of a Genre*, ed. John J. Collins, Semeia 14 (Society of Biblical Literature, 1979), 30; idem, "The Apocalyptic Context of Christian Origins," in *The Bible and Its Traditions*, ed. Michael P. O'Connor and David N. Freedman, MQR 22, no. 3 (1983): 251; Adela Yarbro Collins, "The Early Christian Apocalypses," in *Apocalypse: The Morphology of a Genre*, ed. John J. Collins, Semeia 14 (Society of Biblical Literature, 1979), 70–2; idem, "Apocalypses and Apocalypticism: Early Christianity," ABD 1:290.

21 John J. Collins, "Was the Dead Sea Sect an Apocalyptic Movement?" in *Seers, Sybils, and Sages in Hellenistic-Roman Judaism*, SJSJ 54, ed. John J. Collins and Florentino García Martínez (E. J. Brill, 1997), 262. Cf. Sturm, "Defining the Word 'Apocalyptic,'" 25.

22 Florentino Garcia Martinez, *Qumran and Apocalyptic: Studies on the Aramaic Texts from Qumran*, STDJ (E. J. Brill, 1992), 9:x–xi; Collins, *Apocalyptic Imagination*, 115–6; 140–1; idem, "Was the Dead Sea Sect an Apocalyptic Movement?" 284–5; Frank Moore Cross, *The Ancient Library of Qumran*, 3rd ed. (Fortress Press, 1995), 68–9, n. 3.

23 Lars Hartman, *Prophecy Interpreted: The Formation of Some Jewish Apocalyptic Texts and of the Eschatological Discourse Mark 13 Par*, trans. Neil Tomkinson and Jean Gray, ConBNT 1 (Boktryckeri Aktiebolag, 1966), 28–49; Elisabeth Schüssler Fiorenza, "The Phenomenon of Early Christian Apocalyptic: Some Reflections on Method," in *AMWNE*, ed. David Hellholm (J. C. B Mohr [Paul Siebeck] 1983), 301; Aune, *Literary Environment*, 231; Leon Morris, *Apocalyptic* (Eerdmans, 1972), 73–4; Collins, "The Apocalyptic Context of Christian Origins," 250–64.

24 Frank Moore Cross, "New Directions in the Study of Apocalyptic," in *Apocalypticism*, ed. Robert W. Funk, Journal for Theology and Church (Herder and Herder, 1969), 6:164–5; Joshua Bloch, *On the Apocalyptic in Judaism*, Jewish Quarterly Review, 11 (Dropsie College, 1952), 25–8; Eibert J. C. Tigchelaar, *Prophets of Old and the Day of the End: Zechariah, the Book of Watchers and Apocalyptic* (E. J. Brill, 1996), 13; Paul D. Hanson, *Old Testament Apocalyptic*, Interpreting Biblical Texts, ed. Lloyd R. Bailey Sr. and Victor P. Furnish (Abingdon Press, 1987),

NT examples include the famed "little apocalypse" pericope of Mark 13 and parallels, various Pauline "apocalyptic scenarios,"[25] and numerous scattered references and presuppositions.[26]

APOCALYPTIC ESCHATOLOGY

Defined simplistically as a "set of ideas and motifs that may also be found in other literary genres,"[27] apocalyptic eschatology describes an "ideological basis,"[28] the core "ideational elements,"[29] a "motif-cluster"[30] common to apocalypses. This loosely defined worldview includes such themes as dualism, God's sovereignty, pessimism, paraenesis, judgment, the intervention of a redeemer/judge, the fate of humanity, and an imminent end.[31]

Apocalyptic eschatology's comprehensive dualism divides the cosmos into good and evil forces,[32] history into two ages,[33] and humanity into the righteous and the wicked.[34] At the forefront of this worldview, however, stands an uncompromising confidence in God's sovereignty over every aspect of reality.[35] Related to the dualistic understanding of reality, apocalyptic thought maintains a pessimistic view of human nature and anticipates the increasing

---

35–8; Robert North, "Prophecy to Apocalyptic via Zechariah," in *VTSup* 22 (E. J. Brill, 1972), 47–71; Collins, "Jewish Apocalypses," 29–30.

25 1 Cor 15:20–28; 1 Thess 4:13–5:11; 2 Thess 2:1–12. Perrin and Duling, *Introduction*, 107–11.

26 Myers, "Persistence of Apocalyptic Thought in New Testament Theology," 211–21.

27 Collins, *Apocalyptic Imagination*, 2.

28 Aune, *Literary Environment*, 238.

29 John G. Gammie, "The Classification, Stages of Growth, and Changing Intentions in the Book of Daniel," *JBL* 95, no. 2 (1976): 193.

30 Fiorenza, "Phenomenon of Early Christian Apocalyptic," 301.

31 For lists and discussions of various attributes see, Emil Schürer, *The History of the Jewish People in the Age of Jesus Christ (175 B.C. – A.D. 135* (T&T Clark, 1979), 2:514–47; David C. Sim, *Apocalyptic Eschatology in the Gospel of Matthew* (Cambridge University Press, 1996), 31–53.

32 1 Enoch 6–9; 40:1–10; 2 Enoch 1:4–9; Jub. 2:2; 5:1–11. "Dualism" as used throughout this context refers simply to a bipartite division and does not include notions of philosophical absolutism.

33 1 Enoch 72:1; 4 Ezra 7:50; 2 Bar. 44:8–15.

34 1 Enoch 5:6; 2 Bar. 24:1; 4 Ezra 7:17; Schmithals, *Apocalyptic Movement*, 20–4; Hanson, *Dawn of Apocalyptic*, 127.

35 Dan 11:36; 4 Ezra 6:1–6; T. Mos. 12:1–8; Vielhauer, "Introduction," 590–2; Koch, *Rediscovery*, 29; D. S. Russell, *Divine Disclosure: An Introduction to Jewish Apocalyptic* (Fortress Press, 1992), 86–91; J. Christian Beker, *Paul's Apocalyptic Gospel: The Coming Triumph of God*, Philadelphia: Fortress Press, 1982), 33; Kurt Schubert, *The Dead Sea Community: Its Origins and Teachings*, trans. John W. Doberstein (Adam and Charles Black, 1959), 61, 80–83; J. T. Milik, *Ten Years of Discovery in the Wilderness of Judaea*, trans. J. Strugnell (SCM Press, 1959), 113–5; William R. Murdock, "History and Revelation in Jewish Apocalypticism," *Int* 21, no. 2 (1967): 167–8. From God "stems all there is and all there shall be. Before [the sons of men] existed he made all their plans and when they came into being they will execute all their works in compliance with his instructions, according to his glorious design without altering anything" (1QS 3.15–17).

dominance of evil just before the end of this age.[36] Apocalyptic eschatology's concern with the future does not neglect paraenesis (authoritative moral instruction),[37] demanding instead that the ruling principles of the coming age must "break into the present."[38] At the end of this present evil age, apocalyptic eschatology expects a redeemer/judge figure to intervene, inaugurate God's eternal rule over the cosmos,[39] and execute a final judgment that disseminates reward to the righteous and punishment to the wicked.[40] The expectation of an imminent denouement extant in apocalyptic literature[41] was balanced in the NT by an eschatological prolepsis.[42] Jesus' death and resurrection redefined Jewish interpretations of God's present and future redemptive purposes[43] by inaugurating in part the "age to come"[44] and foreshadowing the redemptive and judgmental second phase of a "two-stage consummation."[45] Apocalyptic eschatology in the NT recognizes in Jesus the embodiment of God's eschatological message: the Redeemer/Judge has come, and he has

---

36 1 Enoch 93:9–10; 4 Ezra 9:14–25; T. Jud. 23:3–4; Jub. 23:14–23; Vielhauer, "Introduction," 589–90; Rowley, *Relevance*, 171; Sim, *Apocalyptic Eschatology*, 42–3.

37 Jürgen C. H. Lebram, "The Piety of the Jewish Apocalyptists," in *AMWNE*, ed. David Hellholm (J. C. B Mohr [Paul Siebeck] 1983), 178–207.

38 1 Enoch 5:4; 94:1–5; 2 Bar. 84:8–9; 4 Ezra 14:27–36; Rowley, *Relevance*, 38; Koch, *Rediscovery*, 25–6; Stephenson Humphries-Brooks, "Apocalyptic Paraenesis in Matthew 6:19–34," in *Apocalyptic and the New Testament*, ed. Joel Marcus and Marion L. Soards, JSNTSup 24 (Sheffield Academic Press, 1989), 95–112.

39 Koch, *Rediscovery*, 31–2; Rowley, *Relevance*, 182; Schürer, *History of the Jewish People*, 517–24; Fiorenza, "Phenomenon of Early Christian Apocalyptic," 300; Sim, *Apocalyptic Eschatology*, 43–5. Cf. Richard B. Hays, "'The Righteous One' as Eschatological Deliverer: A Case Study in Paul's Apocalyptic Hermeneutics," in *Apocalyptic and the New Testament*, ed. Joel Marcus and Marion L. Soards, JSNTSup 24 (Sheffield Academic Press, 1989), 191–215.

40 1 Enoch 1:3–9; 46:3–5; 2 Bar. 29:3; Sib. Or. 3:670–700; Pss. Sol. 17:21–44; Schürer, *History of the Jewish People*, 526–9; Hanson, *Dawn of Apocalyptic*, 160–1, 185; Collins, "Introduction: Towards the Morphology of a Genre," 7; Sim, *Apocalyptic Eschatology*, 45–7; Rowley, *Relevance*, 189–91; Rowland, *Open Heaven*, 158–9; Aune, *Literary Environment*, 238–9.

41 Rev 1:1–3; 22:6–7, 10, 12; 1 Enoch 94:6–7; 4 Ezra 4:50; 2 Bar. 85:10.

42 Brown, *Introduction*, 775; Leander E. Keck, "Paul and Apocalyptic Theology," *Int* 38, no. 3 (1984): 236.

43 N. T. Wright, *The New Testament and the People of God*, Christian Origins and the Question of God 1 (Fortress Press, 1992), 446; idem, *Jesus and the Victory of God*, Christian Origins and the Question of God 2 (Fortress Press, 1996), 473–4; Marcus J. Borg and N. T. Wright, *The Meaning of Jesus: Two Visions* (Harper San Francisco, 1999), 202–3; J. Louis Martyn, "Apocalyptic Antinomies in Paul's Letter to the Galatians," *NTS* 31, no. 3 (1985): 421; J. Christian Beker, *Paul the Apostle: The Triumph of God in Life and Thought* (Fortress Press, 1980), 19–21; idem, *Paul's Apocalyptic Gospel*, 29–53.

44 Kümmel, *Theology of the New Testament*, 36–9; E. Earle Ellis, "Present and Future Eschatology in Luke," *NTS* 12 (1965): 40–1.

45 E. Earle Ellis, *The Old Testament in Early Christianity: Canon and Interpretation in the Light of Modern Research* (Baker Book House, 1991), 103; Werner Georg Kümmel, *Promise and Fulfillment: The Eschatological Message of Jesus*, trans. Dorothea M. Barton (SCM Press, 1961), 154–5; George Eldon Ladd, *The Presence of the Future: The Eschatology of Biblical Realism* (Eerdmans, 1974), 331–9.

come to reconfigure Israel's worldview, replacing their ethno-religious symbols of hope with himself.[46]

Because of its revelatory nature,[47] the theological content of apocalyptic eschatology is not presented as the summary result of tradition, reason, or speculation.[48] Apocalyptic eschatology "purports to be 'revealed' eschatology— revealed, that is, by God."[49] Apocalypses "do not take the stance of a neutral observer, but take and urge a very definite point of view. . . apocalyptic language is *commissive* in character: it commits us to a view of the world for the sake of the actions and attitudes that are entailed."[50] Imbedded in the direct revelation is an implicit claim to divine authority.[51] John, for example, must write exactly what he sees (Rev 1:11): a specific word from the Spirit of God that must be obeyed (2:7) and preserved from corruption (22:18).[52] Such revelation, by definition, is not expressed as the product of religious opinion. Revelation is the "sole epistemic norm of theology,"[53] the historical and propositional[54] objectification of ultimate reality.[55] Apocalyptic eschatology holds the "conviction that God has now given to the elect true perception both of present developments (the real world) and of a wondrous transformation in the near future."[56]

PLURALISTIC CONTEXT

Apocalyptic literature and its complementary eschatological outlook flourishes

46 Wright, *Christian Origins and the Question of God*, 1:224–32; ibid., 2:473–4.

47 See Aune's discussion of "Revelatory Formulas and Genres" (*Prophecy in Early Christianity*, 114–21).

48 Rowland, *Open Heaven*, 1–3; John J. Collins, "From Prophecy to Apocalypticism: The Expectation of the End," in *The Origins of Apocalypticism in Judaism and Christianity*, vol. 1 of *The Encyclopedia of Apocalypticism*, ed. John J. Collins (The Continuum Publishing Company, 1998), 157.

49 Martinus C. de Boer, *The Defeat of Death: Apocalyptic Eschatology in 1 Corinthians 15 and Romans 5*, JSNTSup 22 (JSOT Press, 1988), 21.

50 Collins, *Apocalyptic Imagination*, 215.

51 William Adler, "Introduction," in *The Jewish Apocalyptic Heritage in Early Christianity*, ed. James C. VanderKam and William Adler (Fortress Press, 1996), 20.

52 Ibid.; Rowland, *Open Heaven*, 20.

53 W. P. Abraham, "Epistemology, Religious," in *BEMCT*, ed. Alister E. McGrath (Basil Blackwell, 1993), 158.

54 Richard Swinburne, "Revelation," *Routledge Encyclopedia of Philosophy* 8:297–300.

55 Schmithals, *Apocalyptic Movement*, 71. Cf. John B. Webster, "Revelation, Concept of," in *BEMCT*, ed. Alister E. McGrath (Basil Blackwell, 1993), 557–61. Cf. John Hick, "Revelation," in *The Encyclopedia of Philosophy*, ed. Paul Edwards (MacMillan and the Free Press, 1967), 7:189–91.

56 Martyn, "Apocalyptic Antinomies," 424, n. 28.

36   Jude's Apocalyptic Eschatology as Theological Exclusivism

primarily in the context of crisis.[57] Across the historical spectrum from Isaiah to Revelation, political, social, and cultural crisis appears to be precipitated by invasive and omnipresent theological pluralism.

Pre-exilic Period

Isaiah's apocalyptic eschatology emerged under the cloud of a national capitulation to Canaanite polytheism in the eighth century B.C.[58] Israel's conquest of Palestine failed to eliminate the diluting influence of pluriform and syncretistic Canaanite paganism.[59] By the time of Isaiah's ministry, Samaria and the Northern Kingdom had openly synthesized their own religious heritage with the idolatrous and immoral indigenous fertility cults.[60] By adopting forbidden religious and social practices from the surrounding cultures, the Northern Kingdom invited an invasion stirred by God's judgmental hand.[61] After conquering and destroying Samaria, Assyria's program of deportation, colonization, and forced assimilation further diluted the Northern Kingdom's religious and ethnic identity with a fresh injection of foreign religious influences.[62]

---

57 Hengel, *Judaism and Hellenism*, 1:194; Russell, *Method and Message*, 15–18; Hanson, *Dawn of Apocalyptic*, 433–4; idem, "Apocalypticism," 30; Collins, *Apocalyptic Imagination*, 29–30; Hellholm, "The Problem of Apocalyptic Genre," 27; Adela Yarbro Collins, *Crisis and Catharsis: The Power of the Apocalypse* (Westminster Press, 1984), 84–107.

58 For affirmations of Isaiah's literary unity and pre-exilic date, see Jan Ridderbos, *The Bible Student's Commentary: Isaiah*, trans. John Vriend (Zondervan, 1985), 8–33; J. Alec Motyer, *The Prophecy of Isaiah: An Introduction and Commentary* (InterVarsity Press, 1993), 13–30. Cf. also William LaSor, David Hubbard, and Frederic Bush, *Old Testament Survey: The Message, Form, and Background of the Old Testament* (Eerdmans, 1982), 376: "No reason suffices to reject the view that Isaiah was the dominant personality responsible for the entire prophecy that bears his name." Though he dates the apocalyptic sections later than Isaiah, Ronald E. Clements acknowledges "there is no doubt that their 'message' was felt to have a direct bearing on the earlier prophecies of Isaiah, and, for this reason to belong to the proper interpretation of these" (*Isaiah 1–39*, NCBC [Eerdmans, 1980], 3).

59 Exod 23:23–33; Josh 23:23; Judg 2:1–3. Cf. John Day, *Yahweh and the Gods and Goddesses of Canaan*, JSOTSup 265 (Sheffield Academic Press, 2000), 226–33; John Gray, *The Canaanites*, Ancient Peoples and Places 38 (Frederick A. Praeger, 1964), 119–138; W. F. Albright, *Yahweh and the Gods of Canaan: A Historical Analysis of Two Contrasting Faiths* (The Athlone Press, 1968); Georg Fohrer, *History of Israelite Religion*, trans. David. E. Green (Abingdon Press, 1972), 62–5; Peter C. Craigie and Gerald H. Wilson, "Religions of the Biblical World: Canaanite (Syria and Palestine)," *ISBE* 4:95–101.

60 1 Kgs 12:25–33; 16:26; Hos 4:11–19; Mic 1:7. According to John Bright, "Yahwism was in danger of becoming a pagan religion" (*A History of Israel*, 4th ed. [Westminster John Knox Press, 2000], 260–2).

61 2 Kgs 17:7–23; cf. Josh 23:12–13; 24:20; Isa 9:8–10:6; 28:1–4.

62 2 Kings 17:24–41. H. Jagersma, *A History of Israel in the Old Testament Period*, trans. John Bowden (Fortress Press, 1983), 160; Francois Castel, *The History of Israel and Judah in Old Testament Times*, trans. Matthew J. O'Connell (Paulist Press, 1985), 123.

Isaiah predicted an imminent judgment against Judah for the same viola-tions.[63] The Southern Kingdom's syncretistic trend was already established,[64] eventually degenerating into full blown apostasy with Manasseh who "se-duced them to do evil more than the nations whom the Lord destroyed be-fore the sons of Israel."[65] By 586 B.C., assimilation to surrounding pagan plu-ralism had resulted in total national destruction, the deterioration of Israel's distinctive covenantal identity, and a wholesale deportation to Babylon (2 Kgs 25:1–11).

Exilic Period

Jewish religion and society in the Southern Kingdom were directed and sta-bilized by the temple, the "master symbol" of Israel's exclusive claim to God's presence and protection.[66] With the destruction of Jerusalem and the Bab-ylonian captivity, Jews lost their unifying symbols and faced extinction as a distinct ethno-religious culture.[67] Daniel's apocalyptic eschatology therefore grows out of the looming critical conflict between Israel's ancestral mono-theism and the myriad of religious options provided by the Babylonian pantheon.[68]

While segments of the surviving Judean population embraced the religious

63 Isa 2:8–3:26; 6:9–13; cf. Ezek 16:15–59.

64 Saul M. Olyan, *Asherah and the Cult of Yahweh in Israel*, SBLMS 34 (Scholars Press, 1988), 70–4.

65 2 Kgs 21:1–9; cf. Isa 2:8; 57:4–10.

66 Paul D. Hanson, "Israelite Religion in the Early Postexilic Period," in *Ancient Israelite Religion: Essays in Honor of Frank Moore Cross*, ed. Patrick D. Miller Jr., Paul D. Hanson, and S. Dean McBride (Fortress Press, 1987), 488–9.

67 Ibid., 490; Bright, *History of Israel*, 347–8.

68 A "contest" theme between Yahweh and the gods of the nations runs overtly through-out Daniel (Dan 2:46–47; 3:16–18, 26–30; 5:1–30; 6:25–27; 11:36–45). Cf. Gleason L. Archer Jr., *Daniel*, EBC 7 (Zondervan, 1985), 4; Collins, *Apocalyptic Imagination*, 72. The debate over dating Daniel is complex and arduous. John J. Collins' discussion encapsulates the majority critical (Maccabean) view (*Daniel: A Commentary on the Book of Daniel*, Hermeneia [Fortress Press, 1993], 1–38). The traditional (exilic) view, however, has never been abandoned. Cf. e.g. Robert Dick Wilson, *Studies in the Book of Daniel: A Discussion of the Historical Questions* (G. P. Put-nam's Sons, 1917); R. K. Harrison, *Introduction to the Old Testament* (Eerdmans, 1969), 1110–27; Edward J. Young, *The Prophecy of Daniel: A Commentary* (Eerdmans, 1964), 19–26; the collection of essays in D. J. Wiseman et al., eds., *Notes on Some Problems in the Book of Daniel* (Tyndale Press, 1965); Joyce G. Baldwin, *Daniel: An Introduction and Commentary*, TOTC (InterVarsity Press, 1978), 18–46; Archer, *Daniel*, 4–8; Gerhard F. Hasel, "The Book of Daniel: Evidence Re-lating to Persons and Chronology," *AUSS* 19, no. 1 (1981): 37–49; idem, "The Book of Daniel and Matters of Language: Evidences Relating to Names, Words, and the Aramaic Language," Ibid. 19, no. 3 (1981): 211–25; William H. Shea, "Daniel 3: Extra-Biblical Texts and the Convocation on the Plain of Dura," Ibid. 20, no. 1 (1982): 29–52; idem, "Darius the Mede: An Update," Ibid. 20, no. 3 (1982): 229–47; Arthur J. Ferch, "The Book of Daniel and the 'Maccabean Thesis,'" Ibid. 21, no. 2 (1983): 129–41. As the discussion of the Hellenistic era below will demonstrate, critical

pluralism of their neighbors (Jer 44:15–19), the deported Jewish aristocracy was immersed in a resocialization program designed to transform exemplary young Israelites into productive Babylonian politicos.[69] Because politics and religion were interwoven and indistinguishable in Babylonian society,[70] Daniel and his countrymen were confronted by an assimilation and indoctrination system that threatened to dissolve their theological heritage. Though Mesopotamian religion was "characterized by the absence of any centrality and by a deep-seated tolerance to shifting stresses,"[71] Jews were expected to compromise even the most fundamental tenets of their faith when the divine head of state[72] deemed it compulsory.[73] Israel's survivors were therefore captives of a hostile pagan theocracy where multiple divine loyalties were both presumed, and at times, prescribed.[74] As Daniel's apocalyptic eschatology illustrates, pluralism in Babylon "compelled Israel more and more to emphasize the exclusiveness of its faith. If it did not wish to disappear abroad, it had to reflect upon its own distinctiveness; it preserved the tradition and let its distinctive features come to the fore."[75]

The threat of pluralism, originating both externally and internally, continued with the return from exile. Settlers from the Assyrian colony in Palestine attempted a theological merger with the exiles (Ezra 4:1–5), and leading Israelites, including Levites and princes, compromised ethnic and religious purity by intermarrying with their pagan neighbors (Ezra 9:1). The restoration remnant was a "tiny island in a vast ocean of pagan peoples, without clear boundaries. Unchecked assimilation would mean the end of the community,

---

post-exilic interpretations of Daniel do not invalidate the proposed thesis that his prophecy was written in the context of encroaching religious pluralism.

69 John E. Goldingay, *Daniel*, WBC 30 (Word, 1987), 23–4. According to Dan 1:4, Nebuchadnezzar ordered his steward to teach young Jewish nobles the "literature and language of the Chaldeans" in preparation for service in his court. For general outlines of the possible curriculum and its related religious overtones, see Collins, *Daniel*, 137–9, and the literature cited.

70 Karen Rhea Nemet-Nejat, *Daily Life in Ancient Mesopotamia* (Greenwood Press, 1998), 217–18; J. N. Postgate, *Early Mesopotamia: Society and Economy at the Dawn of History* (Routledge, 1994), 260.

71 A. Leo Oppenheim, *Ancient Mesopotamia: Portrait of a Dead Civilization* (University of Chicago Press, 1964), 182. Cf., however, Haman's complaint that Jewish "laws are different from those of all other people, and they do not observe the king's laws, so it is not in the king's interest to let them remain" (Esth 3:8).

72 Cf. Postgate, *Early Mesopotamia*, 266–7; H. W. F. Saggs, *The Greatness That Was Babylon: A Survey of the Ancient Civilization of the Tigris-Euphrates Valley* (Sidgwick and Jackson, 1988), 311–12.

73 Cf. Dan 1:5 (dietary laws); 3:1–11 (state mandated idolatry). Jeremiah saw Babylonians as a people "mad over fearsome idols" (Jer 50:38).

74 Collins, *Daniel*, 185.

75 Werner H. Schmidt, *The Faith of the Old Testament: A History*, trans. John Sturdy (Westminster Press, 1983), 254.

and along with it the precious heritage it preserved for the world."[76] The Israelite population that remained in Judea during the exile had likely "absorbed so much from the pagan environment that their religion was no longer Yahwism in pure form."[77] Zechariah's apocalyptic eschatology, however, looks forward to the final vindication of Israel's faith in the Messianic kingdom.[78]

Hellenistic Period

In Palestine and the diaspora during the Hellenistic and Roman periods (ca. 332 B.C. – A.D. 70), the bulk of the apocalyptic corpus was written as a Jewish counterpoint, a faith response to the influx of Hellenistic culture, mysticism, mystery religion, and idolatry.[79] Apocalyptic literature and theology, according to Hengel, "is above all a fruit of the Jewish struggle for spiritual and religious self-determination against the invasion of Jerusalem by the Hellenistic spirit."[80]

Alexander's military conquests in the fourth century B.C. accomplished much more than the mere cobbling together of a broad based political kingdom. As part of his grandiose vision for world domination, Alexander exported Greek culture, and, through systematic colonization, transformed the social, political, and religious complexion of the Near East.[81] The "common architecture"[82] of Hellenistic polytheism spreading throughout Palestine and the diaspora demanded religious tolerance,[83] inclusiveness,[84] and a systematic melding of divergent beliefs.[85]

While pious Jews bitterly resisted the process,[86] by the reign of Antiochus

76 LaSor, Hubbard and Bush, *Old Testament Survey*, 656. Cf. the specter of idolatry in Zechariah's apocalyptic judgment pronouncements (Zech 9:7; 10:2; 13:2).

77 Bright, *History of Israel*, 368. Cf. Haggai's denunciation of the ritually unclean (Hag 2:10–14).

78 Zech 9:10–15; 10:6–12; 13:1; 14:1–11.

79 Cf. T. Jud. 23:1–2; 1 Enoch 99:6–7; Russell, *Method and Message*, 16, 36; Hengel, *Judaism and Hellenism*, vol. 1, 253; Frederick J. Murphy, "Apocalypses and Apocalypticism: The State of the Question," *CurBS* 2 (1994): 169; Hanson, "Israelite Religion," 492; Collins, *Apocalyptic Imagination*, 28; idem, "From Prophecy to Apocalypticism," 157.

80 Hengel, *Judaism and Hellenism*, 1:196.

81 Bradford C. Welles, *Alexander and the Hellenistic World* (A. M. Hakkert, 1970), 153–75; Helmut Koester, *History, Culture, and Religion of the Hellenistic Age*, 2nd ed., vol. 1 of *Introduction to the New Testament* (Walter de Gruyter, 1995), 41–5; Erich S. Gruen, *The Hellenistic World and the Coming of Rome*, vol. 1 (University of California Press, 1984), 250–60.

82 Luther Martin, *Hellenistic Religions: An Introduction*, (Oxford University Press, 1987), 10–1.

83 Ramsay MacMullen, *Paganism in the Roman Empire* (Yale University Press, 1981), 2, 90–4.

84 Everett Ferguson, *Backgrounds of Early Christianity*, 2nd ed. (Eerdmans, 1993), 161–5.

85 Cf. Acts 17:1–16; 19:23–28; Helmut Koester, *History, Culture, and Religion*, 156–9; Frederick C. Grant, *Hellenistic Religions: The Age of Syncretism* (Liberal Arts Press, 1953), xiii.

86 1 Macc 2:15–26; 2 Macc 6:11, 18–31.

IV (175–163 B.C.), Hellenism as the culture of the ruling power proved irresistible for many.[87] Greeks and Hellenized Jews participated in nude sports, immorality, and pagan rites in a gymnasium built within Jerusalem.[88] Apostate priests attempted to redefine Judaism as a "Syro-Hellenic cult in which Yahweh would be worshipped in identification with Zeus."[89] Antiochus eventually outlawed Judaism altogether, required Jews throughout Palestine to practice idolatry, and "erected a desolating sacrilege upon the altar of burnt offering" (1 Macc 1:41–54). Those who did not "choose to change over to Greek customs" or the "alien religion" were executed.[90]

Hasmonean Period

Maccabean (ca. 167–141 B.C.) preservation and unification of Israel's traditional faith was hampered both by Hellenism's relative influence among the ruling elite[91] and the resulting popular disaffection. What began with Mattathias as a militant religious purification movement (1 Macc 2:27) quickly evolved into a Hasmonean monarchy willing to entertain Hellenistic ideals[92] and usurp unlawfully the office of high priest.[93] In response, the united front against Hellenistic pluralism collapsed, and pre-revolutionary diversity within Israel fractured into a plurality of interpretations regarding the nature of true Judaism.[94] Disgruntled by the perceived corruption of the temple cult

---

87 1 Macc 1:43, 52, 60–64. Cf. John J. Collins, "Cult and Culture: The Limits of Hellenization in Judea," in *Hellenism in the Land of Israel*, ed. John J. Collins and Gregory E. Sterling (University of Notre Dame Press, 2001), 38–61; W. O. E. Oesterley, *The Jews and Judaism during the Greek Period: The Background of Christianity* (Macmillan, 1941), 19–21; Hengel, *Judaism and Hellenism*, vol. 1, 49–50, 267–72; Russell, *Apocalyptic*, 9–10.

88 1 Macc 1:11–15; Hengel, *Judaism and Hellenism*, vol. 1, 70–8.

89 Bright, *History of Israel*, 422.

90 2 Macc 6:9, 25. Cf. Hengel's conclusion that the bitter persecution was actually orchestrated by extreme Jewish Hellenists in Jerusalem (*Judaism and Hellenism*, vol. 1, 286–90).

91 Collins, "Cult and Culture," 38–61.

92 Driven by political ambition, the Hasmoneans assumed royal authority, courted Hellenists, butchered pious dissenters (Josephus, *Jewish Antiquities* 13; 4QpNah 3–4.i.6–8), assassinated family members, and Hellenized their names (cf. "Alexander Jannaeus"); Elias Bickerman, *From Ezra to the Last of the Maccabees: Foundations of Post-biblical Judaism* (Schocken Books, 1972), 153–82; H. Jagersma, *A History of Israel from Alexander the Great to Bar Kochba* (Fortress Press, 1986), 67, 80–92; John H. Hayes and Sara R. Mandell, *The Jewish People in Classical Antiquity: From Alexander to Bar Kochba* (Westminster John Knox Press, 1998), 80, 93–100; Victor Tcherikover, *Hellenistic Civilization and the Jews*, trans. S. Applebaum (The Jewish Publication Society of America, 1959), 236–57.

93 Although beginning with Jonathon (ca. 161–142 B.C.) the Hasmoneans procured the high priesthood, they were not descendents of Aaron and therefore ineligible according to the Law. Cf. Assumption of Moses 6:1; Pss. Sol. 17:8; Joachim Jeremias, *Jerusalem in the Time of Jesus: An Investigation into Economic and Social Conditions during the New Testament Period*, trans. F. H. Cave and C. H. Cave (Fortress Press, 1969), 188–9.

94 Albert I. Baumgarten, *The Flourishing of Jewish Sects in the Maccabean Era: An Interpre-

and priesthood,[95] the Qumran community took their version of the truth into the desert. "Born out of an intense ideological crisis and at the moment of a theocratic régime's political bankruptcy,"[96] the Qumran community's apocalyptic eschatology repudiated perceived errors[97] in competing "Judaisms."[98]

Roman Period

Conflation of political, cultural, and religious idiosyncrasies precipitated a deep-seated identity crisis in first-century Palestinian society.[99] The first-century Jewish revolt against Rome was cultivated by the gradual intensification of religious and political insensitivity toward conservative Jewish sensibilities.[100] Apocalyptic literature of the era details the shared disposition of "dissent and remnant groups" within Israel who hoped for fulfillment in a future age, convinced that the Jewish masses and the pluriform religious establishment[101] of the age were fundamentally corrupt and subject to judgment.[102] Jesus and his movement clashed with various contemporary Jewish parties,

---

tation, SJSJ 55 (Brill, 1997), 26–28; 112–3; Anthony J. Saldarini, *Pharisees, Scribes and Sadducees in Palestinian Society: A Sociological Approach* (Eerdmans, 1988), 59–62; Plöger, *Theocracy and Eschatology*, 8–9; Koester, *History, Culture, and Religion*, 208–10; Hengel, *Judaism and Hellenism*, vol. 1, 179–80, 252; Gerd Theissen, *Sociology of Early Palestinian Christianity*, trans. John Bowden (Fortress Press, 1978), 87.

95 Milik, *Ten Years of Discovery*, 80–98; Cross, *Ancient Library*, 100–20; John J. Collins, "The Origin of the Qumran Community: A Review of the Evidence," in *Seers, Sybils, and Sages in Hellenistic-Roman Judaism*, SJSJ 54, ed. John J. Collins and Florentino García Martínez (E. J. Brill, 1997), 247.

96 Milik, *Ten Years of Discovery*, 98.

97 Mark Adam Elliott, *The Survivors of Israel: A Reconsideration of the Theology of Pre-Christian Judaism* (Eerdmans, 2000), 57–72.

98 Cf. Gabriele Boccaccini, *Middle Judaism: Jewish Thought, 300 B.C.E to 200 C.E.* (Fortress Press, 1991), 15–21; Marcel Simon, *Jewish Sects at the Time of Jesus*, trans. James H. Farley (Fortress Press, 1967), 14–5.

99 Theissen, *Sociology*, 92–7. Cf. Frederick J. Murphy, *The Religious World of Jesus: An Introduction to Second Temple Judaism* (Abingdon Press, 1991), 345–6.

100 See for examples Pompey's inspection of the Holy of Holies (Pss. Sol. 2:1–3; Tacitus, *Histories* 5.9); Herod's golden eagle (Josephus, *Jewish War* 1.648–650); the Roman cavalry's murder of 3,000 in the temple complex during Passover (Josephus, *Jewish Antiquities* 17.213–219); Pilate's display of busts in Jerusalem bearing the image of Caesar (Josephus, *Jewish War* 2.169–174); and Caligula's plan to erect his own statue in the temple (Josephus, *Jewish War* 2.184–187).

101 Cf. discussions of various second temple religio-political groups in Lester L. Grabbe's chapter "Sects and Violence: Religious Pluralism from the Maccabees to Yavneh" (*The Roman Period*, vol. 2 of *Judaism from Cyrus to Hadrian* [Fortress Press, 1992], 463–554); Jeremias, *Jerusalem in the Time of Jesus*, 233–67; Jacob Neusner, *Judaism in the Beginning of Christianity* (Fortress Press, 1984), 25–8; Gary G. Porton, "Diversity in Postbiblical Judaism," in *Early Judaism and Its Modern Interpreters*, ed. Robert A. Kraft and George W. E. Nickelsburg (Scholars Press, 1986), 57–73.

102 Cf. Matt 3:7–12 (John the Baptist); 4 Ezra 6:19–25; 7:20–27, 37; 8:1–3; 2 Bar. 14:14; 44:2–7; Pss. Sol. 2:1–3; Elliott, *Survivors of Israel*, 561–73, 663–4; Grabbe, *Judaism from Cyrus to Hadrian*, 2:413.

accusing them of feigning fidelity to covenantal Judaism while routinely failing to understand or apply it.[103] Jesus himself claimed to embody the essence
of Israelite religion and castigated all differing opinions as manifestations of
unbelief.[104]

The early church was also "committed to encountering the world in its universal mission to convert it."[105] The pluriformity of Hellenistic cultures, however, presented believer's with an impressive set of philosophical and theological challenges.[106] Inevitably, converts from divergent viewpoints brought
with them various Jewish[107] and Greek syncretistic attitudes that clashed
with Christianity's theological[108] and ethical[109] exclusivism. In cosmopolitan
Corinth for example, Paul encountered bewildering spiritual and moral pluralism[110] where "no taste or sensibility need go unsatisfied,"[111] where sexuality
and the underworld were combined thematically as macabre expressions of
worship.[112] Various elements of Corinthian decadence seeped into the local

---

103 Matt 15:1–20; 16:1–4; 22:15–29; 23:1–39; Luke 20:39–47; John 5:39–47.

104 John 3:18; 8:12–18, 42–45; 14:6–7.

105 Alan F. Segal, *Rebecca's Children: Judaism and Christianity in the Roman World* (Harvard University Press, 1986), 177. Cf. Matt 28:19–20; Acts 1:8; Rom 1:14.

106 Aune, *Literary Environment*, 244–5; Leonard Thompson, "A Sociological Analysis of
Tribulation in the Apocalypse of John," in *Early Christian Apocalypticism: Genre and Social Set-
ting*, ed. Adela Yarbro Collins, Semeia 36 (Scholars Press, 1986), 165–6; Adela Yarbro Collins,
"Vilification and Self-Definition in the Book of Revelation," *HTR* 79, nos. 1–3 (1986): 315–8; G. R.
Beasley-Murray, "Revelation, Book of," in *DLNT*, ed. Ralph P. Martin and Peter H. Davids (Inter-
Varsity Press, 1997), 1028–9, 1035. Cf. Revelation's overt condemnation of Greco-Roman pagan
culture: Eating idol meat (Rev 2:14, 20), worshipping the beast (Rev 13:15–17; 14:9–10; 19:20),
and sexual impurity (Rev 14:4). Compromising "centrists" who abandoned their earlier deeds
(Rev 2:5), whose works are incomplete (Rev 3:2), or who are "lukewarm" (Rev 3:15–16) are condemned by the "apocalyptic tradition of nonconformity and opposition to the insidious influence of the dominant alien culture" (Aune, *Literary Environment*, 245).

107 John J. Collins, *Between Athens and Jerusalem: Jewish Identity in the Hellenistic Diaspora* (Crossroad, 1982), 38–9, 46, 244–6.

108 Acts 4:12; Phil 2:10–11; 1 Tim 2:5.

109 Matt 5:20, 47–8; 1 Cor 6:9–11; Eph 4:17–22; Rev 21:8.

110 Cf. Oscar Broneer, "Paul and the Pagan Cults at Isthmia," *HTR* 64, no. 2–3 (1971): 175–6;
Charles K. Williams II, "Corinth and the Cult of Aphrodite," in *Corinthiaca*, ed. Mario A. Del
Chiaro (University of Missouri Press, 1986), 12–24; idem, "The City of Corinth and Its Domes-
tic Religion," *Hesperia* 50, no. 4 (1981): 408–21; Dennis Edwin Smith, "The Egyptian Cults at
Corinth," *HTR* 70, no. 3–4 (1977): 201–31.

111 Jerome Murphy-O'Connor, "The Corinth that Saint Paul Saw," *BA* 47, no. 3 (1984): 155.

112 The fabled cult of Aphrodite in Corinth was not limited to sexuality or fertility. One
sanctuary to Aphrodite found in north eastern Corinth points to her character as a "divinity
of death and the lower world" (Lewis Farnell, *The Cults of the Greek States*, vol. 2 [Caratzas
Brothers, 1977], 652). Among a series of tombs, one of which was dedicated to the legendary
Corinthian beauty Lais, stood a temple to Aphrodite Melainis, or Dark Aphrodite. This repre-
sentation of the goddess of love emphasized darkness because "human copulations do not
always take place in the daylight like those of cattle but mostly at night" (Pausanias *Description of Greece* 8.6.5, trans. W. H. S. Jones, vol. 3, LCL, ed. G. P. Goold et al. [Harvard University
Press, 1977]). Yet the dark understanding of Aphrodite also depicted her as Aphrodite on the

Christian sub-culture, soliciting Paul's vigorous rebuke.[113]

IDEOLOGICAL FUNCTION

In the context of religious pluralism, apocalyptic eschatology functions as an exclusionary ideological force, the "organizing center" of a "counter-cultural community."[114] The general contours of this function include (1) community identification, (2) explanation of opposition, (3) encouragement for the faithful, and (4) community preservation and control.[115]

Community Identification

The community to which apocalyptic literature is primarily addressed can only exist by establishing and maintaining ideological boundaries that identify its unique culture.[116] Apocalyptic dualism separating the righteous from the wicked provides a defining and exclusive influence by contending that, when beliefs and practices contradict the revealed worldview, such beliefs and practices are necessarily erroneous and untenable.[117] A clear line of demarcation is then drawn between the righteous who meet inclusionary requirements established by the revelation[118] and the wicked who reject such distinctives and are totally excluded.[119] Because, for example, adherence to early Christian apocalyptic eschatology ensured a distinct and exclusive community, believers endured persecution from their former spheres of identity (1 Thess 2:14).[120] In the conflux of worldviews, apocalyptic eschatology broaches an irreconcilable division.

Tomb or Τυμβωρύχος, "Goddess of Graves." At Corinth, therefore, sexual and underworld religious themes were interwoven, typifying the profundity of first-century pluralism (Williams, "Corinth and the Cult of Aphrodite," 12).

113 1 Cor 5; 6:12–20; 2 Cor 2:1–4; 12:21; cf. Gordon Fee, *The First Epistle to the Corinthians*, NICNT (Eerdmans, 1987), 11–4.

114 Wayne A. Meeks, "Social Functions of Apocalyptic Language in Pauline Christianity," in *AMWNE*, ed. David Hellholm (J. C. B Mohr [Paul Siebeck] 1983), 702; Elliott, *Survivors of Israel*, 57–8, 185–6.

115 Cf. the lists of functions in Sim, *Apocalyptic Eschatology*, 64; Meeks, "Social Functions of Apocalyptic Language," 700; Elliott, *Survivors of Israel*, 9.

116 Elliott, *Survivors of Israel*, 9; Wayne A. Meeks, *The First Urban Christians: The Social World of the Apostle Paul* (Yale University Press, 1983), 84.

117 Cf. Carson, *Gagging of God*, 27.

118 See Elliott's emphasis on "exclusivist soteriology" in his chapter "Limits on the Community of Salvation" (*Survivors of Israel*, 115–86).

119 Cf. 2 Bar. 44:1–15; 1QS 1.1–7; 6.12–16; Sim, *Apocalyptic Eschatology*, 65.

120 Meeks, "Social Function of Apocalyptic Language," 691.

Explanation of Opposition

That the faithful community will face opposition in the present age of evil is presupposed by apocalyptic pessimism. Apocalyptic eschatology does not, however, offer an answer to the problems of suffering and theodicy.[121] Suffering is rather offered as a promise, an identifying signal of the community's distinctiveness.[122] The community's obedience to its worldview effects the separation from conflicting viewpoints and stimulates negative reactions from those outside. Suffering "helps to make sense of the separation and thus to reinforce the boundaries between the group and the larger society."[123] By describing suffering in terms of a providential badge of legitimacy, apocalyptic eschatology cultivates confidence in God's sovereign goodness despite painful circumstances.[124]

Encouragement for the Faithful

Apocalyptic eschatology provides encouragement for the righteous who willingly conform to the revealed worldview. Promises of vindication, redemption, role reversal, and fabulous eternal reward bolster the resolve to remain faithful.[125] In light of what is to come, the community's perception of suffering, isolation, and marginalization fades in intensity. In an indirect sense the certainty of reward or punishment in apocalyptic eschatology encourages those who are excluded because of unfaithfulness to become faithful and embrace the truth.[126]

Community Preservation and Control

Apocalyptic eschatology guards the community's theological boundaries and preserves its purity by identifying and de-legitimizing dissidence, unsanctioned innovation, and subversive sub-groups.[127] This paraenetic value encourages "cognitive and behavioral modifications based on the message

---

121 Ibid., 692.

122 Cf. Phil 1:28–29; 1 Thess 3:2–4; 2 Thess 1:4–10.

123 Meeks, "Social Function of Apocalyptic Language," 692.

124 Sim, *Apocalyptic Eschatology*, 66.

125 Cf. Rev 2:9–11; 3:9–13; 1 Enoch 95:3; 96:1–8; 104:1–5; E. P. Sanders, "The Genre of Palestinian Jewish Apocalypses," in *AMWNE*, ed. David Hellholm (J. C. B Mohr [Paul Siebeck] 1983), 456–7; Hellholm, "The Problem of Apocalyptic Genre," 27.

126 Hans Dieter Betz, "The Problem of Apocalyptic Genre in Greek and Hellenistic Literature: The Case of the Oracle of Trophonius," in *AMWNE*, ed. David Hellholm (J. C. B Mohr [Paul Siebeck] 1983), 595–6.

127 Meeks, *Fist Urban Christians*, 177–9; Collins, "Vilification and Self-Definition," 314.

communicated from the transcendent world."[128] As an attempt to standardize or institutionalize[129] "both the understanding and the behavior of the audience by means of divine authority,"[130] apocalyptic eschatology purges doctrinal and ethical threats to the community's identity. Dissolution and dilution of the fellowship's ratified norms by internal or external influences are checked by theological specificity and the threat of judgment.[131]

ELEMENTS OF EXCLUSIVISM

Apocalyptic eschatology as a revelation based worldview presupposes that God has revealed himself in a particular and unique way[132] that provides the special undiscoverable knowledge necessary for achieving social and individual fulfillment[133] and results in a clear antithesis between the sacred and the profane.[134] Apocalyptic eschatology as revealed eschatology stakes a claim to truth. As a truth claim it is therefore inherently particular, divisive, and exclusive[135]—an imposition of ultimate reality on the human spirit[136] that consistently differentiates between good and evil, truth and error, the righteous and the wicked. This overarching characteristic appears in several of its most prominent thematic elements.

Dualism

Various "dimensions" of dualism are evident throughout apocalyptic texts

---

128 Aune, "The Apocalypse of John and the Problem of Genre," 90.

129 Meeks, *First Urban Christians*, 173.

130 Collins, "Early Christian Apocalypticism," 7. Cf. Hellholm, "The Problem of Apocalyptic Genre," 27.

131 Cf. 1 John 4:1–3; Rev 2:14–16, 20–23; 3:1–3; 1 Enoch 108:1–15; 1QS 2.11–17; Lebram, "Piety of the Jewish Apocalyptists," 188–9; Collins, *Crisis and Catharsis*, 124–7; Betz, "Problem of Apocalyptic Genre," 595; Meeks, *First Urban Christians*, 175.

132 Cf. John P. Newport, *Life's Ultimate Questions: A Contemporary Philosophy of Religion* (Scripta, 1989), 10–1; Ronald H. Nash, *Faith and Reason: Searching for a Rational Faith* (Zondervan, 1988), 37.

133 Aune, *Literary Environment*, 231. Cf. Nash, *Faith and Reason*, 32.

134 Cf. Millard J. Erickson, *Where is Theology Going? Issues and Perspectives on the Future of Theology* (Baker, 1994), 73–8; Gordon H. Clark, *Religion, Reason and Revelation*, 2nd ed. (Trinity Foundation, 1986), 183–5; William J. Abraham, *An Introduction to the Philosophy of Religion* (Prentice-Hall, 1985), 216–7; Willem F. Zuurdeeg, *An Analytical Philosophy of Religion* (Abingdon Press, 1958), 24–43.

135 Cf. Keith Ward, "Truth and the Diversity of Religions," in *The Philosophical Challenge of Religious Diversity*, ed. Philip L. Quinn and Kevin Meeker (Oxford University Press, 2000), 110, 125.

136 Herbert H. Farmer, *Revelation and Religion: Studies in the Theological Interpretation of Religious Types*, Texts and Studies in Religion 80 (Nisbet, 1954; repr., Edwin Mellen, 1999), 25.

that undergird a fundamental worldview.[137] Though comprehensive, apocalyptic dualism is not absolute. God remains preeminent,[138] and, beyond the visible realm, God's absolute infinite goodness confronts finite evil.[139] The cosmic division between good and evil is objectified in descriptions of the angelic hosts. "Thousands upon thousands" and "myriads upon myriads" of holy angels minister before God's throne,[140] mediate divine revelations,[141] serve men,[142] rule nations,[143] and battle fallen angels.[144] At the parousia the "holy angels," who belong specifically to the Son of Man, will return with Jesus and facilitate the process of judgment by separating the righteous from the wicked and casting the unrighteous into eternal fire.[145] Satan and his demons, however, corrupt humanity, endanger the earth, and oppose God's work.[146] The Gospel record of satanic and demonic defeat at the hands of Jesus depicts a real but temporary cosmic conflict between good and evil.[147] Though Satan and his minions vigorously oppose his work, Jesus as God incarnate ultimately triumphs.[148]

The two "orbs of power"[149] dividing the cosmos translate into a historical dualism that divides the "two ages." According to the apocalyptic prophets, God has created history in two parts.[150] In Isa 65:17 God declares, "For behold, I create new heavens and a new earth; and the former things shall not be remembered or come to mind."[151] This present age (αἰών) has a definite

---

137 Jörg Frey, "Apocalyptic Dualism" in *The Oxford Handbook of Apocalyptic Literature*, ed. John J. Collins (Oxford University Press, 2014) , 271–294.

138 Col 1:15–17; 1QS 3.15, 24–25.

139 Matt 25:41; Rev 20:10; 1 Enoch 90:24–27; Hartman, *Prophecy Interpreted*, 41.

140 Dan 7:10; 1 Thess 3:13; 2 Thess 1:7; Rev 5:11.

141 Matt 1:20–21; 2:13, 19–20; 28:1–8; 1 Enoch 1:2; 87:3–4; 4 Ezra 4:1–4; Jub. 4:21; Sim, *Apocalyptic Eschatology*, 75.

142 Dan 4:13–14; 10:12; Matt 4:11; Rev 8:3–4; 19:10; 1 Enoch 15:2; 40:9.

143 Dan 10:13, 20–21; 12:1; 1 Enoch 20:1–7.

144 Dan 10:21; Rev 12:7; 20:1–2; 1QS 4.15–26.

145 Matt 13:41–42, 49–50; 16:27; 24:31; Mark 8:38; 25:31; cf. 1 Enoch 54:6; T. Levi 3:2; T. Ab. 12:1–2; Sim, *Apocalyptic Eschatology*, 76.

146 Dan 10:13; Zech 3:1–2; Matt 16:23; Eph 6:11–12; Rev 12:5, 12; 1 Enoch 6:1–3; 9:1; 10:15; 11:4–5; 69:4–5; Russell, *Method and Message*, 240–57; Martinus C. de Boer, "Paul and Jewish Apocalyptic Eschatology," in *Apocalyptic and the New Testament*, ed. Joel Marcus and Marion L. Soards, JSNTSup 24 (Sheffield Academic Press, 1989), 174–5.

147 Matt 4:1–11; 8:16, 28–34; 12:22–30; 16:23; Rev 12:12.

148 Matt 25:41; Rev 20:10. On "that Day" the "Lord will punish the host of heaven" (Isa 24:21).

149 Martyn, "Apocalyptic Antinomies in Galatians," 417.

150 "The Most High has made not one world, but two" (4 Ezra 7:50). Hanson, *Dawn of Apocalyptic*, 127; Martyn, "Apocalyptic Antinomies," 412–14; Keck, "Paul and Apocalyptic Theology," 236.

151 Matt 12:32; Mark 10:30; Luke 18:30; Heb 6:5; Rev 21:1–8; 1 Enoch 91:16; 4 Ezra 7:75.

termination point,[152] but the age to come is eternal.[153] The new order of joy, prosperity, and longevity will replace the fallen and corrupt old heavens and old earth where predators currently devour prey and evil abounds throughout the land.[154] The present order is evil, characterized by murder, deceit, greed, and injustice.[155] The "former things," the "things of the past," will be forgotten when the new "springs forth."[156] This dichotomy developed into an "ontological equation, present era = evil, future era = good (limited to the chosen)," necessitating a cataclysmic supplanting of the old with the new.[157]

Cosmological and historical dualism directly results in the cleavage of humanity into two mutually exclusive categories.[158] In Jesus' explanation of the parable of the wheat and the tares, the "sons of the kingdom" and the "sons of the evil one" are directly identified with cosmic combatants, the "Son of Man" and the "devil" (Matt 13:37–39). The result is an irreconcilable division between the "righteous" who will "shine forth as the sun" and the "lawless" who will be thrown into the "furnace of fire" where there will be "weeping and gnashing of teeth."[159] Jesus came for the purpose of dividing humanity into those who believe and obey him and those who do not.[160] Throughout the literature, the righteous, who can anticipate the blessing of God, are separated from the wicked who can only expect God's curse.[161] In Revelation, humans who worship Satan wage war against the righteous and are permanently eschatologically excluded from God's favor.[162] Only those whose names are recorded in the book of life, before the foundations of the world, will enjoy the new age.[163] Israel itself is divided into the polluted and the pure remnant,[164]

---

152 Dan 8:19; Matt 13:39–40, 49; 24:3; 28:20; 2 Bar. 31:5.

153 Mark 10:30; Luke 18:30; 1 Enoch 45:4–5; 2 Bar. 43:11–12; 4 Ezra 7:112.

154 Isa 65:19–25; 1 Cor 10:11; Gal 1:4; 1 Enoch 45:4–6; 72:1; 91:16.

155 Isa 59:9–15; John 3:19; Rom 12:2; 1 John 2:15–17; 3:13; 5:19.

156 Isa 43:18–19; cf. 1 Cor 7:31; Gal 6:13–14; 2 Bar. 31:5.

157 Zech 14:1–21; 2 Bar. 31:5; 44:8–15; Hanson, *Dawn of Apocalyptic*, 151–2, 158–60; Schmithals, *Apocalyptic Movement*, 82–5.

158 Murdock, "History and Revelation," 173; James H. Charlesworth, "A Critical Comparison of the Dualism in 1QS 3:13–4:26 and the 'Dualism' Contained in the Fourth Gospel," *NTS* 15, no. 4 (1969): 391; Aune, *Literary Environment*, 244; Sim, *Apocalyptic Eschatology*, 40; N. T. Wright, "Jesus," in *Early Christian Thought in Its Jewish Context*, ed. John Barclay and John Sweet (Cambridge University Press, 1996), 52.

159 Matt 13:40–43; cf. 1 Enoch 91:4, 18–19; 94:1–5; 2 Bar. 85:13; 1QS 3.18–4.1.

160 Matt 10:34–36; Luke 12:49–53; cf. T. Ash. 1:4–9.

161 Matt 25:31–46; 1 Cor 6:9–10; 2 Thess 2:11–13; Heb 10:26–31; Rev 22:14–15; 1 Enoch 5:6; 2 Bar. 24:1–2; 48:48; 4 Ezra 7:17; Sib. Or. 4:40.

162 Rev 13:4–8, 16; 17:8; 20:15.

163 Rev 13:8; 21:27.

164 Isa 59:1–15; 65:13–15; 2 Bar. 44:15; Hanson, *Dawn of Apocalyptic*, 151; idem, "Old Testament Apocalyptic Reexamined," in *Visionaries and Their Apocalypses*, ed. Paul D. Hanson, IRT 4 (Fortress Press, 1983), 50.

and in the NT there is no middle ground between believers who embrace Jesus and the wicked who reject him.[165]

Determinism

Apocalyptic eschatology presupposes that God rules history from beginning to end with the "freedom, contingency, and unpredictable character" of the divine will:[166]

> For I am God and there is no other; I am God, and there is no one like me, declaring the end from the beginning and from ancient times things which have not been done, saying, "My purpose will be established, and I will accomplish all my good pleasure." (Isa 46:9–10)

From beginning to end, creation and re-creation, God's sovereign hand has fixed the direction and duration of all things, "for that which is decreed will be done."[167] Daniel's revelatory specificity pertaining to the "appointed time of the end"[168] assumes historical predetermination. God can show Daniel how future kings and kingdoms will rise and fall because the Lord of creation has already established an unalterable time table of "weeks" and "days."[169] Future events are presently "inscribed in the writing of truth" and will be orchestrated "in order to fulfill the vision," God's template for the future.[170] In the NT Jesus' life and work is consistently interpreted as prophecy fulfilled.[171] Essential to Paul's preaching is the conviction that Jesus "died for our sins according to the Scriptures, and that he was buried, and that he was raised on the third day according to the Scriptures" (1 Cor 15:3–4). This fulfillment theme reveals the conviction that "history as a totality is foreordained and unchangeable."[172]

---

165 Matt 7:13–14; 13:36–43; John 3:8–10; 15:18–19; Sim, *Apocalyptic Eschatology*, 79.

166 Schmithals, *Apocalyptic Movement*, 75; Mladen Popovic, "Apocalyptic Determinism," in *The Oxford Handbook of Apocalyptic Literature*, ed. John J. Collins (New York: Oxford University Press, 2014), 255–270.

167 Dan 11:36; cf. 4 Ezra 6:1–6.

168 Dan 8:19; 10:14; 11:29.

169 Dan 8:19–26; 9:24–27; 12:11–12; Rev 11:2; 12:6; Jub. 1:29. God has "weighed the age in the balance, and measured the times by measure, and numbered the times by number, and he will not move or arouse them until that measure is fulfilled" (4 Ezra 4:36–37).

170 Dan 10:21; 11:14; cf. T. Mos. 12:4–6.

171 Matt 1:22–23; 2:5–6; 21:42; John 12:38–40; John 13:18. Jesus was "delivered up by the predetermined plan and foreknowledge of God," subjected to "whatever Thy hand and Thy purpose predestined to occur" (Acts 2:23; 4:28).

172 Sim, *Apocalyptic Eschatology*, 89.

History itself is but the outworking of God's divine plan.[173]

God's rule over history and the cosmos includes the division and categorization of human destinies in advance.[174] Only those whom God himself has destined for glory—the elect, the chosen, the remnant—can anticipate eternal reward. God promises his inheritance to the "chosen ones," leaving only hunger, thirst, and shame for the wicked.[175] According to Jesus, "many are called, but few are chosen."[176] Only God's grace expressed toward the "elect whom he chose" prevents human annihilation in "those days" of final tribulation.[177] All those the Father has given to Jesus will respond and enter the fold (John 6:37, 44), and the elect, blessed before birth, were chosen and recorded in the book of life before the foundation of the world.[178] Repentance and faith are themselves gifts bestowed by the sovereign God.[179]

Despite this apparent rigid determinism, apocalyptic eschatology consistently affirms human responsibility, expressing both points of view "side by side without any intellectual difficulty."[180] God abandons the wicked to judgment "because I called, but you did not answer; I spoke, but you did not hear. And you did evil in my sight, and chose that in which I did not delight" (Isa 65:12). Those who wish to be included among the righteous must freely volunteer, exercising liberty, power of choice, and a reflective self-consciousness.[181]

Pessimism

Apocalyptic pessimism passes judgment on humanity and the present age by the standard of divinely revealed ideals. Encroaching evil in this age infects the

---

173 1 Enoch 81:1–2; 93:1–3; 103:2–3; Russell, *Method and Message*, 205; Murdock, "History and Revelation," 168–9.

174 Russell, *Method and Message*, 233; Schmithals, *Apocalyptic Movement*, 86; Gerhard F. Hasel, "Resurrection in the Theology of Old Testament Apocalyptic," *ZAW* 92, no. 2 (1980): 280; Jacob Licht, "An Analysis of the Treatise of the Two Spirits in DSD," in *Aspects of the Dead Sea Scrolls*, ed. Chaim Rabin and Yigael Yadin, *ScrHier* 4 (Magnes Press, 1958), 89; Cross, *Ancient Library of Qumran*, 153; Helmer Ringgren, *The Faith of Qumran: Theology of the Dead Sea Scrolls*, trans. Emilie T. Sander (Fortress Press, 1963), 53–4, 107–11; Charlesworth, "Dualism," 402.

175 Isa 65:8–16; Zech 13:7–9; 1 Enoch 1:1–2; 5:7–10.

176 Matt 22:14; cf. 4 Ezra 8:1–3.

177 Mark 13:20 and parallels.

178 Rom 8:29–30; 9:11–18; Eph 1:4–5; Rev 13:8; 17:8. God created the "just and the wicked," foreordaining the "judgment of all their deeds" (1QH 12.38; cf. 1QH 9.7–9; 4 Ezra 8:1). God determines the fate of the righteous "from the womb," opening the "narrowness of his soul to eternal salvation. . . . But the wicked you have created for the time of wrath, from the womb you have predestined them for the day of annihilation" (1QH 7.19–21; cf. 1 Enoch 94:2–3).

179 John 6:65; Acts 11:18; 13:48; Phil 1:29; 2 Tim 2:25.

180 Russell, *Method and Message*, 232; Rowley, *Relevance*, 168.

181 Matt 4:17; 11:28; Mark 13:5, 9; Rom 10:13; 1QS 1.7, 11; 2 Enoch 30:15; 53:2–4; 2 Bar. 48:40; 85:7; Russell, *Method and Message*, 232–3.

cosmos itself, hastening the world's deterioration as it wilts under the pressures of sin and ungodliness (Isa 24:4–5). Falsehood, deception, confusion, and mischief characterize the human web of iniquity, and the earth is "polluted by its inhabitants" who are "defiled with blood."[182] Since the Fall the cosmos labors under this "slavery to corruption."[183] Plagues, earthquakes, celestial discord, ecological catastrophe—complete cosmic upheaval—coincide with a quantitative increase in wickedness and foreshadow impending judgment.[184] In the last days difficult times will come:

> For men will be lovers of self, lovers of money, boastful, arrogant, revilers, disobedient to parents, ungrateful, unholy, unloving, irreconcilable, malicious gossips, without self-control, brutal, haters of good, treacherous, reckless, conceited, lovers of pleasure rather than lovers of God.[185]

An increase in lawlessness will lead to murderous hatred for the faithful as the uncommitted abandon the faith and all their pious façades (Matt 24:9–12). Hypocrisy, apostasy, and unbridled evil will lead to unprecedented distress and tribulation.[186] Devastating plagues from the hand of God will not, however, soften the hearts of the wicked, who will not repent of their idolatry, demonic worship, murders, sorceries, immorality, or thievery (Rev 9:20–21; Jub. 23:20–21). Satan incarnate will wage war against God's people, temporarily overcoming them.[187] Wickedness will not be subdued until a catastrophic war on the cosmic and human level exalts good over evil in a final manifestation of righteous force.[188] On "that day" God will "punish the world for its evil, and the wicked for their iniquity" (Isa 13:11).

Judgment

According to Russell, the "doctrine of the last judgment is the most characteristic doctrine of Jewish apocalyptic. It is *the* great event towards which

---

182 Isa 24:5; 59:3–8; cf. T. Jud. 23:1–5. The angel Uriel promises to reveal to Ezra "why the heart is evil" (4 Ezra 4:4).

183 Rom 8:19–22; cf. 4 Ezra 14:10; 2 Bar. 85:10. The world "already is aging and passing the strength of youth" (4 Ezra 5:55).

184 Isa 13:13; 24:19–21; Joel 3:15–16; Matt 24:7, 29; Rev 8:1–9:21; 1 Enoch 91:5–7; Apoc. Ab. 29:15; 4 Ezra 9:1–3; 2 Bar. 27:7; Fiorenza, "Phenomenon of Early Christian Apocalyptic," 300; Russell, *Divine Disclosure*, 92–3.

185 2 Tim 3:2–4; cf. 1 Enoch 91:5–7; 93:9.

186 Dan 11:32–35; 12:1; Matt 24:21; 2 Thess 2:3–7; 1 Tim 4:1; 2 Tim 4:3–4; 1 Enoch 94:5; 1QM 1.2–3. Cf. Elliott, *Survivors of Israel*, 108–3.

187 Dan 7:21, 25; Rev 11:7; 13:7.

188 Dan 11:40–45; Rev 19:11–21; 20:7–8; 1 Enoch 90:10–19.

the whole universe is moving and which will vindicate once and for all God's righteous purpose for men and all creation."[189] The impending judgment is universal and inescapable. On "that day" the earth will be "completely laid waste," those who flee will not escape, and the celestial bodies, sun and moon, will be caught up in the judgment.[190] Creation in its totality will be subjected to the flames of judgment and retribution:

> But the present heavens and earth by his word are being reserved for fire, kept for the day of judgment and destruction of ungodly men. . . But the day of the Lord will come like a thief, in which the heavens will pass away with a roar and the elements will be destroyed with intense heat, and the earth and its works will be burned up.[191]

All the dead and all the living will face God's tribunal.[192] Men are "appointed" for judgment at the "consummation of the ages" (Heb 9:27), and angels will not be exempt. The Lord will "punish the host of heaven, on high, and the kings of the earth on earth. And they will be gathered together like prisoners in the dungeon, and will be confined in prison."[193] For the righteous, judgment leads to eternal life characterized by peace, joy, contentment, fulfillment, and intimacy with God.[194] Excluded from this kingdom, however, are the wicked who reject God. Their condemnation brings weeping, gnashing of teeth, flaming torment, eternal darkness, and isolation from all that is good.[195]

The criteria for judgment in apocalyptic eschatology has been predetermined by God who "demands the obedience of mankind to his will, which he has made known to them."[196] At issue is the interdependent duality of doctrine and ethics. Theological accuracy and specificity are non-negotiable. Idolaters who "set a table for Fortune and who fill cups with mixed wine for

---

189 Russell, *Method and Message*, 380; Dale C. Allison, Jr., "Apocalyptic Ethics and Behavior," in *The Oxford Handbook of Apocalyptic Literature*, ed. John J. Collins (Oxford University Press, 2014), 296–297.

190 Isa 24:3–5, 18, 23; cf. Sib. Or. 2:196–213.

191 2 Pet 3:7, 10; cf. Matt 24:29; Heb 1:11–21; 12:26–29; Rev 6:12–17; 20:11; 21:1.

192 Dan 7:9–14; Matt 25:31; Rev 20:12–13.

193 Isa 24:3–5, 21–22; cf. 1 Enoch 56:1–4; 61:8. The imprisonment theme here raises the possibility that the same motif in 1 Enoch 10:4–12 originates from an earlier and broader Jewish tradition. See John J. Collins, "The Place of Apocalypticism in the Religion of Israel," in *Ancient Israelite Religion: Essays in Honor of Frank Moore Cross*, ed. Patrick D. Miller Jr., Paul D. Hanson, and S. Dean McBride (Fortress Press, 1987), 548.

194 Isa 65:17–25; Zech 14:6–8; Dan 12:2; Matt 13:43; 25:46; Luke 16:25; Rev 21:2–7; 22:1–5; 4 Ezra 7:33–38.

195 Isa 24:1–13; 66:4, 24; Zech 14:12–15; Dan 12:2; Matt 8:12; 13:41–42, 49–50; 22:13; 25:46; Luke 16:19–26; 2 Thess 1:9; Rev 20:15; 21:8; 22:15; 4 Ezra 7:33–38; 2 Bar. 44:15.

196 Hartman, *Prophecy Interpreted*, 41. Cf. Russell, *Method and Message*, 380.

Destiny" have rejected the covenant's revealed monotheistic creationism and are destined for the sword (Isa 65:11). In Daniel the prototypical saint who will inherit the kingdom (Dan 7:21–22, 27) will not deviate from strict conformity to covenantal monotheism (Dan 3:1–30). The wicked, however, will be annihilated for their idolatrous abominations and blasphemous violation of the covenant.[197]

The standard for theological purity becomes more restricted in the NT. God's wrath is directed against those who suppress the truth of his revealed "attributes, his eternal power and divine nature" (Rom 1:18–19). Condemnation is averted and the kingdom inherited only by those who believe specifically in Jesus Christ (John 14:6). Jesus declared, "He who believes in [the Son] is not judged; he who does not believe has been judged already, because he has not believed in the name of the only begotten Son of God" (John 3:18). Jesus condemned his opponents to face judgment because they refused to embrace the Christological correction of their theological systems.[198] Eschatological curse is pronounced against any who distort the received gospel (Gal 1:8–9) in all of its particularity. Antichrists who have emerged at the "last hour" of this age will be destroyed because they embrace lies, reject truth, and distort Christology.[199] In Revelation the testimony of Jesus is the hallmark of righteousness, and a person's vindication in the face of judgment is inseparably linked to this distinction.[200]

Judgment in apocalyptic eschatology critiques not only what people believe but also what they do. Because the wicked "transgressed laws, violated statutes, and broke the everlasting covenant," the day of judgment will bring destruction and misery (Isa 24:1–13). The Redeemer, when he comes to Zion, comes with retribution: "According to their deeds, so he will repay, wrath to his adversaries, recompense to his enemies" (Isa 59:18). Idolatry and theological error leads to immorality which in turn solicits judgment.[201] Books containing the catalogue of human iniquity will be opened at the judgment, and God will repay each person according to his or her works, whether good or evil.[202]

Paraenesis

Prophetic emphasis on paraenesis meshed with apocalyptic expectations of

---

197 Dan 3:1–7; 7:25–26; 11:31–32, 36–38; 12:10–11; cf. Zech 13:1–3.
198 Matt 21:33–46; John 8:23–26; 12:48.
199 2 Thess 2:10–12; 1 John 2:18–23; 4:1–3.
200 Rev 1:9; 2:7, 11, 17, 26–27; 3:5, 12, 21; 12:10–11; 19:10.
201 Isa 57:1–10; 59:1–8; Rom 1:18–24.
202 Dan 7:10; Matt 16:27; 25:31–46; Rev 20:12

the end reveal a genetic line of ideological continuity.[203] God's will, perfectly realized in the age to come, must be obeyed in the age that is ending. The revelation of an impending judgment and cosmic denouement naturally generates interest in how best to prepare.[204] "Ethics," according to Amos N. Wilder, "was inextricably implied in the best apocalyptic; it was assumed. The eschatological hope was only for those who were righteous. And it was the ethical consciousness which in the first place demanded the Kingdom."[205] In light of God's revealed will and sovereignty over the cosmos, apocalyptic eschatology calls for individual responsibility.[206] God commands Israel, "Preserve justice, and do righteousness, for my salvation is about to come and my righteousness to be revealed."[207] To those who "loosen the bonds of wickedness, to undo the bands of the yoke, and to let the oppressed go free," God promises eschatological guidance, satisfaction, strength, and delight.[208] God's enemies and God's people alike are expected to obey his commands.[209]

When "that Day" arrives, many making a claim to godliness will be rejected for failing to perform the will of God (Matt 7:21–23). The Son of Man separates the sheep from the goats at judgment based on the presence or absence of concrete compassionate deeds.[210] In light of the fact that the "night is almost gone, and the day is at hand," Paul commands the Romans to pay what they owe, fulfill the law of love, and lay aside the deeds of darkness including carousing, drunkenness, sexual promiscuity, sensuality, strife, and jealousy (Rom 13:7–13). The "revelation of Jesus Christ" is introduced by a lengthy paraenetic discourse encouraging believers to repent of complacency, endure suffering and persecution, turn from doctrinal error, spurn immorality, stir from spiritual indifference, and cultivate humility.[211] Keeping God's

203 Russell, *Method and Message*, 100–3; Fiorenza, "Phenomenon of Early Christian Apocalyptic," 300–2;

204 Meyers, "Apocalyptic Thought in the New Testament," 220; Allison, "Apocalyptic Ethics and Behavior," 295–311.

205 Amos N. Wilder, *Eschatology and Ethics in the Teaching of Jesus*, rev. ed. (Harper and Brothers, 1950), 32. Cf. W. D. Davies, *Torah in the Messianic Age and/or the Age to Come*, Journal of Biblical Literature Monograph Series 7 (Society of Biblical Literature, 1952), 3, n. 4; George Foot Moore, *Judaism in the First Centuries of the Christian Era: The Age of the Tannaim*, vol. 1 (Harvard University Press, 1927), 271; R. Travers Herford, *Talmud and Apocrypha: A Comparative Study of the Jewish Ethical Teaching in the Rabbinical and Non-rabbinical Sources in the Early Centuries* (Soncino Press, 1933), 171, 178. There will be a "great contest for entry to the heavenly city" (Sib. Or. 2:38–39).

206 Isa 26:7–19; 1 Enoch 91:4–11. Hasel, "Resurrection," 283.

207 Isa 56:1; cf. 2 Enoch 9:1; Sib. Or. 2:56–78.

208 Isa 58:6–14; cf. 1 Enoch 94:1–10.

209 Dan 4:27; 9:9–14; 1 Enoch 5:4; Russell, *Method and Message*, 102.

210 Matt 25:31–46; cf. 2 Enoch 10:1–6; Sib. Or. 2:80–94; 4 Ezra 2:20–23.

211 Rev 2:5, 10, 14–16, 20; 3:2, 17–19.

commandments and overcoming every form of corruption are the distinguishing characteristics of heirs to the kingdom.[212] The eschatological hope of "conquering" is dependent on perseverance[213] and obedience.[214]

Redeemer/Judge

As the corrective to evil and suffering, apocalyptic eschatology anticipates the appearance of a divine redeemer/judge: "Oh, that Thou wouldst rend the heavens and come down, that the mountains might quake at they presence" (Isa 64:1).[215] In response to human depravity God will assume the role of Divine Warrior, arrayed for judgment against his enemies (Isa 59:15–19). At that time a "redeemer will come to Zion, and to those who turn from transgression in Jacob."[216] His judgment is cosmic in reach, stretching from east to west and unconstrained by human opposition or political structure.[217]

The "little apocalypse" in Zechariah 14 depicts an apocalyptic theophany fully assimilated by later Christian messianic expectation. On "that Day" Yahweh the Divine Warrior will battle the wicked nations and stand on the Mount of Olives, splitting it down the "middle from east to west" (Zech 14:3–4). Accompanied by angelic hosts,[218] he will create a new order signified by the flow of living water from Jerusalem and the archetypal transformation of day and night into perpetual light.[219] It is at this time that God will establish his permanent and uncompromising authority: "And the Lord will be king over all the earth; in that day the Lord will be the only one, and his name the only one" (Zech 14:9).[220]

The Messiah's return in the NT specifies much of the OT apocalyptic language and imagery. Seated on the Mount of Olives, the scene of Zechariah's theophany, Jesus describes the nature of his second advent. The Son of Man will return with irresistible power to wage war and execute judgment against the wicked.[221] With Jesus' return will come a new heaven, a new earth, and a new Jerusalem where light is provided by the presence of God, where a "river of

---

212 Rev 2:7, 11, 17, 26; 3:5, 12, 21; 14:10.
213 Rev 2:2, 19; 13:10; 14:12.
214 Rev 1:3; 2:10; 3:8; 12:17; 14:12; 22:7, 9; Aune, *Literary Environment*, 244.
215 Cf. 4 Ezra 9:1; 2 Bar. 30:1–5.
216 Isa 59:20; cf. 2 Bar. 29:3; Pss. Sol. 17:26–34.
217 Hanson, *Dawn of Apocalyptic*, 129–34.
218 Zech 14:5; Matt 24:31; Rev 19:14; 1 Enoch 1:9.
219 Zech 14:6–8; cf. 1 Enoch 45:4–5; 53:7; 4 Ezra 7:36–44; T. Dan 5:12.
220 Cf. 2 Bar. 70:9; 72:1–6.
221 Matt 24:27–31; 25:13–46; Rev 19:11–21; 20:11–15; cf. Pss. Sol. 17:21–25; Apoc. Ab. 30:2–8; CD 7.19–20.

the water of life" flows freely, and where joy and contentment endure forever.[222] Upon his return Jesus' omnipotent work[223] and new name, "King of Kings and Lord of Lords," declare his unequivocal, singular, and universal authority.[224]

CONCLUSION

From at least the pre-exilic period through the New Testament era, theological pluralism threatened Judaism and Christianity with annihilation by assimilation. The very nature of polytheistic pluriformity demanded a philosophical and theological syncretism that explicitly contravened biblically mandated exclusivism. As a resistive front against this encroaching pluralism, apocalyptic eschatology developed as an inherently exclusivistic worldview, dictating acceptable belief and practice in an effort to control and preserve a faithful community. Apocalyptic eschatology's discernable thematic cluster maintains a strict division between what is inside or outside the true faith. At the most fundamental levels, apocalyptic dualism divides the cosmos between God's immutable good and finite evil, this present evil age and the coming age of righteousness, and the people of God or the children of Satan. By insisting on the absolute sovereignty of the biblical God, apocalyptic eschatology excludes every other claim to ultimate self-determination. Apocalyptic pessimism indicts fallen human nature, the present age, and those who hope in either. Although theological pluralism assumes even contradictory truth claims and ethical standpoints may be ultimately acceptable, the apocalyptic expectation of eschatological judgment excludes all compromise with divinely revealed standards. As a revelation-based worldview, apocalyptic eschatology imposes a divinely prescribed ethic that rejects alternative standards and forbids compromise. Finally, the one true redeemer/judge's anticipated arrival is a supremely exclusionary event, the climactic ἀποκάλυψις ("revelation") that permanently divides the redeemed from the doomed, cosmic good from evil, and this fallen age from fully realized eternal life.

---

222 Rev 21:1, 23; 22:1–2; cf. Jub. 23:29–30; 1QS 4.7–8; 1QM 17.6–8.

223 Rev 19:19–21; 20:11; 21:5–6; 22:12–13; cf. Dan 7:13–14; Col 1:16–17.

224 Rev 19:16; Phil 2:9–11; cf. 1 Enoch 10:21; 1QM 14.15–16.

CHAPTER 3

APOCALYPTIC ESCHATOLOGY IN JUDE

AT CONTEXTUAL, LITERARY, AND THEMATIC LEVELS, the epistle of Jude is dependent on apocalyptic eschatology. Consistent with early Jewish and Christian responses to ubiquitous theological pluralism, Jude confronts a similar community crisis by following the same exclusionary worldview pattern established in apocalyptic literature. Apocalyptic elements of exclusivism saturate the letter's message, calling Christians to "contend for the faith once for all delivered to the saints" (v. 3).

PLURALISTIC CONTEXT

The very existence and nature of Jude's short epistle testify to its origination in a pluralistic context. Discourse is solicited and controlled by its occasion, or its "rhetorical situation." This situation involves a "complex of persons, events, objects, and relations presenting an actual or potential exigence which can be completely or partially removed if discourse, introduced into the situation, can so constrain human decision or action as to bring about the significant modification of the exigence."[1] As argued in the previous chapter, apocalyptic eschatology responds to the "exigence" or crisis of theological pluralism. When ideological suppositions contrary to the sanctioned worldview threatened to dilute the community's theological continuity, apocalyptic theologians responded with an aggressive defense and promotion of "the truth." Confronted by an influx of antinomian syncretistic sympathies, Jude responds with his own exposition of apocalyptic eschatology.[2] Jude's relationship to apocalyptic materials therefore extends beyond the merely literary.

---

1 Lloyd Bitzer, "The Rhetorical Situation," in *Rhetoric: A Tradition in Transition*, ed. Walter R. Fisher (Michigan State University Press, 1974), 252.

2 Achtemeier, *Introducing the New Testament*, 532; Charles, "Literary Artifice," 109–110.

Jude's apocalyptic eschatology is no artificial rhetorical tool.[3] According to Bauckham, "it is the worldview within which he naturally thinks and which he takes it for granted his readers accept."[4]

Community Infiltration

Jude identifies τινες ἄνθρωποι ("some men") in the church as the source of opposing theological pluralism (v. 4). These men apparently παρεισέδυσαν ("crept in") the church on the strength of their convincing Christian façades. The verb παρεισδύνω is a NT *hapax legomenon*[5] that generally refers to infiltration by stealth.[6] The verbal image depicts a certain specific (τινες) group of men slipping into Jude's community from the outside. The NT frequently uses similar language to describe itinerant prophets or teachers who oppose the apostolic mission with theological and ethical error.[7] An unfortunate fulfillment of the Israelite wilderness typology, Jude's audience included an apostate faction destined for eschatological judgment (v. 5). The factional membership was not, however, passive but aggressive and insidious. They were false teachers, comparable to the archetypal heretics Cain, Balaam, and Korah, who garnered positions of authority and influence only to spread corruption and destruction (v. 11).[8] Like dangerous reefs (σπιλάδες) that threaten ships at sea, Jude's opponents boldly participated in the church's fellowship meals and posed a threat to anyone who ventured too close (v. 12).[9] By

---

3 Cf. Rowston who interprets Jude as a post-apostolic attempt to revive Pauline apocalyptic eschatology in response to encroaching gnosticism ("Most Neglected Book," 561–2).

4 Bauckham, *Jude, 2 Peter*, 11.

5 "*Hapax legomenon*" refers to a word that is used only once in a corpus of literature.

6 Cf. Josephus, *Jewish War* 1.468; Plutarch, *Agis and Cleomenes* 3.1; idem, *Moralia* 216b; Horst Balz and Gerhard Schneider, "παρεισδύω," *EDNT* 3:37; the noun form παρείσδυσις with reference to the devil (Epistle of Barnabas 2:10; 4:9); Vögtle, *Judasbrief*, 26; Bauckham, *Jude, 2 Peter*, 35.

7 Cf. Matt 7:15; 2 Cor 11:3–15; Gal 2:4, 10; 2 Tim 3:6; Titus 1:11; 1 John 4:1; 2 John 10; 2 Pet 2:1; Vögtle, *Judasbrief*, 25; Ellis, "Prophecy and Hermeneutic in Jude," 230–2; idem, "Paul and his Opponents," in *Prophecy and Hermeneutic in Early Christianity* (Baker, 1993), 115; Ralph P. Martin, *The Theology of the Letters of James, Peter, and Jude* (Cambridge University Press, 1994), 84.

8 Cf. Balaam's prophetic leadership status (Num 22:5–6; 31:16) and Korah's priestly/princely heritage (Num 16:1–2); Jacob Milgrom, *Numbers*, The JPS Torah Commentary (The Jewish Publication Society, 1990), 471–3; Baruch A. Levine, *Numbers 1–20: A New Translation with Introduction and Commentary*, AB 4a (Doubleday, 1993), 410–3. Cain's reputation as both the "arch-sinner" and "first heretic" is more obscure but already extant in the first-century A.D.; cf. Matt 23:34–35; 1 Enoch 85:3–4; and Josephus, *Jewish Antiquities* 1.61 where Cain is labeled the first "instructor (διδάσκαλος) in wicked practices" (trans. H. St. J. Thackeray, vol. 4, LCL, ed. G. P. Goold et al. [Harvard University Press, 1978]); Geza Vermes, "The Targumic Versions of Genesis 4:3–16," in *Post Biblical Studies*, Studies in Judaism in Late Antiquity 8, ed. Jacob Neusner (E. J. Brill, 1975), 116.

9 Mayor, *Jude*, 40–41; Reicke, *Jude*, 207; Vögtle, *Judasbrief*, 67.

"shepherding themselves" (ἑαυτοὺς ποιμαίνοντες) they engaged in pastoral activity that was purely self-serving.[10] The results, according to Jude's vivid imagery,[11] are predictable. Just as waterless clouds and barren uprooted trees produce nothing of value, their "ministry" was devoid of true spiritual fruit (v. 12). These heretics were like waves that "toss up refuse and mud,"[12] managing to produce only "shameful deeds" (αἰσχύνας, v. 13).[13] The importation of their ideas was already weakening the fellowship, necessitating aggressive intervention and accountability (vv. 22–23).

Ethical and Theological Antinomianism

By identifying these ἄνθρωποι ("men") as ἀσεβεῖς ("ungodly"), Jude provides a fitting blanket summarization of their antinomian character (v. 4): "Unrighteous behavior stemming from an irreverent rejection of the moral authority of God's commandments."[14] These two aspects of their error, practical and theoretical,[15] are outlined by two attributive participial phrases modifying ἄνθρωποι. These men, first of all, "turn the grace of God into licentiousness" (τὴν τοῦ θεοῦ ἡμῶν χάριτα μετατιθέντες εἰς ἀσέλγειαν). They redefine grace, the Christian doctrine of freedom and forgiveness, as license for immorality.[16] Secondly, as those who "deny our only master and Lord, Jesus Christ," (τὸν μόνον δεσπότην καὶ κύριον ἡμῶν Ἰησοῦν Χριστὸν ἀρνούμενοι), they justify their lawless behavior by rejecting the constraints of divine authority. They specifically reject Christ's lordship (τὸν μόνον δεσπότην καὶ κύριον), his authority to command virtuous living.[17] As leaders in the community they openly declare their allegiance to the Christian gospel. Yet as antinomians they redefine the

---

10 Jude's shepherding language in Christian vernacular is unmistakably pastoral. Cf. Ezek 34:2–3; John 21:16; Acts 20:28; 1 Cor 9:7; Eph 4:11; 1 Pet 5:2; Knoch, *Judasbrief*, 184–5; Vögtle, *Judasbrief*, 67–8.

11 Cf. Num 16:24, 26–27, 34; Ps 1:3; 52:5; Prov 2:22; 25:14; Isa 8:14–15; 57:20 Jer 17:6; 1 Enoch 18:14–16; 80:2–8; Osburn, "1 Enoch 80:2–8 (67:5–7) and Jude 12–13," *The CBQ* 47, no. 2 (1985): 296–303; idem, "Discourse Analysis and Jewish Apocalyptic in the Epistle of Jude," in *Linguistics and New Testament Interpretation: Essays on Discourse Analysis*, ed. David Alan Black (Broadman Press, 1992), 301–3.

12 Isa 57:20. For other instances of this metaphorical description of the wicked see 1QH 2.12–13, 27–28; 6.23; 8.15.

13 Cf. Luke 14:9; 2 Cor 4:2; Phil 3:19; Heb 12:2; Rev 3:18; Josephus, *Jewish Antiquities* 4.260; Axel Horstmann, "αἰσχύνομαι," *EDNT* 1:43.

14 Bauckham, *Jude, 2 Peter*, 38. Cf. the stem ἀσεβ- in the LXX and its connections with false teachers (Prov 28:4; Jer 3:13). In the NT see 1 Tim 1:9–10; 2 Tim 2:16; 2 Pet 2:5–6; Sellin, "Häretiker des Judasbriefes," 211–2; Peter Fiedler, "ἀσεβέω," *EDNT* 1:169.

15 Martin, *Theology of Jude*, 73.

16 Osburn, "1 Enoch 80:2–8 (67:5–7) and Jude 12–13," 300; E. M. Sidebottom, *James, Jude and 2 Peter*, The Century Bible: New Edition (Thomas Nelson and Sons, 1967), 83–4.

17 Osburn, "Discourse Analysis," 291.

gospel to accommodate their own predilections.[18] The result is a syncretistic[19] anti-gospel that ebbs and flows with the tide of human self-authentication.

As the connotations of ἀσέλγειαν ("sensuality") in v. 4 reveal,[20] their most overt behavioral errors involve sexual impurity. Just as the fallen angels and the Sodomites transgressed God's ordained sexual boundaries (vv. 6–7),[21] Jude's opponents "defile the flesh" (σάρκα μὲν μιαίνουσιν, v. 8).[22] In v. 10 their moral corruption (φθείρονται)[23] is compared to the instinctive (φυσικῶς) irrational (ἄλογα) behaviors of brute beasts (ζῷα). They are only committed to pursuing their own desires (τὰς ἐπιθυμίας ἑαυτῶν, v. 16) which include a passion for wicked deeds (τὰς ἑαυτῶν ἐπιθυμίας τῶν ἀσεβειῶν, v.18).[24]

Their immoral behavior, however, is merely the logical outcome of a more insidious spiritual flaw: They reject the Lord's authority and its objective manifestations.[25] Jude's central exhortation in v. 3 indirectly levels this accusation by demanding conformity to "the faith once for all delivered to the saints" (τῇ ἅπαξ παραδοθείσῃ τοῖς ἁγίοις πίστει). The objective use of πίστις here and in the Pauline literature refers to the content of Christian belief: the "gospel" or the corpus of authentic Christian ideas.[26] "The faith," the "gospel," is a fixed whole defined by correct intellectual content and correct practical behavior.[27] By placing the attributive participial phrase ἅπαξ παραδοθείσῃ τοῖς ἁγίοις in an emphatic position between πίστει and its definite article τῇ, Jude makes a deliberate rhetorical effort to document this faith's inviolate status. The adverb ἅπαξ ("once and for all") anchors the faith temporally; at one particular time one particular body of normative Christian truth was permanently fixed.[28] As

18 Osburn, "1 Enoch 80:2–8 (67:5–7) and Jude 12–13," 300–1; Rowston, "Most Neglected Book," 555;

19 Cf. Rowston, "Most Neglected Book," 561–2.

20 Cf. Rom 13:13; 2 Cor 12:21; 1 Pet 4:3; T. Jud. 23:1; Sellin, "Häretiker des Judasbriefes," 211–2; Horst Goldstein, "ἀσέλγεια," EDNT 1:169–170.

21 Cf. 1 Enoch 9:8; 12:4; T. Naph. 3:1–4:2; Jub. 20:5; 3 Macc 2:4–5.

22 Jude's verb μιαίνω appears repeatedly in connection with the angelic Watcher's sexual sin (1 Enoch 7:1; 9:8; 10:11; 12:4; 15:3–4; cf. Jub. 16:5 [Sodom]); Mayor, Jude, 33; Bauckham, Jude, 2 Peter, 56; Fuchs and Reymond, Jude, 166–7.

23 Cf. Gen 6:11 (LXX); Hos 9:9 (LXX); 1 Cor 15:33; 2 Cor 7:2; 11:3; Eph 4:22; Rev 19:2; T. Jud. 19:4; Günther Harder, "φθείρω, κτλ.," TDNT 9:99–103.

24 Cf. T. Jud. 13:2; T. Iss. 6:2; CD 2:16–21; 3:2–6; Reicke, Jude, 213; Knoch, Judasbrief, 189.

25 Martin, Theology of Jude, 74.

26 1 Cor 16:13; Gal 1:23; 3:23; 6:10; Eph 4:5; Phil 1:25; Col 1:23; cf. Rom 10:16; 2 Thess 1:8; 1 Pet 4:17; Rudolf Bultmann, "πιστεύω, κτλ.," TDNT 6:213; Anthony C. Thiselton, The First Epistle to the Corinthians: A Commentary on the Greek Text, NIGTC (Eerdmans, 2000), 1336; Hans Dieter Betz, Galatians: A Commentary on Paul's Letter to the Churches in Galatia, Hermeneia (Fortress Press, 1979), 81, n. 235; 176, n. 120; Bauckham, Jude, 2 Peter, 32–3.

27 1 Tim 3:9–10; 4:1–2, 6–7; 2 Tim 4:7 in the context of vv. 1–5.

28 In vv. 3 and 5 ἅπαξ draws a clear connection between the "once for all" exodus event that defined Jewish self-understanding and the "once for all" Jesus event that defines Christi-

a Jewish technical term, παραδίδωμι refers to the methodical, controlled, and accurate "delivering" or "handing over" of authoritative "holy word" traditions.[29] Paul received the traditions he delivered, not from other people, but "by means of revelation" (δι' ἀποκαλύψεως, Gal 1:12). The Corinthians were praiseworthy because they held "firmly to the traditions" (παραδόσεις)" just as he had "delivered (παρέδωκα) them" (1 Cor 11:2). He "delivered" (παρέδωκα) a creed that was at every point in unity with the Scriptures (κατὰ τὰς γραφὰς, 1 Cor 15:3–4).[30] Paul could in fact identify the traditions he delivered with Scripture as "word of God" equivalents:[31]

> When you received from us the word of God's message, you accepted it not as the word of men, but for what it really is, the word of God." (1 Thess 2:13)

It is for the preservation of this objective body of doctrine that Jude's audience must strive.[32]

Jude's opponents, however, exhibit a fundamental disregard for divine authority that is illustrated by three typological examples of sin and judgment

anity. Cf. Ps 88:35 (LXX); Heb 10:2; Pss. Sol. 12:6; Philo, *On Drunkenness* 198: "traditions delivered once for all" (τοῖς ἄπαξ παραδοθεῖσι); Josephus, *Jewish Antiquities* 4.140; idem, *Jewish War* 2.158: the Essenes "irresistibly attract all who have once (ἄπαξ) tasted their philosophy" (trans. H. St. J. Thackeray, vol. 2, LCL, ed. G. P. Goold et al. [Harvard University Press, 1976]).

   29 Cf. 1 Cor 11:23; 15:3; Gal 1:19; Phil 4:9; Col 2:6; 1 Thess 2:13; 2 Thess 2:15; 3:6; Birger Gerhardsson, *Memory and Manuscript: Oral Tradition and Written Transmission in Rabbinic Judaism and Early Christianity*, trans. Eric J. Sharpe (C. W. K. Gleerup, 1961), 93–121; 288–306; James I. H. McDonald, *Kerygma and Didache*, 101–25; Oscar Cullmann, "The Tradition," in *The Early Church: Studies in Early Christian History and Theology*, ed. A. J. B. Higgins (Westminster Press, 1956), 63–9; E. Earle Ellis, *The Making of the New Testament Documents*, BibInt 39 (E. J. Brill, 1999), 22, 26–27, 47.

   30 Fee, *1 Corinthians*, 725–8; Hans Conzelmann, *1 Corinthians: A Commentary on the First Epistle to the Corinthians*, trans. James W. Leitch, Hermeneia (Fortress Press, 1975), 255.

   31 Cf. 2 Thess 2:15; 3:6; Ernest Best, *A Commentary on the First and Second Epistles to the Thessalonians* (Hendrickson, 1986), 111; Charles A. Wanamaker, *The Epistles to the Thessalonians: A Commentary on the Greek Text*, NIGTC (Eerdmans, 1990), 110–1; F. F. Bruce, *1 and 2 Thessalonians*, WBC 45 (Word Books, 1982), 44–5; James D. G. Dunn, *The Epistles to the Colossians and to Philemon: A Commentary on the Greek Text*, NIGTC (Eerdmans, 1996), 286. According to E. Earle Ellis, Paul "regards his writing as divine revelation and commands it to be read in church which, in the Jewish context, gives it the status of canonical Scripture" (*Making of the New Testament*, 220); cf. idem, "New Directions in the History of Early Christianity," in *Early Christianity, Late Antiquity and Beyond*, vol. 2 of *Ancient History in a Modern University*, ed. T. W. Hillard et al. (Eerdmans, 1998), 89–90; 1 Cor 14:37; Col 4:16; 1 Thess 5:27; Philip S. Alexander, "Jewish Aramaic Translations of Hebrew Scriptures," in *Mikra: Text, Translation, Reading and Interpretation of the Hebrew Bible in Ancient Judaism and Early Christianity*, ed. Martin Jan Mulder (Fortress Press, 1988), 238–9; Martin Hengel, regarding John's apocalypse, *The Johannine Question* (SCM Press, 1989), 126.

   32 Gerhard Dautzenberg, "ἀγών," *EDNT* 1:27.

(vv. 5–8). The faithless Israelites (v. 5) were condemned because they did not believe God's word, his immutable promises:

> Then they despised the pleasant land; they did not believe in his word, they grumbled in their tents; they did not listen to the voice of the Lord. (Ps 106:24–25)

Angels and Sodom and Gomorrah were doomed because they violated God's order, God's law, and, therefore, God himself (vv. 6–7).[33] Related apocalyptic tradition describes these examples with this precise charge in mind:

> Sun, moon, and stars do not alter their order; thus you should not alter the Law of God by the disorder of your actions.... . do not become like Sodom, which departed from the order of nature. Likewise the Watchers departed from nature's order. (T. Naph. 3:2–5)

Just as (ὁμοίως) all three OT types flouted God's revealed will, Jude's opponents reject divine standards in favor of their own subjective self-inflicted delusion (v. 8).[34] In v. 8 the participle ἐνυπνιαζόμενοι ("dreaming") establishes the cause of three finite verbal descriptions of rebellious behavior.[35] Ἐνυπνιάζομαι, commonly used in the LXX for the pseudo-revelations of false prophets, therefore identifies the opponents' rebuttal to the revealed faith.[36] Their authority source is subjective and internal, dependent entirely on ecstatic experience.[37] "On the strength of their dreams" they justify immorality (σάρκα μὲν μιαίνουσιν) by rejecting divine authority (κυριότητα ἀθετοῦσιν) and insulting the angelic representatives of God's ordained moral and created order (δόξας βλασφημοῦσιν, v. 8).[38] By embracing the license of self-verification, they reject Christ's authority by default and "end up with only their own self-regarding autonomy."[39]

---

33 Paulsen, *Judasbrief*, 63; Frankemölle, *Judasbrief*, 124.

34 Spitta, *Brief des Judas*, 342.

35 Mayor, *Jude*, 33; Grundmann, *Brief des Judas*, 35; Cantinat, *Jude*, 308; cf. Daniel B. Wallace who notes that the "causal participle normally *precedes* the verb it modifies. Thus, form follows function (i.e., the cause of an action precedes the action)" (*Greek Grammar Beyond the Basics: An Exegetical Syntax of the New Testament* [Zondervan, 1996], 631).

36 Deut 13:2, 3, 5; Isa 56:10; Jer 23:25; 36:8; cf. Jer 23:32; Zech 10:2; 1 Enoch 99:8; Vögtle, *Judasbrief*, 49.

37 Hans Windisch, *Die Katholischen Briefe*, HNT 15 (J. C. B. Mohr [Paul Siebeck], 1951), 41; Sellin, "Häretiker des Judasbriefes," 216–7; Bauckham, *Jude, 2 Peter*, 64.

38 According to Jewish tradition, God employed the angels (δόξας) to mediate Mosaic law. Cf. Jub. 1:27–29; Acts 7:38, 53; Heb 2:2; Josephus, *Jewish Antiquities* 15.136; The Shepherd of Hermas, Similitudes 8.3.3; Bauckham, *Jude, 2 Peter*, 55; Schrage, *Der Judas Brief*, 232.

39 Martin, *Theology of Jude*, 74, 84.

Jude's woe-oracle in v. 11 further exposes the false teachers' antinomian-ism by identifying them with three notorious rebels from Jewish history. Ac-cording to tradition, Cain's argument with Abel was a theological denial of God's moral authority to judge the world justly. Cain contends:

> There is no judgment, there is no judge, there is no other world, there is no gift of good reward for the righteous, and no punishment for the wicked.[40]

Balaam abandoned God's commandments and his own prophecies in order to lead the Israelites away from the law.[41] Korah and his companions, offended by distinctions within the priesthood, challenged God's law by challenging its representatives (Moses and Aaron).[42] Like Cain, Balaam, and Korah, Ju-de's opponents boldly reject God's revealed will. In their teaching they speak harshly against God and his word (τῶν σκληρῶν ὧν ἐλάλησαν κατ᾽ αὐτοῦ), murmuring and complaining (γογγυσταί μεμψίμοιροι)[43] like the faithless Isra-elites who despised the Lord's will for their lives (vv. 15–16).[44] Their teachings are boastful and arrogant, affronts to God's authority[45] designed to endear them to antinomian financiers (v. 16).[46] Fulfilling an apostolic prophecy, these "scoffers" (ἐμπαῖκται) repudiate the constraints of piety and authoritarian religion (v. 18)[47] and create divisions (ἀποδιορίζοντες) that exalt antinomian elitists (v. 19).[48]

IDEOLOGICAL FUNCTION

Consistent with apocalyptic eschatology in general, Jude's message is de-signed to "bring about a separation between the original community and

---

40 Targum Pseudo-Jonathan Gen 4:8, translated by Michael Maher, *Targum Pseudo-Jona-than: Genesis, Translated, with Introduction and Notes*, The Aramaic Bible 1b (Liturgical Press, 1992); cf. also Targum Neofiti 1 Gen 4:8; Vermes, "Targumic Versions," 116.

41 Num 22–24; 31:16; Deut 23:4; Neh 13:2; Rev 2:14.

42 Num 16:1–11, 40; 26:9; Martin Noth, *Numbers: A Commentary*, trans. James D. Martin, OTL (Westminster, 1968), 125, 130; Timothy R. Ashley, *The Book of Numbers*, NICOT (Eerdmans, 1993), 295–7.

43 Cf. the "grumbling" of Israel (Num 14:2, 27, 29, 36; Deut 1:27; Ps 106:25; CD 3.8) and Korah (Num 16:11).

44 Mayor, *Jude*, 45; Paulsen, *Judasbrief*, 77; Bauckham, *Jude, 2 Peter*, 97–8.

45 Cf. Ps 12:3–4; Dan 7:8, 20; 11:36; Rev 13:5–6; 1 Enoch 5:4; 101:3; T. Mos. 7:1–10; Martin, *The-ology of Jude*, 71.

46 Cf. Deut 10:17; 16:19; 2 Chr 19:7; Prov 28:21; Mal 2:9; Sir 35:12–13; T. Mos. 7:9–10; "[Jerusa-lem's] leaders pronounce judgment for a bribe, her priests instruct for a price, and her proph-ets divine for money" (Mic 3:11); Bauckham, *Jude, 2 Peter*, 99–100.

47 Cf. Ps 1:1; Prov 1:22; 9:7–8; 13:1; 4 Ezra 7:79, 81; Cantinat, *Jude*, 325; Bauckham, *Jude, 2 Pe-ter*, 104.

48 Bigg, *Jude*, 339; Windisch, *Katholischen Briefe*, 46; Cantinat, *Jude*, 327..

the newcomers,"[49] functioning as an exclusionary force that demands clear distinction between one legitimate ideology and its competition.[50] "Jude's language is a language of social and religious control" that not only reflects "certain beliefs and social processes" but also "actively establishes and maintains" them.[51]

COMMUNITY IDENTIFICATION

Jude's apocalyptic eschatology establishes and maintains ideological boundaries within the community by clearly differentiating between those faithful to the revealed worldview and apostate syncretists who have abandoned it.[52] The faithful are addressed directly in the first or second person plural[53] and embraced as the "beloved"[54] who enjoy a common salvific experience (v. 3). Their character and eschatological destiny are preserved by God (vv. 1, 24), and they have been well schooled[55] in "the faith," the normative Christian worldview.[56] By cultivating and maintaining fidelity to the sacrosanct ideology,[57] they can anticipate eternal purity and life in the new age to come (vv. 20–21, 24). The false teachers, however, are labeled "ungodly" (ἀσεβεῖς)[58] and identified by a derogatory use of the third person[59] that completely excludes them from the blessed fellowship. This "negative labelling" technique "serves as a social distancing device, underscoring differences and thus dividing social categories into polarities such as the good and the wicked, heroes and villains, believers and infidels or the honorable and the shameful. Such labelling serves to underscore societal values by setting apart those who lack or flaunt them."[60] The error of Jude's opponents is an abandonment of the revealed

---

49 Webb, "Eschatology of the Epistle of Jude and Its Rhetorical and Social Functions," 150; Koester, *History and Literature of Early Christianity*, 247.

50 Neyrey, *Jude*, 37–9. Cf. Meeks, "Social Functions of Apocalyptic Language," 702; Elliott, *Survivors of Israel*, 57–8, 185–6; Dunnett, "Hermeneutics of Jude," 287–92.

51 Joubert, "Language, Ideology, and the Social Context," 347

52 Joubert, "Language, Ideology, and the Social Context," 342–7; Watson, *Invention, Arrangement, and Style*, 31–2, 79; Achtemeier, *Introducing the New Testament*, 532.

53 Cf. vv. 3, 4, 5, 12, 17, 18, 20–21, 24–25.

54 Cf. vv. 1, 3, 17, 20.

55 Theodor Zahn, *Introduction to the New Testament*, vol. 2, trans. John Moore Trout et al.(1909; repr., Klock and Klock, 1977), 241–2; Neyrey, *Jude*, 33.

56 Cf. vv. 3, 17, 20.

57 Cf. the superlative τῇ ἁγιωτάτῃ ὑμῶν πίστει ("your most holy faith," v. 20).

58 Cf. the stem ἀσεβ-, vv. 4, 15 (3x), 18.

59 Cf. οὗτοι ("these," vv. 8, 10, 12, 16, 19); αὐτοῖς ("them," v. 11); τούτοις ("these," v. 14); Cantinat, *Jude*, 307; Bauckham, *Jude, 2 Peter*, 45; Charles, "'Those' and 'These,'" 110–1; Neyrey, *Jude*, 31.

60 Bruce J. Malina and Jerome H. Neyrey, *Calling Jesus Names: The Social Value of Labels in Matthew*, FF (Polebridge Press, 1988), 37–8.

"faith" (v. 4) that separates them from the regenerate[61] and identifies them as objects of divine invective and eschatological doom.[62] They are the embodiment of apostasy in the last days (vv. 14–15, 17–18), and their errors must be disclosed and rejected with warlike intensity.[63]

EXPLANATION OF OPPOSITION

Jude's paraenetic sections (vv. 3, 20–23) reveal that the genuine church body was besieged and opposed by factions from within. The faith in its traditional form must be defended (v. 3) because it was threatened by antinomian compromise (v. 4). The effects of this seditious influence were already rippling through the community and generating divisions (v. 19), disputes, waffling, and carnality (vv. 22–23). In order to explain this dissonance, Jude turns to apocalyptic prophecies (vv. 14–15, 17–18) that predict the inevitable conflict between ungodliness and God's program of redemption at the end of the age.[64] God's judgment is leveled against sinners whose words and deeds are directed first and foremost against him (κατ' αὐτου, v. 15). The heretics are fundamentally "ungodly" (ἀσεβεῖς) and therefore opposed to God's will and way.[65] Their commitment to ungodliness therefore naturally leads to "mocking" and contradicting the truth (v. 18), bringing them into direct opposition to those who champion the truth.

ENCOURAGEMENT FOR THE FAITHFUL

For those who willingly conform to the revealed world view, Jude promises divine preservation (vv. 1, 24) and eternal life (v. 21).[66] The faithful can entrust themselves to the God who calls them, loves them, and provides them with mercy and peace (v. 1–2). They can depend on God's faithfulness to defend his own name, vindicate their ideology, and execute judgment against the unrighteous at the parousia.[67] The object of their worship and obedience is a benevolent savior, supremely powerful and worthy of devotion (vv. 24–25). Those tottering on the brink of apostasy and eschatological exclusion can indirectly benefit from the certainty of judgment and vindication. Motivated

---

61 Cf. vv. 4, 8, 10–12, 16, 19, 22–23.
62 Cf. vv. 4, 5–7, 11, 13, 15, 23.
63 Cf. vv. 3, 5, 23.
64 Neyrey, *Jude*, 40.
65 Cf. vv. 4, 15 (3x), 18; Fiedler, "ἀσεβέω," 168–9.
66 Webb, "Eschatology of the Epistle of Jude and Its Rhetorical and Social Functions," 140–2, 150.
67 Cf. vv. 4, 5–7, 13, 14–15.

by threat and hope, they might still receive mercy and be "snatched from the fire" (v. 23).

COMMUNITY PRESERVATION AND CONTROL

Jude's apocalyptic eschatology is a conduit of authority and control and elim-inates the possibility for peaceful coexistence of antithetical Christian view-points.[68] There is, according to Jude, one unified and immutable standard for Christian belief and practice. Conformity to "the faith which was once for all delivered to the saints" (v. 3) identifies the legitimate community and pre-serves its boundaries.[69] The faithful contend for this authoritative faith and build their lives on it (vv. 3, 20). This careful attention to doctrinal purity pro-vides a "bulwark" against apostasy,[70] forcing Jude's readers to be critical of the ideology of the antinomians and to reject them as ungodly.[71] Rooted in a re-vealed authority structure,[72] Jude's message excludes theological innovation and threatens the dissident and subversive with eschatological judgment.[73]

ELEMENTS OF EXCLUSIVISM

Authority

With the title Ἰούδας ... ἀδελφὸς Ἰακώβου (v. 1) Jude subtly asserts his author-ity as a "brother of the Lord"[74] and a keeper of revelation. In defense of his own unique status, Paul cites the "brothers of the Lord" as complimentary examples of apostolic privilege and authority (1 Cor 9:5).[75] The strength of this comparison for Paul's argument depends on the well known and indisputable authenticity of an apostolic ministry belonging to a special leadership class

---

68 Joubert, "Language, Ideology and the Social Context," 338–47; Koester, *History and Lit-erature of Early Christianity*, 247.

69 Watson, *Intervention, Arrangement, and Style*, 31–2.

70 Martin, *Theology of Jude*, 75–81; Vögtle, *Judasbrief,* 3.

71 Webb, "Eschatology of the Epistle of Jude and Its Rhetorical and Social Functions," 149–50; Joubert, "Language, Ideology and Social Context," 344–5.

72 Cf. Collins, "Early Christian Apocalypticism," 7.

73 Cf. vv. 4, 5–7, 13, 15, 23.

74 See Chapter One, "Author, Date, Destination," above.

75 Hans Lietzmann, *An die Korinther, I–II*, rev. Werner Georg Kümmel, HNT 9 (J. C. B. Mohr [Paul Siebeck], 1949), 40–1; Christian Wolff, *Der erste Brief des Paulus an die Korinther,* THKNT 7/2 (Evangelische Verlangsanstalt, 1982), 22, n. 126; Archibald Robertson and Alfred Plummer, *A Critical and Exegetical Commentary on the First Epistle of St. Paul to the Corinthians,* ICC (T&T Clark, 1914), 181–2; Fee, *First Corinthians,* 403; C. K. Barrett, *A Commentary on the First Epistle to the Corinthians,* HNTC (Harper and Row, 1968), 203.

related by blood to Jesus.[76] Though ἀπόστολος in the NT is used in a very broad sense with various qualifiers,[77] it also describes a unique preaching and teaching fraternity set apart by a "dominical commission" from the risen Christ.[78] Entrusted with God's revelation in Christ, these apostles occupy the church's preeminent office (1 Cor 12:28) and provide the "authentic interpretation" of Jesus, the standards for doctrine and preaching, and the very foundation of the church itself.[79] For Paul, apostolic authority is absolute, derived from the message received directly from Christ, making the apostle the "direct mediator of the gospel and its authoritative interpreter."[80] Apparently, "brothers of the Lord" was an established appellation for those in Jesus' family who exercised this apostolic authority but were reverentially distinguished from the apostolic college.[81]

Neither James nor Jude, however, explicitly emphasize their status as "brothers of the Lord." Both use Ἰησοῦ Χριστοῦ δοῦλος ("slave of Jesus Christ"),[82] a more subtle but equally weighty self-designation. In both OT and NT use, δοῦλος often accompanied by genitive qualifiers (θεοῦ, κυρίου, Χριστοῦ [Ἰησοῦ]) identifies men appointed by God to a particular position of leadership, authority, and service.[83] Jude's claim to be a "slave of Jesus Christ," a quasi-technical term, signifies both his humble submission before God and his role as a chosen and authorized representative of God's will to the people.[84]

---

76 Bauckham, "Relatives of Jesus," 59.

77 Andrew C. Clark, "Apostleship: Evidence from the New Testament and Early Christian Literature," in *Vox Evangelica* 19, ed. Harold H. Rowdon (The London Bible College, 1989), 49–75.

78 E. Earle Ellis, "Paul and his Co-Workers," in *Prophecy and Hermeneutic in Early Christianity* (Eerdmans, 1978; repr., Baker Books, 1993), 12–3; Walter Schmithals, *The Office of Apostle in the Early Church*, trans. John E. Steely (Abingdon Press, 1969), 24–32. Cf. 1 Cor 9:1; 15:3–10; Gal 1:1–24.

79 Cf. Acts 2:42; 1 Cor 3:11; Gal 2:2, 9; Eph 2:20; Rev 21:14; William Childs Robinson, "Apostle," *ISBE* 1:193–5; Adolf Schlatter, *The Church in the New Testament Period*, trans. Paul P. Levertoff (SPCK, 1955), 9–10, 25, 76.

80 Beker, *Paul the Apostle*, 6; Schmithals, *Office of Apostle*, 31–40; Peter R. Jones, "1 Corinthians 15:8: Paul the Last Apostle," *TynBul* 36 (1985): 3–7, 28–34. Cf. the apostles' disciplinary authority in Acts 5:1–11; 1 Cor 5:1–7; 2 Cor 2:1–10; 2 Thess 3:6; 1 Tim 1:20.

81 Bauckham, *Jude, 2 Peter*, 23–4. Cf. 1 Cor 15:7; Gal 1:19.

82 Jas 1:1 is more expansive: θεοῦ καὶ κυρίου Ἰησοῦ Χριστοῦ δοῦλος ("a slave of God and of the Lord Jesus Christ").

83 Cf. in the LXX, Abraham (Ps 104:42); Jacob (Gen 32:10; Isa 41:8; 48:20; Jer 26:27); Moses (4 Kgdms 18:12; Neh 9:14; Ps 104:26; Dan 9:11; Mal 4:4); Joshua (Judg 2:8); David (2 Kgdms 7:5; Ps 88:3, 20); Zerubbabel (Hag 2:24); and the prophets (Amos 3:7; Jer 51:4). In the NT see Acts 16:17; Rom 1:1; Gal 1:10; Phil 1:1; Titus 1:1; 2 Pet 1:1; Rev 15:3. Gerhard Sass, "Zur Bedeutung von δοῦλος bei Paulus," *ZNW* 40 (1941): 26, 30–2; Karl Heinrich Rengstorf, "δοῦλος, κτλ.," *TDNT* 2:276–77; Franz Mußner, *Der Jakobsbrief*, HThKNT 13/1 (Herder, 1975), 60.

84 Knoch, *Judasbrief*, 169; Samuel Benetreau, *La deuxième épître de Pierre et l'épître de Jude*, CEB 16 (Édifac, 1994), 259–60. Cf. Mußner, *Jakobusbrief*, 61; Martin Dibelius, *James: A*

If Bauckham's assessment of the Jerusalem bishop lists[85] is correct, Jude exercised a prominent leading role in the earliest Jerusalem church along with his brothers (James and Joseph/Josis) and a few of the remaining Twelve (John, Matthias, and Philip).[86]

In continuity with the apostolic mission, Jude was charged by the risen Lord with proclaiming, interpreting, and preserving God's revelation in Christ, the "faith which was once for all delivered to the saints" (v. 3), the "most holy faith" (v. 20). Though he does not offer a doctrinal statement, Jude nevertheless assumes that ἡ πίστις ("the faith") is definitive, recognizable, and objective. His theme matches that found in Paul where ἡ πίστις can describe the comprehensive and monolithic corpus of teaching and doctrine that defines authentic Christianity[87] and specifies the "divinely appointed norm which determines every theological statement and every aspect of Christian conduct."[88] Jude's faith is an "inseparably interwoven matrix of doctrine and practice, and he is quick to condemn deviation from true faith in all its dimensions – thought, word, and deed."[89]

In order to advance his polemic for the faith, Jude resorts to Scripture as the authority base, the "touchstone not only of the New Testament writers' religious teachings but also of their total life and culture."[90] As Ellis has pointed out, Jude 5–19 is a refined exposition of several biblical "texts." Though the texts themselves are actually summaries of OT teaching (vv. 5–7, 11), "apocryphal elaborations" on the OT (vv. 9, 14–15), and an apostolic prophecy (v. 18), their use reflects the NT exegetical principle that "faithful interpretations of (canonical) Scripture are equivalent to Scripture. That is, like Scripture the interpretations mediate God's teaching although, unlike Scripture, they do not

---

Commentary on the Epistle of James, rev. Heinrich Greeven, trans. Michael A. Williams, Hermeneia (Fortress Press, 1976), 65; Peter Davids, *The Epistle of James: A Commentary on the Greek Text*, NIGTC (Eerdmans, 1982), 63.

85 See the lists from Eusebius and Epiphanius compiled by Adolf Harnack, *Geschichte der altchristlichen Litteratur bis Eusebius II: Die Chronologie der altchristlichen Litteratur bis Eusebius*, vol. 1 (J. C. Hinrichs, 1897), 223–5.

86 Bauckham, "Relatives of Jesus," 71–6.

87 Rom 1:5; 12:6; Gal 3:23–25; 1 Tim 1:19; 4:1, 6; 6:10, 21; 2 Tim 2:18; 4:7; Rom 1:5; 12:6; Gal 3:23–25; 1 Tim 1:19; 4:1, 6; 6:10, 21; 2 Tim 2:18; 4:7; Gerhard Barth, "πίστις, εως, ἡ," *EDNT* 3:94; Leon Morris, "Faith," in *DPL*, ed. Gerald F. Hawthorne and Ralph P. Martin (InterVarsity Press, 1993), 290. According to Bultmann, "πιστεύω, κτλ.," 213–4, ἡ πίστις can refer to the Christian "message, teaching or principle" (Eph 4:5); a "norm or principle" in contrast to the Law (Rom 3:31; 4:14); an "independent entity" (Gal 3:23, 25); orthodoxy (2 Pet 1:1); or Christianity as a whole (1 Tim 1:2, 4; Titus 1:1–4).

88 Otto Michel, "Faith: πίστις," *NIDNTT* 1:601–5; Paulsen, *Judasbrief*, 51.

89 Wolthuis, "Jude and Jewish Traditions," 40.

90 E. Earle Ellis, "Biblical Interpretation in the New Testament Church," in *The Old Testament in Early Christianity: Canon and Interpretation in the Light of Modern Research* (Baker, 1991), 78; Wendland, "Comparative Study of 'Rhetorical Criticism,'" 219.

in themselves have canonical status."[91] As a prophetic Ἰησοῦ Χριστοῦ δοῦλος ("slave of Jesus Christ"), Jude upholds the faith by providing inspired interpretations of these texts, applying biblical revelation to contemporary circumstances.[92] Biblical revelation combined with Jude's authoritative interpretation provide the standard for determining authentic Christianity.

Dualism

Jude's apocalyptic dualism depicts a righteous and omnipotent God whose cosmic order is temporarily fractured by confrontation with evil and rebellion. God expresses his righteous benevolence by loving (ἠγαπημένοις) and preserving (τετηρημένοις) his people (v. 1). The "divine passive"[93] blessing pronouncement in v. 2 (ἔλεος ὑμῖν καὶ εἰρήνη καὶ ἀγάπη πληθυνθείη, "may mercy and peace and love be multiplied to you") is a tacit acknowledgement of dependence on God as the source of all good.[94] The blessing Jude desires for his audience in v. 2 is a composite picture of God's redemptive work[95] including faithfulness and forgiveness (ἔλεος),[96] spiritual wellbeing (εἰρήνη),[97] and love (ἀγάπη).[98] All three are critical needs in the context of human depravity and guilt and are revealed supremely in the salvation provided by Jesus Christ.[99]

---

91 Ellis, "Prophecy and Hermeneutic in Jude," 224; idem, "The Old Testament Canon in the Early Church," in *The Old Testament in Early Christianity: Canon and Interpretation in the Light of Modern Research* (Baker, 1991), 33–4; idem, "Biblical Interpretation in the New Testament Church," 96. Cf. Paul's use of rabbinic interpretations (1 Cor 10:4; Gal 3:19; 2 Tim 3:8) and his commentary on commentary (1 Cor 2:6–16 [Isa 64:4; 65:16; Isa 40:13]; 1 Cor 10:1–31 [Exodus 13–14; Num 14:16; Exod 32:6]); Dunnett, "Hermeneutics of Jude," 290; E. Earle Ellis, "How the New Testament Uses the Old," in *Prophecy and Hermeneutic in Early Christianity* (Eerdmans, 1978; repr., Baker, 1993), 156. See also m. 'Abot 1:1 and Jacob Neusner's introductory comments on the relationship between Mishnah and Scripture (*The Mishnah: A New Translation* [Yale University Press, 1988], xxxviii–xl).

92 Cf. Edward G. Selwyn, *The First Epistle of St. Peter: The Greek Text with Introduction, Notes and Essays*, 2nd ed. (Baker, 1981), 266–7; E. Earle Ellis, "The Role of the Christian Prophet in Acts," in *Prophecy and Hermeneutic in Early Christianity* (Eerdmans, 1978; repr., Baker Books, 1993), 132–8; idem, "Biblical Interpretation in the New Testament Church," 116–21.

93 The voluntative optative without an expressed agent is rhetorically charged, calling attention to God's supremacy even when he is not mentioned explicitly (cf. Wallace, *Grammar*, 438).

94 Cf. 1 Pet 1:2; 2 Pet 1:2; Fuchs and Reymond, *Jude*, 155.

95 Vögtle, *Judasbrief*, 18.

96 Rudolf Bultmann, "ἔλεος, κτλ.," *TDNT* 2:482–485.

97 Werner Foerster, "εἰρήνη, κτλ.," *TDNT* 2:411–417; Ceslas Spicq, "εἰρηνεύω, κτλ.," *TLNT* 1:434.

98 Cf. the combination of ἔλεος and ἀγάπη in vv. 21–22.

99 Cf. σωτηρία ("salvation," v. 3. In v. 25, God is the savior (σωτήρ) by means of Jesus Christ (διὰ Ἰησοῦ Χριστοῦ).

God is forgiving and just, giving grace and executing judgment.[100]

Jude's application of uniqueness and mastery to both God the Father and Jesus Christ reveals a unified omnipotence[101] presiding over the universe with eternal power and authority (κράτος καὶ ἐξουσία πρὸ παντὸς τοῦ αἰῶνος καὶ νῦν καὶ εἰς πάντας τοὺς αἰῶνας, v. 25). Divine rule has established a universal order in which created angelic beings have a specific authoritative function (τὴν ἑαυτῶν ἀρχὴν, v. 6)[102] and a designated realm of existence (τὸ ἴδιον οἰκητήριον, "their own dwelling," v. 6).[103] As Michael's deference to God's authority illustrates (v. 9), these beings are in every way subordinate to the Lord. In v. 14 the possessive genitive αὐτοῦ ("his") identifies the angelic host (ἅγιαι μυριάδες, "myriads of holy ones") as the Lord's own property, accompanying and serving him in the work of judgment.

The negative aspect of Jude's cosmic dualism is evident in the conflict between God and angelic evil. Certain angels rejected their privileged positions, rebelled against God's order, and engaged in immorality.[104] Two contingents represented by Michael and the devil, the holy and the fallen, strive with one another over the outworking of God's will (v. 9). Opposition to God's order is perceived as opposition to God himself.[105] God has therefore already prepared and preserved a corresponding condemnation for insurrectionists. As the perfect tense-form of τετήρηκεν... δεσμοῖς ἀϊδίοις indicates (v. 6), they exist in a state of condemnation that was sealed in the past and continues through the present.[106] They enjoy a limited freedom to spread corruption, but God

---

100 Cf. χάρις ("grace," v. 4) and the overwhelming judgment vocabulary: κρίμα ("judgment," v. 4); ἀπόλλυμι ("destroy," vv. 5, 11); κρίσις ("judgment," vv. 6, 15); δεσμός ἀΐδιος ("eternal chains," v. 6); ζόφος ("gloom," vv. 6, 13); πῦρ ("fire," v. 7, 23); δίκη ("penalty," v. 7); σκότος ("darkness," v. 13); ἐλέγχω ("convict," v. 15).

101 Cf. μόνος ("only," vv. 4, 25); κύριος ("Lord," vv. 4, 9, 14, 17, 21, 25); δεσπότης ("Master," v. 4); Matthew Black, "The Christological Use of the Old Testament in the New Testament," *NTS* 18, no. 1 (1971): 6–11; Osburn, "The Christological Use of 1 Enoch 1:9," 337, 341. The NA28 and UBS5 reveal Jude's high Christology more explicitly than previous printed edititions of the Greek NT. In v. 5 of the NA27 and UBS4 printed texts, ὁ κύριος destroys the unbelieving during the exodus wanderings. Recent editorial committees, however, have decided that Ἰησοῦς is the correct reading and thus directly identifies Christ pre-incarnate with Yahweh. The third-century papyrus 𝔓72c makes this juxtaposition more explicit with the reading θεος Χριστος ("God who is Christ").

102 Cf. Rom 8:38; Eph 1:21; 3:10; 6:12; Col 1:16; 2:15; 1 Enoch 82:10–20; 2 Enoch 20:1; T. Levi 3:7–8; Jub. 2:2; 5:6; 1QM 10.11–12; 1QH 1.10–11; Bauckham, *Jude, 2 Peter*, 52.

103 Cf. Eph 2:2; 3:10; Col 1:16; 1 Enoch 12:4; 15:3, 7; Schelkle, *Judasbrief*, 154; Knoch, *Judasbrief*, 179.

104 Jude 6–7; cf. Gen 6:1–4; Isa 14:5–23; Ezek 28:1–19; 1 Enoch 12:4–6; 15:3–5.

105 Peter Müller, "Judasbrief," 277; Paulsen, *Judasbrief*, 63.

106 Τετήρηκεν is interpreted here as a "consummative perfect," emphasizing a present state of being with particular stress on its actualization in the past (James A. Brooks and Carlton L. Winbery, *Syntax of New Testament Greek* [University Press of America, 1979], 105). Cf. 1 Enoch 10:4–22; 14:5–7.

has already chained these cosmic rebels to their fate. Despite the current rift in his cosmic order, God remains supreme and his will is accomplished.

Jude's message is essentially provoked by the apocalyptic distinction between two ages. According to the apostolic prophecy in v. 18, the appearance of ungodly scoffers has signaled the arrival of the "last time" (ἐπ᾽ ἐσχάτου [τοῦ] χρόνου). In the NT ἐπ᾽ ἐσχάτου [τοῦ] χρόνου and related flexible terminology point to an era bracketed by Christ's first and second advents.[107] Jude's audience lives during the final segment of an evil age and must contend with its characteristic ungodliness while waiting (προσδεχόμενοι, v. 21) for its eventual displacement by a new age of eternal life (ζωὴν αἰώνιον, v. 21), pure character (ἀμώμους, v. 24), and joy (ἀγαλλιάσει, v. 24). Jude's concluding doxology acknowledges and anticipates God's eternal rule (εἰς πάντας τοὺς αἰῶνας, "for all the ages," v. 25) that is yet to be fully realized.

Jude's cosmic division between good and evil is directly reflected by division between the righteous and the wicked in the human sphere.[108] The author indirectly asserts his audience's positional righteousness in v. 24. God's ability to guard or protect[109] them from stumbling[110] in their obedient defense of the faith until the consummation assumes their current state of steadfastness. Jude writes to those who enjoy an intimate relationship with God and Jesus Christ, to those whom God has called (τοῖς ... κλητοῖς, v. 1)[111] to partake of his goodness. They are clearly members of an elect community, and the objects of God's love,[112] preservation,[113] and salvation.[114] Jude's audience shares his relational possession of God. He is "our" (ἡμῶν) God (v. 4), ἡμῶν Lord Jesus Christ (vv. 4, 7, 21, 25), and ἡμῶν savior (v. 25).

The wicked, however, are singled out with particularly invective language;

---

107 Hans-Christoph Hahn, "Time: χρόνος," *NIDNTT* 3:843–44; cf. ἐν ὑστέροις καιροῖς ("in the later times," 1 Tim 4:1); ἐν ἐσχάταις ἡμέραις ("in the last days," 2 Tim 3:1); ἐπ᾽ ἐσχάτου τῶν ἡμερῶν τούτων ("in these last days," Heb 1:2); ἐπὶ συντελείᾳ τῶν αἰώνων ("at the consummation of the ages," Heb 9:26); ἐν καιρῷ ἐσχάτῳ ("in the last time," 1 Pet 1:5); ἐπ᾽ ἐσχάτου τῶν χρόνων ("in the last times," 1 Pet 1:20); ἐσχάτη ὥρα ("the last hour," 1 John 2:18).

108 Koester, *Introduction*, 2:247.

109 BAGD, "φυλάσσω," 1068.

110 Ἄπταιστος, "without stumbling" is a NT *hapax legomenon*. Cf. 3 Macc 6:39; Sib. Or. 3:289: "There is a certain royal tribe whose race will never stumble." Ptolemy II asks of the Septuagint translators, "How can one keep his kingdom without offense to the end?" (Letter of Aristeas 187).

111 Cf. οἱ κλητοί ("the called," in 3 Kgdms 1:49 (LXX); Rom 1:6; 8:28; 1 Cor 1:24; Rev 17:14; Sib. Or. 8:92.

112 They are ἐν θεῷ πατρὶ ἠγαπημένος ("loved in God the father," v. 1); ἀγαπητοί ("loved," v. 3, 17, 20); ἐν ἀγάπῃ θεοῦ ("in the love of God," v. 21).

113 Cf. τηρέω ("keep," v. 1) and φυλάσσω ("guard," v. 24).

114 Cf. κοινός ἡμῶν σωτηρία ("our common salvation," v. 3). They are promised τὸ ἔλεος ... εἰς ζωὴν αἰώνιον ("the mercy ... to eternal life," v. 21).

the bulk of Jude's text centers on their condemnation (vv. 4–19). Segments of the polemic are structured by employing the demonstrative and impersonal οὗτοι to specify them.[115] "These" are defiled, rebellious, and blasphemous (vv. 8, 10). "These" are polluted, worthless, and corrupt (v. 12–13). "These" are arrogant, "mouthy," and manipulative (v. 16). "These" are divisive and carnal (v. 19). This methodical recurrence of οὗτοι snaps a rhetorical mugshot, pointing the finger of accusation with steely intensity. According to Jude, the depravity of their character extends beyond the bounds of natural human proclivities to include a cosmic and archetypal quality. With οὗτοι,[116] the comparative adverb ὁμοίως ("likewise") in v. 8, and the woe-oracle[117] (οὐαί) in v. 11, Jude connects "these" to several of Judaism's apocalyptic and paradigmatic symbols of reprobation. With their encyclopedic catalogue of errors and their certain doom, Jude's opponents personify the faithless exodus wanderers, demons, and Sodom and Gomorrah (vv. 5–7).[118] Kindred spirits with Cain,[119] Balaam,[120] and Korah[121] (v. 11), they fulfill the blackest apocalyptic prophecies of eternal destruction (vv. 14–15, 17–18).

Determinism

Jude's deterministic language appears at the very outset when he addresses

115 Cf. vv. 8, 10, 12, 16, 19; Cantinat, *Jude*, 267–8; Ellis, "Prophecy and Hermeneutic in Jude," 225.

116 According to Bauckham, the interjection of οὗτοι is a common formula in apocalyptic literature used to shift into pivotal interpretive material (*Jude, 2 Peter*, 45). Cf. Dan 5:25–26; Zech 1:10, 19; 4:10, 14; Rev 7:14; 11:4; 14:4; 1 Enoch 46:3.

117 Cf. the "maledictions" in anticipation of impending doom (Isa 3:11; 5:20; Jer 13:27; Hos 7:13; Sir 2:12, 13, 14); against the Pharisees (Matt 23:13–16, 23, 25, 27, 29; Luke 11:42–44, 46, 52); against Judas Iscariot (Matt 26:24; Mark 14:21; Luke 22:22); and against the ungodly in general (1 Enoch 94:6–8; 95:4–7; 96:4–8); George W. E. Nickelsburg, "The Apocalyptic Message of 1 Enoch 92–105," *CBQ* 39, no. 3 (1977): 310–2; Ceslas Spicq, "μακάριος, οὐαί," *TLNT* 2:443–44; Rudolf Bultmann's section "Prophetic and Apocalyptic Sayings" in *The History of the Synoptic Tradition*, trans. John Marsh (Harper and Row, 1963), 108–18.

118 Cf. the wanderers (Num 14:26–35; Ps 95:8–11; 1 Cor 10:5–11; Heb 3:17–19; CD 3.7–12; Sir 16:10); fallen angels (Gen 6:1–4; 2 Pet 2:4; 1 Enoch 10:6; 12:4; 22:11); Sodom and Gomorrah (Gen 19:4–25; Deut 29:23; Isa 1:9; 13:19; Matt 10:15; Mark 6:11; 2 Pet 2:6; Sir 16:8; Jub. 16:6; T. Levi 14:6).

119 Cf. Gen 4:8; 1 John 3:12; 1 Enoch 22:7–8; Adam and Eve (Apocalypse) 2:2–3; 3:2; T. Benj. 7:5.

120 Cf. Num 31:16; Deut 23:4; Neh 13:2. Balaam is the "Wicked Man *par excellence*" in Jewish interpretive tradition (Geza Vermes, "The Story of Balaam – The Scriptural Origin of Haggadah," in *Scripture and Tradition in Judaism: Haggadic Studies*, Studia Post-Biblica 4 [Brill, 1961], 174). See also Louis Ginzberg, *Bible Times and Characters from the Exodus to the Death of Moses*, vol. 3 of *The Legends of the Jews*, trans. Paul Radin (The Jewish Publication Society of America, 1911), 354–82. Balaam's only three appearances in the NT are in overtly apocalyptic contexts (2 Pet 2:15; Jude 11; Rev 2:14), but his name never appears in the Greek OT Pseudepigrapha.

121 Cf. Num 16:1–35; 26:9–10; Ps 106:16–18; 2 Tim 2:19; Sir 45:18–19; Ginzberg, *Bible Times and Characters*, 286–300; G. H. Boobyer, "The Verbs in Jude 11," *NTS* 5, no. 1 (1958): 46–7.

the letter τοῖς ... κλητοῖς ("to the called," v. 1). Although the semantic range of the adjective κλητός can refer to those who are merely "invited" to participate,[122] the NT application of κλητός to identify Christians specializes and strengthens this vernacular sense. Through various grammatical connections κλητός points to God's effectual and irresistible call[123] and can be indistinguishable from ἐκλεκτός ("chosen").[124] In contexts such as Jude 1, κλητός and its semantic relatives transcend the mere communication of an invitation to effect a "new relationship to the one who does the calling."[125] This calling is "pretemporal," and is applied to those "whose lives had been determined by God's summons, who had been drawn into God's ongoing purpose by the power of that call."[126]

God's work of "keeping" (τηρέω, vv. 1, 13) and "preserving" (φυλάσσω, v. 24) asserts his sovereignty over both positive and negative final destinies. In v. 1, the recipients of God's calling are further defined by their experience of divine preservation. According to the perfect passive participle τετηρημένοις, God "keeps" them in a continuous state "for Jesus Christ" (Ἰησοῦ Χριστῷ), "i.e. for his eschatological reign."[127] This theme appears again in v. 24 and clarifies the nature of this state of preservation. God can and will preserve (φυλάξαι) his people from stumbling (ἀπταίστους) in this age until they reach a blameless (ἀμώμους) and joyous (ἀγαλλιάσει) state in the next.[128] By asserting his audience's existence within a state that anticipates perfection backed by divine power for its realization, Jude identifies an implicit, predetermined, eschato-

---

122 Cf. Matt 22:14, "For many are called (κλητοί) but few are chosen"; 3 Kgdms 1:41, 49 (those invited [οἱ κλητοί] to a meal); 3 Macc 5:14 (invited guests [τοὺς κλητούς] for a banquet).

123 For κλητός ("called") used adjectively see with ἅγιοι ("saints"), Rom 1:7; 1 Cor 1:2; with ἀπόστολος ("apostle"), Rom 1:1; 1 Cor 1:1; for substantival uses see Rom 1:6; 8:28 (with divine πρόθεσις, "purpose"); 1 Cor 1:24; Rev 17:14 (in connection with ἐκλεκτός, "chosen"). The cognate verb καλέω ("call") in particular can signify the "process by which God calls those, whom he has already elected and appointed, out of their bondage to this world" (Lothar Coenen, "Call: καλέω," *NIDNTT* 1:275); cf. Rom 8:29–30; 9:11; 1 Cor 7:15; Gal 1:6, 15; Otto Michel, *Der Brief an die Römer*, 67–8; Judith M. Gundry Volf, *Paul and Perseverance: Staying in and Falling Away*, WUNT 2/37 (J. C. B. Mohr [Paul Siebeck], 1990), 12; Thomas R. Schreiner, *Romans*, BECNT 6 (Baker, 1998), 450–1.

124 K. L. Schmidt, "καλέω, κτλ.," *TDNT* 3:494; Wand, *Jude*, 195; Cantinat, *Jude*, 291; Schrage, *Der Judas Brief*, 227.

125 L&N, "Communication: Call," 1:424.

126 James D. G. Dunn, *Romans 1–8*, WBC 38a (Word Books, 1988), 8, 482; Schelkle, *Judasbrief*, 146; "Dieu a l'initiative, c'est son amour qui est à la fois l'instrument et le but de l'appel qu'il adresse aux hommes" ("God takes the initiative; it is his love that is both the instrument and the goal of the call he addresses to men," my translation) (Fuchs and Reymond, *Jude*, 155); Jost Eckert, "καλέω, κτλ.," *EDNT* 2:252; cf. Rom 4:17; 1 Cor 1:9; 7:17–24; Gal 5:8, 13.

127 Harald Riesenfeld, "τηρέω, κτλ.," *TDNT* 8:142; cf. L&N, "Be, Become, Exist, Happen: State," 1:153.

128 Cf. 1 Thess 5:23; Rev 3:10; "Love truth and she will preserve (φυλάξει) you" (T. Reu. 3:9).

logical guarantee.[129] God has their ultimate end in mind before the fact and will ensure its actualization.

Jude's opponents, however, suffer a parallel[130] negative fate. After a string of rhetorically charged accusations (v. 12), Jude declares their sure and unequivocal condemnation (v. 13). As the perfect tense τετήρηται indicates, God has already reserved the gloom of eternal darkness for them. It is not, perhaps, surprising that God would prepare punishments for the guilty in advance of final judgment.[131] According to the relative pronoun in v. 13, however, God's advance preparations are for a particular group's disadvantage (οἷς).[132] Before death has permanently confirmed their apostasy, their eschatological doom is already certain in the mind of God.[133]

Jude's overt dependence on prophecies of the future stems from the prophetic and apocalyptic conviction that God has designed and therefore predetermined history in detail.[134] God can disclose the future because history, from God's perspective, exists before him in its fixed and final form. He possesses history, including the future, in totality and as it is. Jude's opponents fulfill an earlier apostolic prophecy predicting the arrival of licentious mockers

---

129 Schrage, *Der Judas Brief,* 227; Fuchs and Reymond, *Jude,* 155; I. Howard Marshall, *Kept by the Power of God: A Study of Perseverance and Falling Away* (Bethany Fellowship, 1969), 167; Charles, "The Use of Tradition-Material," 5–6. By rejecting the deterministic tone of τηρέω ("Bewahrung," "protect"), Vögtle unnecessarily weakens the very thrust of the consolation (*Judasbrief,* 18). Cf. the similar promise speech with an eschatological tone: "But the Lord is faithful, and he will strengthen and protect (φυλάξει) you from the evil one" (2 Thess 3:3); Georg Bertram, "φυλάσσω, φυλακή," *TDNT* 9:241.

130 Vögtle, *Judasbrief,* 69.

131 Cf. Jesus' warning, "He who believes in [the Son] is not judged; he who does not believe has been judged already" (John 3:18).

132 The explicit personal nature of the dative case is made even more overt when used, as in this case, to emphasize disadvantage. Cf. Stanley E. Porter, *Idioms of the Greek New Testament* (Sheffield Academic Press, 1992), 97–8; H. E. Dana and Julius R. Mantey, *A Manual Grammar of the Greek New Testament* (Macmillan, 1955), 84–5; James Hope Moulton and Nigel Turner, *Syntax,* vol. 3 of *A Grammar of New Testament Greek* (T&T Clark, 1963), 236; Wallace, *Grammar,* 143; the "dative has a distinctive personal touch" (A. T. Robertson, *A Grammar of the Greek New Testament in the Light of Historical Research* [Broadman Press, 1934], 536).

133 Along with their angelic mentors (v. 6) they are "destinés aux ténèbres" (Cantinat, *Jude,* 318).

134 The "book of life of the Lamb" was written "from the foundation of the world" (Rev 13:8). God has known "everything (even) before it came to existence" (1 Enoch 9:11)," and according to 1 Enoch 81:2, heavenly tablets contain "all the deeds of humanity and all the children of the flesh upon the earth for all the generations of the world." Cf. Isa 4:3; Ps 139:16, where in "Thy book they were all written, the days that were ordained for me, when as yet there was not one of them." See John Barton's chapter on "Prophecy and the Divine Plan for History" (*Oracles of God: Perceptions of Ancient Prophecy in Israel after the Exile* [Darton, Longman, and Todd, 1986], 214–34); idem, "Prophecy (Postexilic Hebrew)," *ABD* 5:493–94; A. Berkeley Mickelsen's discussion of "Prophecy and History" (*Interpreting the Bible* [Eerdmans, 1963], 289–92); Franz Schnider, "προφητεύω, κτλ.," *EDNT* 3:183.

(vv. 17–19). These ungodly intruders are described in this context as οἱ πάλαι προγεγραμμένοι εἰς τοῦτο τὸ κρίμα ("those who were designated long ago for this condemnation," v. 4). The verb προγράφω from which Jude's substantival participle προγεγραμμένοι derives can refer to the basic ideas of "write earlier,"[135] or "portray publicly" (Gal 3:1). In Jude 4, however, the author theologizes προγεγραμμένοι by appending two pivotal adverbial modifications. Typical of its NT meaning, the temporal adverb πάλαι establishes the implied action of the participle in the distant past: "Long ago."[136] The accusative prepositional phrase εἰς τοῦτο τὸ κρίμα denotes the action's definitive purpose or goal at the final judgment.[137] Jude's opponents were therefore "marked out," "designated,"[138] or "appointed"[139] for specific judgment "long ago." By appointing them to eschatological judgment long ago, God, the implied agent, predestined[140] their fate before their actual appearance in Jude's historical context.

Two instances of the rare prophetic, proleptic, or futuristic aorist further document God's determination of history. Jude's woe-oracle in v. 11 shifts the emphasis abruptly from a present tense description of the heretics' errors in v. 10[141] to a subtly stylized non-linear declaration of the historical past. The first two aorist verbs, ἐπορεύθησαν ("they walked") and ἐξεχύθησαν ("they dedicated themselves"), emphasize either the constative or ingressive nature of their participation in the errors of Cain and Balaam. The aorist ἀπώλοντο ("they perished"), however, interjects an eschatological event into the past. Jude's opponents, alive and operative in his contemporary circumstances, are

135 Paul reminds the Ephesians "that by revelation there was made known to me the mystery, as I wrote before (προέγρψα) in brief" (Eph 3:3). Cf. Rom 15:4; Josephus, *Jewish Antiquities* 12.30, 33, "mentioned earlier."

136 BAGD, "πάλαι," 605. Cf. Matt 11:21; Luke 10:13; Heb 1:1; 2 Pet 1:9. For less temporal distance see 2 Cor 12:19; Mark 15:44, and the variant insertion of πάλαι at Mark 6:47 (P45, D, *f*1, 28, 2542, *pc*, it, vgmss).

137 Cf. the following examples of judgment (vv. 5–11) which are specific expressions of the final universal judgment (vv. 14–15); Kelly, *Jude*, 249. According to Fuchs and Reymond, προγεγραμμένοι carries an overt judicial tone: "On peut aussi remarquer que le vocabulaire de cette phrase est tout entier emprunté au langage juridique. Προγράφειν a un sens pénal précis, il désigne l'acte d'accusation publique porté contre des criminels" ("It can also be noted that the entire vocabulary of this sentence is borrowed from judicial language. Προγράφειν has a precise legal meaning; it refers to the public prosecution of criminals," my translation) (*Jude*, 159).

138 BAGD, "προγράφω," 704; cf. Reinhold Mayer, "Scripture, Writing: γραφή," *NIDNTT* 3:490.

139 Josephus, *Jewish Antiquities* 11.283; Gottlob Schrenk, "γράφω, κτλ.," *TDNT* 1:771–772. Cf. the ideas of proscription or conscription in Polybius 32.5.12; 32.6.1; Strabo, *Geography* 5.2.6; Dio Cassius, *Roman History* 47.13; Plutarch, *Brutus* 27.6; 1 Macc 10:36.

140 Horst Balz, "προγράφω," *EDNT* 3:154. Their "names have been registered for condemnation" (*LSJ*, "προγράφω," 1473). Charles connects the term to the prophetic speech in vv. 14 and 17 and defines it as a past word spoken "prophetically to the present, finding fulfillment, in 'these' ungodly" ("The Use of Tradition-Material," 6).

141 Οὐκ οἴδασιν ("they do not understand"), βλασφημοῦσιν ("they blaspheme"), ἐπίστανται ("they understand"), φθείρονται ("they are destroyed").

associated prophetically with Korah's destruction in the past. As Bateman observes, this "proleptic or prophetic rendering" of the aorist ... retains the perspective of an event completed in the past while drawing attention to the in-
evitability of the destruction of the godless" at the parousia.[142] In v. 14, Jude's
deliberate emendation of 1 Enoch 1:9 shifts verbal tenses from the futuristic
present (ἔρχεται, "he will come")[143] to the proleptic aorist (ἦλθεν, "he came"),[144]
locating the Lord's future judgmental parousia in the past: "The Lord *came* ...
to execute judgment." Verbal aspect in the aorist portrays action externally,
"in summary, viewed as a whole from the outside."[145] The semantics of a proleptic aorist parallel the Semitic "prophetic perfect"[146] and views an "event
that is not yet past as though it were already completed."[147] These Greek and
Semitic perspectives combined in the context of Jude 11 and 14[148] reflect an
apocalyptic panoramic view of history where, in God's providence, the future is so certain it can be described in terms of the past. God stands outside
of history and decrees or predestines the end from the beginning.[149] Here the

---

142 Bateman, *Jude*, 269.

143 Cf. Matthew Black's collation of 1 Enoch 1:9 with Jude 14–15. Direct verbal parallels are
italicized: ὅτι ἔρχεται σύν ταῖς μυριάσιν αὐτοῦ καὶ τοῖς ἁγίοις αὐτοῦ, ποιῆσαι κρίσιν κατὰ πάντων,
καὶ ἀπολέσει πάντας τοὺς ἀσεβεῖς, καὶ ἐλέγεξει πᾶσαν σάρκα περὶ πάντων ἔργων τῆς ἀσεβείας αὐτῶν
ὧν ἠσέβησαν καὶ σκληρῶν ὧν ἐλάλησαν λόγων, [[καὶ περὶ πάντων ὧν κατελάλησαν]] κατ᾽ αὐτοῦ
ἁμαρτωλοὶ ἀσεβεῖς (*Apocalypsis Henochi Graece*, PVTG [E. J. Brill, 1970]).

144 Osburn, "The Christological Use of 1 Enoch 1:9," 336–7; idem, "Discourse Analysis,"
304–5; James VanderKam, "The Theophany of Enoch I 3b–7, 9," *VT* 23, no. 2 (1973): 148.

145 Buist M. Fanning, *Verbal Aspect in New Testament Greek*, Oxford Theological Monographs (Clarendon Press, 1990), 97; K. L. McKay, "Time and Aspect in New Testament Greek,"
NovT 34, no. 3 (1992): 225.

146 Isa 5:13; 9:1–3; 10:28; 11:9; 19:7; Job 5:20; 2 Chr 20:37; "The prophet so transports himself
in imagination into the future that he describes the future event as if it had been already seen
or heard by him" (Wilhelm Gesenius, *Gesenius' Hebrew Grammar*, ed. E. Kautzsch, trans. A. E.
Cowley [Clarendon Press, 1910], 312–3); J. C. L. Gibson, *Davidson's Introductory Hebrew Grammar: Syntax*, 4th ed. (T&T Clark, 1994), 68; C. L. Seow, *A Grammar for Biblical Hebrew* (Abingdon Press, 1987), 93.

147 Wallace, *Grammar*, 563; Fanning, *Verbal Aspect*, 269–74; Stanley E. Porter, *Verbal As-
pect in the Greek of the New Testament, with Reference to Tense and Mood*, Studies in Biblical
Greek 1 (Peter Lang, 1989), 232–3; Brooks and Winbery, *Syntax*, 103–4. Cf. John 13:31–32; 17:18;
Rev 14:8. See in particular the deterministic implications of the example in Rom 8:30 where
Paul depicts God's eschatological glorification of the elect in the aorist tense: "Those whom
God justified, these he also glorified (ἐδόξασεν)." According to C. E. B. Cranfield, the aorist
ἐδόξασεν in this context points to a "glorification that has already been foreordained by God (cf.
v. 29); the divine decision has been taken" (*A Critical and Exegetical Commentary on the Epistle
to the Romans*, ICC [T&T Clark, 1987], 1:433); Gundry Volf, *Paul and Perseverance*, 12; Dunn, *Romans 1–8*, 485–6; Schreiner, *Romans*, 454.

148 Cf. Knoch, *Judasbrief*, 183, 187; Vögtle, *Judasbrief*, 64, 72–3; Grundmann, *Brief des Judas*, 42.

149 Fanning, *Verbal Aspect*, 274; cf. Angelo Lancellotti's "L'aoristo di 'predestinazione"
("the aorist of predistination," my translation) (*Uso delle forme verbali*, vol. 1 of *Sintassi ebraica
nel greco dell'Apocalisse*, Collectio Assisiensis 1 [Studio Teologico "Porziuncola," 1964], 50–1).

final judgment of the wicked is an absolute supra-historical fact, a "fulfilled *future* event."¹⁵⁰ In the mind of God, and according to his absolute grasp of historical reality, "their destiny is already sealed."¹⁵¹

Pessimism

The most overt examples of Jude's apocalyptic pessimism appear in three prophecies tied conspicuously together by the stem ἀσεβ- ("ungodly," vv. 4, 14–15, 18). Since the Adamic catastrophe, ungodly men have no doubt populated the earth: "Sin entered into the world, and death through sin, and so death spread to all men, because all sinned" (Rom 5:12). In these three contexts, however, Jude points to a unique category and quantity of ungodliness anticipated and now manifest at the end of the age. In v. 4 the uniqueness of an ungodly class is revealed by its foreordination to judgment. All ungodly men will someday face judgment, but Jude's opponents in particular were appointed for judgment long ago,¹⁵² and their surreptitious arrival in Jude's present circumstances signals the beginning of a pessimistic fulfillment.

Jude's edited citation of 1 Enoch 1:9 looks ahead to a distinctive manifestation of wicked men and their deeds:

> Behold the Lord came with myriads of his holy ones in order to execute judgment against all and to convict every soul concerning all of their ungodly (ἀσεβείας) deeds which they committed in an ungodly way (ἠσέβησαν) and concerning all the harsh words which ungodly (ἀσεβεῖς) sinners have spoken against him. (Jude 14–15)

In its own context, the theophany of 1 Enoch 1:9 occurs on the "day of tribulation at (the time of) the removal of all the ungodly ones" (1 Enoch 1:1). At that time the "state of violence will intensify upon the earth," and "every (form of)

---

150 James Charlesworth, *The Old Testament Pseudepigrapha and the New Testament: Prolegomena for the Study of Christian Origins* (Cambridge University Press, 1985), 73–4. Cf. Bauckham, *Jude, 2 Peter*, 84; Schelkle, *Judasbrief*, 164; Matthew Black, "The Maranatha Invocation and Jude 14, 15 (1 Enoch 1:9)," in *Christ and Spirit in the New Testament*, ed. Barnabas Lindars and Stephen S. Smalley (Cambridge University Press, 1973), 189–96; Osburn, "The Christological Use of 1 Enoch 1:9," 336.

151 Schelkle, *Judasbrief*, 161.

152 Cf. the subsection "Determinism" above for an exposition of the adjectival clause οἱ πάλαι προγεγραμμένοι εἰς τοῦτο τὸ κρίμα ("those who were designated long ago for this condemnation"). Moulton and Turner argue that using the articular participial modifier οἱ πάλαι προγεγραμμένοι further amplifies the identity of the anarthrous antagonists τινες ἄνθρωποι ("certain men"), by reminding the readers of some well known information (*Syntax*, 152).

oppression, injustice, and iniquity shall infect (the world) twofold" (1 Enoch 91:5–6). Enoch prophesies the advent of final destruction and redemption (1 Enoch 108:3–15) after the "time of those who work evil is completed" (1 Enoch 108:2). Jude assimilates Enoch's multi-layered condemnation of a climactic increase in wickedness by applying it to his adversaries. Those in Jude's time who live according to their own lusts (κατὰ τὰς ἐπιθυμίας ἑαυτῶν πορευόμενοι, v. 16) display the ungodly deeds prophesied by Enoch. Harsh words from the end-time-wicked flow from the mouths of Jude's opponents. They are (εἰσιν), in the present tense, verbally corrupt; they are grumblers and complainers who boast and flatter (v. 16).

Jude's citation of an apostolic prophecy (v. 18) makes his apocalyptic pessimism still more explicit. Here again the types of evil men identified by the apostles, in this case "mockers" or "scoffers" (ἐμπαῖκται) who "live according to their own desires for ungodly deeds (τῶν ἀσεβειῶν),"[153] have existed throughout history.[154] The apostles, however, particularized the subjects of their prophecy with a time designation typical of apocalyptic discourse; these reprobates will appear ἐπ᾽ ἐσχάτου [τοῦ] χρόνου (v. 18).[155] "At the last time," "at the end of the age," the apostles envisioned the emergence of a caste apparently distinguishable from the masses of historical degenerates by the quantity and intensity of their wickedness.[156] What the apostles foresaw in the "eschatological future,"[157] Jude found fulfilled in the divisive and unspiritual objects of his scorn (v. 19).

The consolation of God's keeping and preserving power is an indirect cosmological and anthropological indictment. The simple hope for a new age, in Jude's language τὸ ἔλεος τοῦ κυρίου ἡμῶν Ἰησοῦ Χριστοῦ εἰς ζωὴν αἰώνιον ("the mercy of our Lord Jesus Christ to eternal life," v. 21), condemns the substance of the present age. God's ability to guard, keep, or protect believers

---

153 Cf. the oblique verbal parallels between Jude's descriptive application of the Enoch prophecy to his opponents (κατὰ τὰς ἐπιθυμίας ἑαυτῶν πορευόμενοι, "those who live according to their own lusts", v. 16) and the apostles' prophetic description (κατὰ τὰς ἑαυτῶν ἐπιθυμίας πορευόμενοι τῶν ἀσεβειῶν, "those who live according to their own ungodly lusts", v. 18).

154 The word group including Jude's ἐμπαῖκται points to those who reject spiritual truth and its moral implications, characterizing "scoffers" as men "hostile to revelation" (Georg Bertram, "παίζω, ἐμπαίζω, κτλ.," *TDNT* 5:630–636); cf. Ps 1:1; Prov 1:22; 9:7–8; 13:1; 2 Pet 3:3; 4 Ezra 7:79–81. The verb form ἐμπαίζω ("scoff") occurs in the NT almost exclusively in the Synoptic passion narratives depicting the mocking of Jesus (Mark 15:13 and parallels; Matt 20:19 and parallels; 27:27–31; Luke 23:11).

155 Vögtle, *Judasbrief*, 88–90; Schrage, *Judas*, 236; cf. CD 4.4; 6.11; 1QSa 1.1; 1QpHab 9.6; 2 Bar. 6:8; 41:5; 78:5. In contexts similar to Jude 18 see 1 Tim 4:1; 2 Tim 3:1; 1QpHab 2.5–6; Did. 16:3; Ascension of Isaiah 3:30.

156 Cf. Mark 13:6, 22, and parallels; 1 Tim 4:1–3; 2 Tim 3:1–9. "And because lawlessness is increased, most people's love will grow cold" (Matt 24:12); 1 Enoch 89:61–71; 98:7; 104:7.

157 Bauckham, *Jude, 2 Peter*, 104.

(vv. 1, 24) provides comfort and peace only in response to the definite threat posed by their residual sinful condition: "The general sense is that God will protect Jude's readers from the dangers of falling into the sinful ways of the false teachers and thereby failing to attain to final salvation."[158] The hope of reaching the new age "without stumbling" and "blameless" (v. 24) depends on the underlying presupposition that stumbling and blame remain dreaded alternatives.

Jude's command to exercise mercy toward the faltering in v. 23 is qualified by the sobering warning to diligently curb the human propensity for evil. As the bulk of Jude's polemic illustrates, wickedness solicits God's judgment with all of its attending severity and eschatological permanence. Jude's audience must, therefore, show mercy ἐν φόβῳ ("with fear"), with solemn recognition that God will judge false teachers and any who join them in vice.[159] In characteristically Pauline language, σάρξ ("flesh"), the metaphysical principle of human depravity and the internal source[160] of corruption,[161] presents a very real obstacle (v. 23). Believers are not impervious to its infectious power and must hate (μισοῦντες), in Jude's hyperbolic language, even the clothing worn by those under its control. Those who carelessly forfeit perseverance and entertain those carnal errors on vivid display in the lives of the false teachers (cf. vv. 8, 10) risk sharing their fate.

Judgment

The centrality of judgment to Jude's short document is vividly illustrated by the density of judgment related terminology: κρίμα ("condemnation," v. 4); ἀπόλλυμι ("destroy," vv. 5, 11); κρίσις ("judgment," vv. 6, 15); πῦρ ("fire," vv. 7, 22); δίκη ὑπέχω ("undergo punishment," v. 7); ζόφος and σκότος ("gloom" and "darkness" vv. 6, 13); and ἐλέγχω ("convict," v. 15). The letter's structure, outlined by the bipartite admonition in vv. 3–4,[162] hints at this preoccupation with judgment. First, Jude identifies the purpose of his letter by issuing the command to contend for the faith (v. 3). Second, Jude supports his command with an explanatory ground or basis (γάρ): abominable traitors who have infiltrated the church are destined εἰς τοῦτο τὸ κρίμα ("for this condemnation," v. 4).

---

158 Ibid.

159 Kelly, *Jude*, 23; Green, *Jude*, 204.

160 Cf. Jude's ablative of source construct ἀπὸ τῆς σαρκὸς ἐσπιλωμένον (v. 23).

161 Cf. Rom 7:18; 8:6–13; Gal 5:16–21; Eph 2:3; Robert Jewett, *Paul's Anthropological Terms: A Study of Their Use in Conflict Settings*, AGJU 10 (E. J. Brill, 1971), 114–6. According to Jewett, Paul's use of σάρξ ("flesh") "as a sphere of evil influence in the personal and cosmic realms" is "entirely apocalyptic in nature" (94, 115).

162 Osburn, "Discourse Analysis," 288–9; Watson, *Invention, Arrangement, and Style*, 47–8.

What follows in the letter's foundational section (vv. 5–16) is an explication of the controlling motif τοῦτο τὸ κρίμα.[163] Between the introductory exhortation in vv. 3–4 and the companion imperatives in vv. 17–23, Jude articulates an apocalyptic judgment theology by applying Jewish tradition material to contemporary circumstance with a view toward the parousia. Jude's apocalyptic message is from beginning to end an exhortation to the faithful in light of the certainty of eschatological judgment.

In vv. 5–7 Jude provides three typological examples drawn from a core Jewish judgment tradition,[164] which he then applies to his contemporary opponents (vv. 8–10). The first example (v. 5) refers to God's displeasure with the unbelieving Israelites who refused to enter the promised land. In both contexts the issue (unbelief) and the devastating result (death) are the same. In Num 14:11, "The Lord said to Moses, 'How long will this people spurn Me? And how long will they not believe in me, despite all the signs which I have performed in their midst?'" God sentenced them to destruction for their unbelief (Num 14:22–23), and all but two from an entire generation died in the desert as a result (Num 26:64–65). Jude 5 takes over this judgment tradition and reminds the readers that, though God had redeemed Israel as a whole from Egypt, identification with God's people (λαόν) provided no insulation for the faithless (τοὺς μὴ πιστεύσαντας). Subsequent (τὸ δεύτερον) to the original redemption and reaffirmation of the covenant community (cf. Ex 19:1–8), God destroyed (ἀπώλεσεν) those who did not in fact believe. Consistent with other NT applications,[165] Jude employs this tradition typologically as a warning for the eschatological community of faith. Dissent and corruption within the community ἐπ' ἐσχάτου [τοῦ] χρόνου ("in [the] last time," v. 18) will certainly be purged.

Through a stylistic catchword connection, the divine work of destruction appears again in v. 11 where Jude's woe-oracle issues a "Yahweh-centered" curse against "covenantal apostasies."[166] The same verbal root used to describe

---

163 Grundmann, *Brief des Judas*, 29; Cantinat, *Jude*, 297; Ellis, "Prophecy and Hermeneutic in Jude," 226.

164 Cf. 2 Pet 2:4–7; Sir 16:5–11; 3 Macc 2:3–7; Wis 10:6–7; T. Naph. 3:4–4:5; CD 2.14–3.12; Klaus Berger, "Hartherzigkeit und Gottes Gesetz, die Vorgeschichte des antijüdischen Vorwurfs in Mc 10:5," *ZNW* 61, nos. 1/2 (1970): 27–42; Bauckham, *Jude, 2 Peter*, 46.

165 The eschatological significance of the wilderness judgment in NT interpretive tradition is highlighted by two other prominent references. In 1 Cor 10:11 Paul interprets the event as a negative typological example (τυπικῶς) written to exhort those "upon whom τὰ τέλη τῶν αἰώνων ('the end of the ages') has come." In Hebrews 3–4 Israel's failure at the edge of Canaan is an eschatological warning to enter God's rest "today" (σήμερον, 3:7, 13, 15; 4:7) and remain firm "until the end" (μέχρι τέλους, 3:14).

166 Erhard Gerstenberger, "The Woe-Oracles of the Prophets," *JBL* 81, no. 3 (1962): 263; David E. Garland, *The Intention of Matthew 23*, NovTSup 52 (E. J. Brill, 1979), 78.

God's destructive action against the rebellious Israelites in v. 5 (ἀπόλλυμι) is applied to Jude's opponents with a slightly different nuance. There the heretics are identified as those who "perished" (ἀπώλοντο) with Korah in his rebellion. With the proleptic aorist ἀπώλοντο Jude summarizes in one word a very vivid OT judgment event and its eschatological implications:

> The ground that was under them split open; and the earth opened its mouth and swallowed them up, and their households, and all the men who belonged to Korah, with their possessions. So they and all that belonged to them went down alive to Sheol; and the earth closed over them, and they perished (ἀπώλοντο, LXX) from the midst of the assembly. (Num 16:31–33)

According to Jude's rare aorist construction,[167] the wicked's identification with Korah's destruction involves more than mere physical death. Participation in a catastrophic judgment from the past foreshadows an incalculable devastation still to come for the ungodly.

Jude's account of the fallen angels in v. 6 relies on an ancient judgment tradition surrounding the sins of the OT antediluvian "sons of God." As the human race multiplied, "the sons of God saw that the daughters of men were beautiful; and they took wives for themselves, whomever they chose" (Gen 6:2). Until the second century A.D. Jewish exegetes uniformly interpreted these "sons of God" as angelic, demonic, spiritual beings who married human women.[168] First Enoch 6:1–19:3 expands in detail[169] the cryptic Genesis text, depicting a clan of renegade angels (οἱ ἄγγελοι υἱοὶ οὐρανοῦ, 6:2) so consumed with lust they "abandoned" (ἀπολείπω) heaven and "defiled themselves with women" (1 Enoch 12:4).[170] Clearly dependent on 1 Enoch,[171] Jude's indictment also includes the angels (ἀγγέλους) who abandoned (ἀπολιπόντας) their own

---

167 Cf. Porter, *Verbal Aspect*, 232–3.

168 Jub. 4:15, 22; 5:1; T. Reu. 5:6, 7; T. Naph. 3:5; 2 Enoch 18:3–5; 2 *Bar* 56:11–14; Philo, *On the Giants* 6; idem *Questions and Answers on Genesis* 1.92; Josephus, *Jewish Antiquities* 1.73; 1QapGen 2.1–16; CD 2.17–19; cf. 1 Cor 11:10; Philip S. Alexander, "The Targumim and Early Exegesis of 'Sons of God' in Genesis 6," *JJS* 23, no. 1 (1972): 60–1; Gordon J. Wenham, *Genesis 1–15*, WBC 1 (Word Books, 1987), 139–41.

169 Cf. Milik who contends that the fragments of Genesis 4–8 interwoven throughout 1 Enoch 6–19 are actually "earlier than the definitive version of the first chapters of Genesis" (*Books of Enoch*, 31).

170 The term ἀπολείπω shared with Jude 6 appears again in 15:3: "For what reason have you abandoned (ἀπελίπετε) the high, holy, and eternal heaven; and slept with women and defiled yourselves with the daughters of the people?"

171 Bauckham, *Jude, 2 Peter*, 51.

dwelling[172] in pursuit of sexual sin.

In each recitation of the angel tradition—Genesis, 1 Enoch, and Jude—descriptions of evil provide background support for the overarching theme of judgment. The sins of the sons of God in Genesis led directly to the flood (Gen 6:5–7), a unique expression (Gen 8:21–22) of catastrophic judgment within the terrestrial realm. First Enoch's exposition of the Genesis judgment explicitly draws cosmic forces of evil into the fray and focuses ultimately on the "final obliteration of evil" at the eschaton.[173] In language reminiscent of Jude 6, Enoch observes the Lord commanding one angel to entomb another until the arrival of an all important date:

> And to Raphael [the Lord] said, "Go, Raphael, and bind Asael; fetter (δῆσον) him hand and foot and cast him into darkness (σκότος); make an opening in the desert which is in the desert of Dudael, and there go and cast him in. And place upon him jagged and rough rocks, and cover him with darkness (σκότος) and let him abide there for all time (εἰς τούς αἰῶνας), and cover his face that he may not see the light. And on the day of great judgment (τη̑ ἡμέρᾳ τῆς μεγάλης τῆς κρίσεως) he will be led off to the blazing fire."[174]

Asael's incarceration in darkness "for all time" is actually only temporary, implying "for all time" leading up to the "day of great judgment."[175] It is this "great day of judgment," the "judgment which is for ever and ... becomes absolute"[176] that preoccupies the theology of 1 Enoch and Jude.[177]

According to Jude, God keeps fallen angels "in eternal chains" (δεσμοῖς ἀϊδίοις) under the gloom of darkness (ζόφον) "for the purpose of the judgment of the great day" (εἰς κρίσιν μεγάλης ἡμέρας, v. 6). Though biblical tradition

---

172 Jude's term for "dwelling" (οἰκητήριον) shares a lexical relationship with that found in 1 Enoch's statement, "For the dwelling (ἡ κατοίκησις) of the spiritual beings of heaven is heaven" (15:7).

173 George W. E. Nickelsburg, *1 Enoch 1: A Commentary on the Book of 1 Enoch, Chapters 1–36; 81–108*, Hermeneia (Fortress Press, 2001), 167; Matthew Black, *The Book of Enoch or 1 Enoch: A New English Edition with Commentary and Notes*, SVTP 7 (E. J. Brill, 1985), 134–5.

174 1 Enoch 10:4–6, translated by Black, *1 Enoch*, 30.

175 Black, *1 Enoch*, 134.

176 1 Enoch 10:12, τελεσθῇ τὸ κρίμα τοῦ αἰῶνος τῶν αἰώνων, translated by Black, *1 Enoch*, 31; cf. his comments pp. 137–8.

177 Cf. 1 Enoch 15:4; 16:1; 19:1; 22:4, 11; 54:6; 84:4; 91:15; 94:9; 98:10; 99:15; 104:5. According to Nickelsburg, "All the major sections of 1 Enoch and many of their component parts either provide background for this theme [of the coming judgment] or elaborate on it and give it prominence" (*1 Enoch 1*, 37); VanderKam, "Theophany of Enoch 1:3b–7, 9," 131; Schelkle, *Judasbrief*, 152; Kelly, *Jude*, 249.

does include a note of joy for the righteous,[178] the "day of judgment" is generally directed toward the wicked and characterized by vengeance, calamity, terror, accountability, separation, and exclusion:[179]

> A day of wrath is that day,
> A day of trouble and distress,
> A day of destruction and desolation,
> A day of darkness and gloom,
> A day of clouds and thick darkness ... (Zeph 2:15).

All of history leads up to the day of God's holy war[180] when the angels, Jude's opponents, and all creation will face the moment of separation and retribution.[181] Like the angels, God has reserved the "gloom of eternal darkness" (ὁ ζόφος τοῦ σκότους εἰς αἰῶνα) for Jude's adversaries (v. 13).

Jude's third typological example, Sodom and Gomorrah (v. 7), is perhaps the most common paradigmatic example in the history of divine judgment traditions.[182] The destruction of those cities, demanded by their gross immorality, "is set before the eyes of the world as a sample [δεῖγμα] of divine retribution."[183] Jude's use of the present tense πρόκεινται ("they are exhibited") highlights the ongoing relevance of the example; Sodom and Gomorrah's judgment provides a permanent pattern illustrating God's full eschatological response to wickedness. Though Sodom and Gomorrah's annihilation was a single punctiliar event in redemptive history, Jude's typology includes an eternal quality: πυρὸς αἰωνίου δίκην. The "punishment of eternal fire" extends the historical judgment event to include the apocalyptic theme of Hell.[184] Sodom's total devastation by fire prefigures eschatological devastation by eternal fire awaiting Jude's opponents and all those who adopt their errors.

---

178 Amos 5:18–20; Zech 14:3–11; Mark 14:25; cf. T. Mos. 10:8–10; K. D. Schunck, "Strukturlinien in der Entwicklung der Vorstellung vom 'Tag Jahwes,'" *VT* 14, no. 3 (1964): 322.

179 Cf. Deut 32:35; Jer 30:7; Joel 2:11, 31; Amos 5:18, 20; Mal 4:5; Luke 21:22, 34; Rev 6:12–17; 16:14; Wolfgang Trilling, "ἡμέρα," *EDNT* 2:121.

180 Cf. K. D. Schunck, "'Tag Jahwes,'" 330.

181 Matt 7:21–23; 25:31–32; Georg Braumann, "Present: ἡμέρα," *NIDNTT* 2:887–88.

182 Deut 29:23; Isa 1:9; 13:19; Jer 23:14–15; Lam 4:6; Amos 4:11; Zeph 2:9; Matt 10:15; 11:23–24; Luke 10:12; 17:29; Rom 9:29; Sir 16:8; 3 Macc 2:5; Jub. 16:6, 9; 20:5; 22:22; 36:10; T. Ash. 7:1; Philo *Questions and Answers on Genesis* 4.51; Josephus, *Jewish War* 5.566; Vögtle, *Judasbrief*, 42; Bauckham, *Jude, 2 Peter*, 53.

183 E. Kenneth Lee, "Words Denoting 'Pattern' in the New Testament," *NTS* 8, no. 2 (1962): 167.

184 Isa 66:24; Matt 5:22; 13:42, 50; 18:8–9; Rev 19:20; 20:10, 14–15; 21:8; 1 Enoch 18:11–16; 21:7–10; 3 Bar. 4:16; 4 Macc 12:12; T. Levi 25:3; wicked men "of the lot of Belial" will endure the "gloom of everlasting fire" (1QS 2.4–8); Wolthuis, "Jude and Jewish Traditions," 39–40; Hermann Lichtenberger, "πῦρ," *EDNT* 3:200.

The common apocalyptic judgment symbol fire[185] appears again implicitly with Korah's destruction (v. 11) and explicitly in Jude's concluding series of exhortations (v. 23). In addition to the hole that swallowed his family, fire from the Lord blazed against Korah's illegitimate priestly representatives and consumed them (Num 16:35). Jude's command to "snatch some from the fire" (v. 23) resembles OT judgment phraseology: "I overthrew you as God overthrew Sodom and Gomorrah, and you were like a firebrand snatched from a blaze" (Amos 4:11). A similar image occurs in Zech 3:2 where God's purification of Joshua the high priest, in the context of Satanic accusation, makes him "a brand plucked from the fire."[186] Extending these images eschatologically, Jude's fire is here the flame of eternal Hell that threatens those in the church who waver between apostasy and the "faith once for all delivered to the saints."[187]

Jude's judgment discourse reaches its climax with the redacted quotation of an apocalyptic prophecy from 1 Enoch 1:9 (vv. 14–15).[188] Enoch's theophany prophecy serves Jude as a summary statement encapsulating the means and mode of eschatological judgment.[189] As in other NT appropriations of theophany texts,[190] and numerous theophanies in general,[191] "theophany and judgment merge in response to the ungodly."[192] This observation is confirmed syntactically in v. 15 by two infinitival clauses designating the purposes for the Lord's arrival.[193] He will come,[194] first of all, "in order to execute judgment" (ποιῆσαι κρίσιν, v. 15a).[195] The Lord will also come, secondly, to "convict every

185 Cf. Isa 33:12; 64:2; Matt 3:10, 12; 7:19; 1 Cor 3:13; Rev 19:11; 1 Enoch 10:13; 17:1–5; 18:11, 15; 21:3; 91:9; T. Ab. 10:11; T. Zeb. 10:3; Pss. Sol. 12:4; 1QS 4.13; 1QH 4.13; 11.29–36; Nickelsburg, 1 Enoch 1, 222; Lichtenberger, "πῦρ," 198–9; Friedrich Lang, "πῦρ, κτλ.," TDNT 6:937–938; Hans Bietenhard, "Fire: πῦρ," NIDNTT 1:655–56.

186 Schelkle, Judasbrief, 171.

187 Knoch, Judasbrief, 192; Fuchs and Reymond, Jude, 186.

188 Vögtle, Judasbrief, 71; Bauckham, Jude, 2 Peter, 100.

189 In its own context, 1 Enoch 1:9 serves a similar proem like function for the rest of the work; VanderKam, "Theophany of Enoch 1:3b–7, 9," 131; Nickelsburg, 1 Enoch 1, 149; Watson, Invention, Arrangement, and Style, 64–6.

190 Cf. Isa 40:10 quoted in Rev 22:12; Isa 63:1–6 quoted in Rev 19:13, 15; Isa 66:15 quoted in 2 Thess 1:7; Zech 14:5 quoted in 1 Thess 3:13.

191 Cf. the judgment theophanies in Ps 18:9–15; 46:8–9; 76:8–9; 96:13; Isa 19:1; 64:1–2; Mic 1:2–5; Hab 3:3–15; T. Mos. 10:1–7; Jörg Jeremias, Theophanie: Die Geschichte einer alttestamentlichen Gattung, WMANT 10 (Neukirchener Verlag des Erziehungsvereins, 1965), 1–2.

192 Charles, "The Use of Tradition-Material," 5; idem, "Jude's Use of Pseudepigraphal Source-Material," 141–2; VanderKam, "Theophany of Enoch 1:3b–7, 9," 134–6, 148.

193 The Greek version of 1 Enoch 1:9 includes a third purpose: ἀπολέσει πάντας τοὺς ἀσεβεῖς ("he will destroy all the ungodly").

194 Jude's use of the proleptic aorist ἦλθεν ("he came") includes both past and future aspects. See Wallace, Grammar, 563–4.

195 In similar language Jesus himself looked forward to this hour of universal judgment: "And [the Father] gave him authority to execute judgment (κρίσιν ποιεῖν) ... for an hour is com-

soul" (ἐλέγξαι πᾶσαν ψυχήν, v. 15b).

The judicial character of Jude's verb ἐλέγχω ("convict") is clarified by its uses in 1 Enoch. It occurs four times, first in Jude's source text (1 Enoch 1:9) and three more times in a scene depicting a "formal convocation, in which the sentence of the heavenly courtroom is read in the presence of those who have been sentenced."[196] Though Enoch interceded on behalf of the fallen angels (the Watchers) in hope of securing their forgiveness and restoration (13:4–7), God in return commissioned him to "reprimand" (ἐλέγχω) them (13:8, 10). Enoch was destined to deliver a message of hopelessness: "So he created and destined me to reprimand (ἐλέγξασθαι) the Watchers, the sons of heaven" (14:3). The content of this reprimand, in the form of a judgment oracle, details the nature of their sin (15:2–7a; 16:2–3c) and the consequences (15:7b–16:1; 16:3d–4).[197] God has decreed, "Your prayers will not be heard throughout all the days of eternity; and judgment is passed upon you" (14:4). "Therefore," as their sentence reads, "you will have no peace" (16:4). In this context ἐλέγχω moves beyond rebuke, correction, or exposure of error[198] to include the idea of final intractable condemnation.[199]

Jude's selection of the Enoch text and its judicial overtones was likely driven by its comprehensive and pinpointed rhetorical focus on the ungodly as evidenced by the repetition of πᾶς ("all/every") and the stem ἀσεβ-.[200] What Jude means by "against all" (κατὰ πάντων) and "every soul" (πᾶσαν ψυχήν) is qualified by the concluding emphatic placement of ἁμαρτωλοὶ ἀσεβεῖς ("ungodly sinners") at the end of v. 15.[201] God's judgmental arrival is therefore directed against the souls of all ungodly sinners. The judgment will canvass every aspect of their ungodly character including all their ungodly deeds (πάντων τῶν ἔργων ἀσεβείας), impious behavior (ἠσέβησαν) and harsh words (πάντων τῶν σκληρῶν). When the Lord comes to convict every ungodly soul

---

ing, in which all (πάντες) who are in the tombs shall hear his voice, and shall come forth; those who did the good deeds to a resurrection of life, those who committed the evil deeds to a resurrection of judgment" (John 5:27).

196 Nickelsburg, *1 Enoch 1*, 250; Hans-Georg Link, "Guilt: ἐλέγχω," *NIDNTT* 2:141.

197 Nickelsburg, *1 Enoch 1*, 251, 269.

198 Cf. Prov 3:11; 9:7; Matt 18:15; Luke 3:19; 1 Tim 5:20; 2 Tim 4:2; Titus 1:13; 2:15; Sir 18:13; T. Gad 1:9; Adam and Eve (Apocalypse) 11:2; Joseph and Aseneth 10:10; Felix Porsch, "ἔλεγχος," *EDNT* 1:427–28.

199 Cf. Hos 5:9; John 3:20; 16:8; 2 Bar. 55:8; 83:3; T. Benj. 10:7–10; T. Ab. 13:3–7; Pss. Sol. 17:25; Friedrich Büchsel, " ἐλέγχω, κτλ.," *TDNT* 2:275; Link, "Guilt: ἐλέγχω," 141; Paul Volz, *Die Eschatologie der jüdischen Gemeinde im neutestamentlichen Zeitalter: Nach den Quellen der rabbinischen, apokalyptischen und apokryphen Literatur* (Georg Olms Verlagsbuchhandlung, 1966), 214, 302.

200 Watson, *Invention, Arrangement, and Style*, 65–6; Osburn, "The Christological Use of 1 Enoch 1:9," 339–41; Nickelsburg, *1 Enoch 1*, 149; Wolthuis, "Jude and Jewish Traditions," 39.

201 Bauckham, *Jude, 2 Peter*, 97.

on the great day of judgment (v. 6), the sentence will include destruction (vv. 5, 11) and eternal fire (vv. 7, 23).

Paraenesis

As the epistle's paraenetic material proves, Jude's apocalyptic determinism must not be confused with static philosophical fatalism.[202] Jude affirms the eschatological security of his audience while simultaneously exhorting them to live obediently. This characteristically apocalyptic tension between pre-destination and individual responsibility preserves a theological balance at the heart of Jude's polemic.[203]

Structurally, Jude's letter is primarily paraenetic. The appeal in v. 3 introduces the principal purpose for writing that is then further elaborated in vv. 5, 17, and 20–23.[204] The participial phrase παρακαλῶν ἐπαγωνίζεσθαι ("appealing to contend") follows an established petition form that includes (1) background information, (2) a verb of petition, and (3) the desired action. Jude's selection of the very "personal and intense" petition verb παρακαλέω ("appeal") marks the urgency of the message and the severity of the circumstances.[205]

The desired action of this appeal is summarized by the infinitive ἐπαγωνίζεσθαι ("to contend"). Though Jude's compound verb ἐπαγωνίζομαι is a NT hapax legomenon, it belongs in the lexical family with ἀγωνίζομαι ("struggle") and its lengthy history of application in paraenetic contexts. Classical examples used the image of "struggling" in athletic contest to illustrate diligence and self-mastery in the pursuit of virtue.[206] References in later Judaism

---

202 Cf. David W. Bebbington, *Patterns in History: A Christian View* (InterVarsity Press, 1979), 29–31; Ronald H. Nash, *The Meaning of History* (Broadman and Holman, 1998), 31–5; Newport, *Ultimate Questions*, 44–6;

203 Fuchs and Reymond, *Jude*, 184; Windisch, *Katholischen Briefe*, 47.

204 Cf. John Lee White, *The Form and Function of the Body of the Greek Letter: A Study of the Letter-Body in the Non-Literary Papyri and in Paul the Apostle*, 2nd ed., SBLDS 2 (Scholars Press, 1972), 18–9; Osburn, "Discourse Analysis," 292–3; Wendland, "Comparative Study of 'Rhetorical Criticism,'" 210–3. Bauckham concludes, perhaps too narrowly, that the "petition itself is not further explained until" the closing exhortations in vv. 20–23 (*Jude, 2 Peter*, 29). His proposal identifies a tidy imperative "bracket" that unnecessarily overlooks the "reminders" in vv. 5 and 17.

205 In several NT contexts this appeal form with παρακαλέω also includes a phrase establishing divine authority for the instruction. Cf. Rom 12:1; 1 Cor 1:10; 2 Cor 5:20; 6:1 (implied); 10:1; Eph 4:1; 1 Thess 4:1; 2 Thess 3:12; 1 Pet 5:1; Terence Y. Mullins, "Petition as a Literary Form," *NovT* 5, no. 1 (1962): 48–54.

206 Cf. Plato *Gorgias* 526, d–e; idem *Phaedrus* 247b; Epictetus *Dissertations* 1.24 superscription; 2.18.28; 3.22.51; 3.25.2–3; Victor C. Pfitzner, *Paul and the Agon Motif: Traditional Athletic Imagery in the Pauline Literature*, NovTSup 16 (Brill, 1967) 23–35.

denote the literal act of war[207] or the figurative life and death battles for truth and piety against deception and evil.[208] NT examples are confined almost exclusively to the Pauline corpus[209] where "fighting" and "striving" have in view the preservation and advancement of a pristine traditional doctrine and ethic.[210] According to Ethelbert Stauffer, "There seems to belong to the whole concept ... the thought of obstacles, dangers and catastrophes through which the Christian must fight his way."[211] Believers must fight for the benefit of the traditional faith, defending it and preserving it from corruption or dilution.

The battle for the faith is accomplished by filtering the complexities of life through an authoritative belief system. The unalterable faith has already been delivered τοῖς ἁγίοις ("to the saints," v. 3) and received by them. With the concessive participial phrase εἰδότας [ὑμᾶς] πάντα ("though you know all things") Jude acknowledges that they have already been exposed to God's complete revelation (v. 5) through the Church's practice of carefully instructing converts.[212] Biblical religion, however, calls people to consistently remember and reflect on this revelation, subjecting themselves and their experiences to its authority.[213] At pivotal junctures, at the beginning and end of his discourse on judgment, Jude appeals to their intellectual catalogue, turning their attention back to sacred tradition (vv. 5, 17). Beginning in v. 5 Jude seeks to remind (ὑπομνῆσαι) them of certain judgment lessons from redemptive history. At least three grammatical tags in v. 17 mark both the conclusion of the letter's judgment section and the beginning of overt paraenesis. The second person pronoun ὑμεῖς ("you"), the adversative δέ ("but"), and the vocative ἀγαπητοί ("beloved") all lead to the letter's first imperative mood verb: "But you, beloved, remember (μνήσθητε) the words spoken before by the apostles." To "fight for the faith" therefore includes the habitual practice of recalling revealed truth and scrutinizing belief and behavior by its light.

---

207 Letter of Aristeas 273; cf. John 18:36.

208 Cf. 2 Macc 13:14; Sir 4:28; 4 Macc 17:10–13; T. Ash. 6:1–2; T. Jos. 2:2.

209 Cf. Luke 13:24; John 18:36. The noun form ἀγών, "fight," "struggle," or "contest," occurs only in Phil 1:30; Col 2:1; 1 Thess 2:2; 1 Tim 6:12; 2 Tim 4:7; Heb 12:1.

210 1 Cor 9:25; Col 1:29; 4:12; 1 Tim 4:10; 6:12; 2 Tim 4:7; cf. Rom 15:30; Pfitzner, *Paul and the Agon Motif*, 128, 193–5; Stauffer, " ἀγών, κτλ.," 137–9; Dautzenberg, "ἀγών," 27.

211 Ethelbert Stauffer, " ἀγών, κτλ.," *TDNT* 1:138; It is a "continuous, costly and agonizing" defense which invites violent resistance (Green, *Jude*, 172).

212 Cf. Luke 1:4; Sidebottom, *Jude*, 85; Schelkle, *Judasbrief*, 153. Grundmann, however, concludes that πάντα ("all things") refers merely to knowledge of the judgment examples to follow (*Brief des Judas*, 32–3).

213 Num 15:39–40; Deut 4:23; 8:11; Mal 4:4; Luke 24:6, 8; John 2:17; 12:16; 14:26; Rom 15:15; 1 Cor 11:2; 2 Tim 2:8, 14; Titus 3:1; 2 Pet 1:12; 3:1–2; Rev 3:3; cf. Jub. 6:22; 2 Bar. 84:1–11; Brevard S. Childs, *Memory and Tradition in Israel*, SBT 37 (SCM Press, 1962), 50–65; Kelly, *Jude*, 254; Vögtle, *Judasbrief*, 35–6; Fuchs and Reymond, *Jude*, 162–3.

The same introductory construction found in v. 17, ὑμεῖς δέ ἀγαπητοί ("but you beloved"), appears again in v. 20 and signals the transition into the letter's final paraenetic section. The mixture of imperatives and imperatival participles that follow in vv. 20–23 serve to complete the original exhortation to "fight for the faith" (v. 3).[214] The first command, ἐποικοδομοῦντες ἑαυτοὺς τῇ ἁγιωτάτῃ ὑμῶν πίστει ("build yourselves up on your most holy faith"), turns again to the "ensemble of apostolic teaching" articulated in v. 3.[215] In sharp contrast to those who divide (ἀποδιορίζοντες) and destroy the church through false teaching (v. 19), Jude's audience must instead cooperatively pursue the church's edification (ἐποικοδομοῦντες ἑαυτοὺς).[216] The basis or foundation of the project is the pure teaching of the traditional gospel, their "most holy faith."[217]

The somewhat ambiguous finite imperative ἑαυτοὺς ἐν ἀγάπῃ θεοῦ τηρήσατε ("keep yourselves in the love of God," v. 21) continues this emphasis on adherence to "the faith." The genitive θεοῦ identifies ἀγάπη as the love God has for believers.[218] In the Johannine literature similar descriptions of this love connote relational intimacy maintained by obedience to the "commandments."[219] These include both the commandment to believe accurately and the commandment to behave appropriately.[220] The process according to Jude must be accompanied by Spirit led prayerfulness (ἐν πνεύματι ἁγίῳ προσευχόμενοι, v. 20) and a patient waiting that actively orients the "whole of life toward the eschatological hope" for final redemption (προσδεχόμενοι τὸ ἔλεος τοῦ κυρίου ἡμῶν Ἰησοῦ Χριστοῦ εἰς ζωὴν αἰώνιον, v. 21).[221]

Jude's final series of three finite imperatives forms a composite interpersonal admonition (vv. 22–23).[222] Believers contend for the faith by confronting those in error with truth.[223] Rebuke that leads to repentance is an act of

214 Watson, *Invention, Arrangement, and Style*, 40; Bauckham, *Jude, 2 Peter*, 29.

215 Kelly, *Jude*, 285; Vögtle, *Judasbrief*, 99–100. The participial imperative form may itself carry traditional overtones. Cf. David Daube, "Participle and Imperative in 1 Peter," appendix to *The First Epistle of St. Peter: The Greek Text with Introduction, Notes, and Essays*, 2nd ed., by Edward G. Selwyn (Baker, 1981), 467–88; W. D. Davies, *Paul and Rabbinic Judaism: Some Rabbinic Elements in Pauline Theology* (Fortress Press, 1980), 130–45.

216 Bauckham, *Jude, 2 Peter*, 113.

217 Cf. 1 Cor 3:9–15; Eph 2:19–22; 1 Pet 2:5; Fuchs and Reymond, *Jude*, 183.

218 Bigg, *Jude*, 340; Fuchs and Reymond, *Jude*, 184; Vögtle, *Judasbrief*, 100.

219 Sidebottom, *Jude*, 92; Cantinat, *Jude*, 330; Knoch, *Judasbrief*, 190–1.

220 John 14:15, 21; 15:9–12; 1 John 3:23–24; 4:15–21.

221 Cf. Isa 30:18; Dan 12:12; Mic 7:7; Hab 2:3; Zeph 3:8; Mark 15:43; Luke 2:25; Titus 2:13; Schelkle, *Judasbrief*, 169–70; Bauckham, *Jude, 2 Peter*, 114.

222 See Chapter One, "Textual Criticism," above for a summary of the complex text critical issues surrounding vv. 22–23.

223 Cf. Matt 18:15–17; Luke 17:3; Gal 6:1; 2 Thess 3:15; 1 Tim 5:20; Titus 3:10; Jas 5:19–20; Bauckham, *Jude, 2 Peter*, 115.

mercy (ἐλεᾶτε) toward those who dispute²²⁴ the faith in its "once for all de-livered" form or indulge the flesh (ἀπὸ τῆς σαρκὸς ἐσπιλωμένον). These must be restored to orthodoxy and orthopraxy and thus saved, snatched from the precipice of Hell (σῴζετε ἐκ πυρὸς ἁρπάζοντες). Through doctrinal militancy, fervent prayer, and eschatological anticipation (all hallmarks of Jude's Chris-tian worldview) believers avoid the pitfalls of their doomed opponents.²²⁵

Redeemer/Judge

Jude's short message depends completely on the expectation that an apoca-lyptic redeemer/judge will come (vv. 14–15) and bring to an end the ungod-liness that thrives ἐπ' ἐσχάτου [τοῦ] χρόνου ("in the last time," v. 18). Jude's Christian audience is identified solely in relationship to this redeemer. They are those "beloved in God the father" (τοῖς ἐν θεῷ πατρὶ ἠγαπημένοις). God's love for his people is defined most clearly by his redemption of enslaved Is-rael at the exodus and his redemption of enslaved humanity through Christ.²²⁶ By employing the locative of sphere ἐν θεῷ ("in God") instead of the expected ablative of agency ὑπὸ θεοῦ,²²⁷ Jude describes a new love relationship "in God." This familial intimacy (πατρί) includes a reciprocal fellowship where believ-ers are "embraced and enfolded" by God's love.²²⁸

The ultimate realization of this love looks forward to God's coming when he will claim his eschatological inheritance (vv. 1, 24–25). Jude's readers are "those ... kept for Jesus Christ" (τοῖς... Ἰησοῦ Χριστῷ τετηρημένοις, v. 1). Though Χριστῷ could express the rare instrumental of agency ("kept by Christ"), the more natural sense points to advantage ("for the benefit of Christ").²²⁹ As the

---

224 The majority of commentators interpret the participle διακρινομένους (v. 23) "those who waver," "hesitate," or "vacillate" between two conflicting viewpoints (Schelkle, *Judasbrief*, 166, 171; Paulsen, *Judasbrief*, 78, 84; Cantinat, *Jude*, 332–3; Knoch, *Judasbrief*, 190; Grundmann, *Brief des Judas*, 44; Fuchs and Reymond, *Jude*, 185; Kelly, *Jude*, 288). This can fit the context, but the same verb is used in v. 9 (διακρινόμενος) to describe Michael's dispute with the devil. This meaning is attested elsewhere (cf. Ezek 20:35–36 [LXX]; Joel 3:2 [LXX]; Acts 11:2) and both occurrences are connected by allusions to Zech 3:2–4 (Bauckham, *Jude, 2 Peter*, 115; Neyrey, *Jude*, 84).

225 Martin, *Theology of Jude*, 84.

226 Cf. Deut 7:7–8; Hos 11:1; John 3:16; Rom 5:8; Eph 1:4–5; 5:25; 2 Bar. 78:3; Bauckham, *Jude, 2 Peter*, 25.

227 Agency is only rarely expressed by ἐν and the dative; cf. F. Blass and A. Debrunner, *A Greek Grammar of the New Testament and other Early Christian Literature*, trans. Robert W. Funk (University of Chicago Press, 1961), 102–3; Wallace, *Grammar*, 163–6.

228 Cf. Jude 21; John 17:21; 1 John 2:24; 3:24; 4:13–16; Bauckham, *Jude, 2 Peter*, 26.

229 Wallace, *Grammar*, 144. Cf. τηρέω with the dative of disadvantage (Jude 13; 2 Pet 2:17; 3:7). In a similar "inheritance" context it appears with εἰς and the accusative of advantage: "an inheritance ... reserved in heaven for you" (τετηρημένην ἐν οὐρανοῖς εἰς ὑμᾶς, 1 Pet 1:4).

implied agent of the passive τετηρημένοις ("those who are kept"), God sets aside the universal Christian community as Christ's own eternal possession. God alone is the believer's savior (μόνῳ θεῷ σωτῆρι) who keeps his people from stumbling (ἀπταίστους) in order to present them to himself in a blameless condition (ἀμώμους, vv. 24–25). In similar Pauline imagery God predestines Christians to "adoption as sons through Jesus Christ to himself" (Eph 1:5). He gives the Spirit as a pledge of inheritance, "with a view to the redemption of God's own possession" (Eph 1:14). In Eph 5:27 Christ is the redeemer who sacrificed himself "that he might present to himself the church in all her glory, having no spot or wrinkle or any such thing; but that she should be holy and blameless (ἄμωμος)." According to 1 Thess 5:23, the redeemer's preserving work should be understood primarily in light of the parousia:[230] "Now may the God of peace himself sanctify you entirely; and may your spirit and soul and body be preserved (τηρηθείη) complete, without blame (ἀμέμπτως) at the coming (ἐν τῇ παρουσίᾳ) of our Lord Jesus Christ."

While the theme of preservation until the eschaton hints at God's coming, Christological references and the main body of the letter look specifically to Jesus' parousia as the coming of the apocalyptic redeemer/judge. Every occurrence of the name Ἰησοῦς ("Jesus") is also accompanied by the title Χριστός ("Christ") and its transparent messianic significance.[231] As the Christ, the Messiah, Jesus functions as the agent sent by God to perform his twofold eschatological purpose: liberate God's people and execute judgment from the throne of universal authority.[232] The theme of a coming redeemer/judge appears most clearly, however, through Jude's application of apocalyptic theophany language to Jesus the κύριος ("Lord").

In v. 4 Jesus is given the very exclusive title τὸν μόνον δεσπότην καὶ κύριον ("the only master and lord"). By ascribing to Jesus the roles of δεσπότης and κύριος Jude unequivocally declares the redeemer's deity. Individually, δεσπότης and κύριος were interchangeable titles for God that the earliest Christians

---

230 Cf. Best, *Thessalonians*, 242–3; I. Howard Marshall, "Pauline Theology in the Thessalonian Correspondence," in *Paul and Paulinism: Essays in Honour of C. K. Barrett*, ed. M. D. Hooker and S. G. Wilson (SPCK, 1982), 179–80; Wanamaker, *Thessalonians*, 206–7.

231 Cf. vv. 1, 4, 17, 21, 25. In the Palestinian church especially, the messianic connotations of Χριστός were unavoidable; Oscar Cullmann, *The Christology of the New Testament*, rev. ed., trans. Shirley C. Guthrie and Charles A. M. Hall (Westminster Press, 1963), 112, 133; W. C. van Unnik, "Jesus the Christ," *NTS* 8, no. 2 (1962): 113.

232 S. Mowinckel, *He that Cometh*, trans. G. W. Anderson (Abingdon Press, 1954), 261–79; Nils Alstrup Dahl, *Jesus the Christ: The Historical Origins of Christological Doctrine* (Fortress Press, 1991), 20–1; Richard J. Bauckham, "Jude's Christology," in *Jude and the Relatives of Jesus in the Early Church* (T&T Clark, 1990), 300–1; Ferdinand Hahn, "Χριστός," *EDNT* 3:478–80, 485–86; Cullmann, *Christology*, 113–17; cf. 1 Enoch 45:3; 46; 55:4; 69:27–29; 4 Ezra 12:31–33; 13:26, 37–38; 2 Bar. 40:1; 72:2.

adopted and applied Christologically.[233] In a few instances they are combined in the LXX to translate the divine name "Lord God" (יְהוִה אֲדֹנָי)[234] or to qualify the nature of his authority.[235] The attributive adjective μόνον appended by a Jewish Christian to such overt divine titles would make the Christological implications unmistakable. In a near parallel to Jude's phraseology, Josephus recounts a Jewish sect's passion for autonomy that is driven by the conviction that "God alone is their leader and master" (μόνον ἡγεμόνα καὶ δεσπότην τὸν θεόν).[236]

The name κύριος ("Lord") appears again in Jude's quotation of 1 Enoch 1:9 (vv. 14–15) and "undoubtedly denotes Jesus as the eschatological redeemer who is to triumph eventually as the Judge of all mankind."[237] The Enoch text itself is an apocalyptic adaptation of OT "day of the Lord" texts which anticipate redemption and judgment at the eschatological coming of God:[238]

> The God of the universe, the Holy Great One, will come … Behold, he will arrive with ten million of the holy ones in order to execute judgment upon all. He will destroy the wicked ones and censure all flesh on account of everything that they have done, that which the sinners and the wicked ones committed against him. (1 Enoch 1:3, 9)

Contextually, the subject of 1 Enoch 1:9 is borrowed from v. 3: "The God of the Universe, the Holy Great One." At this point Jude's insertion of κύριος into his version of Enoch's "curse" or "ban formula"[239] makes an "unmistakable prediction" of Jesus' coming in judgment:[240]

---

233 Cf. Matt 3:3; Luke 2:29; Acts 4:24; Rom 10:9; 1 Cor 12:3; 1 Pet 3:14–15; Rev 6:10; 17:14; 19:16. See in particular Phil 2:7–10 where Jesus Christ as κύριος ("Lord") is given the "name above every name," the "sacred name of Jahweh, the *Kyrios* of the Greek Old Testament" (Black, "Christological Use," 7); F. F. Bruce, "Jesus is Lord," in *Soli Deo Gloria: New Testament Studies in Honor of William Childs Robinson*, ed. J. McDowell Richards (John Knox Press, 1968), 32–6; Günter Haufe, "δεσπότης," *EDNT* 1:290–92; Joseph A. Fitzmyer, "κύριος," *EDNT* 2:329–31.

234 Gen 15:2, 8; Isa 1:24; 3:1; 10:33; Jer 1:6; 4:10; cf. Josephus, *Jewish Antiquities* 20.90; T. Ab. 4:5–6; 9:6.

235 Cf. Job 5:8; Jonah 4:3; Karl Heinrich Rengstorf, "δεσπότης, κτλ.," *TDNT* 2:45–47.

236 Josephus, *Jewish Antiquities* 18.23; cf. idem, *Jewish War* 7.323, 410; Bauckham, "Jude's Christology," 307.

237 Osburn, "The Christological Use of 1 Enoch 1:9," 341; D. G. Wohlenberg, *Der erste und zweite Petrusbrief und der Judasbrief*, KNT 15 (A. Deichert'sche, 1915), 318; Schelkle, *Judasbrief*, 164; Kelly, *Jude*, 276.

238 Cf. Deut 33:2; Isa 40:10; 66:15–16; Micah 1:3–4; Zech 14:5; Hartman, *Prophecy Interpreted*, 112–8; Bauckham, "Jude's Christology," 288–9; VanderKam, "Theophany of Enoch 1:3b–7, 9," 129–50.

239 Black, "Christological Use," 10–11; cf. C. F. D. Moule, "A Reconsideration of the Context of *Maranatha*," *NTS* 8, no. 4 (1960): 307–10.

240 Osburn, "Discourse Analysis," 305; Fuchs and Reymond, *Jude*, 176; Vögtle, *Judasbrief*, 77–8.

Behold, the Lord (κύριος) came with myriads of his holy ones, to execute judgment upon all, and to convict all the ungodly of all their ungodly deeds which they have done in an ungodly way, and of all the harsh words which ungodly sinners have spoken against him. (vv. 14–15)

The contention that Jude applies κύριος and Enoch's theophany prophecy to Jesus is supported by the NT's repeated "referential shift of 'Lord' from God to Christ"[241] in adaptations of OT theophany texts. For example, Zech 14:5 in the LXX reads: καὶ ἥξει κύριος ὁ θεός μου, καὶ πάντες οἱ ἅγιοι μετ' αὐτοῦ ("and the Lord my God shall come, and all the holy ones with him"). Paul, however, can pray in almost identical language that the Lord would perfect Christians "at the coming of our Lord Jesus with all his saints" (ἐν τῇ παρουσίᾳ τοῦ κυρίου ἡμῶν Ἰησοῦ μετὰ πάντων τῶν ἁγίων αὐτοῦ, 1 Thess 3:13).[242] Jesus therefore fulfills the dual redeemer/judge role anticipated in OT and apocalyptic theophany tradition.

According to 1 Enoch 1:8, when the "Great Holy One, the eternal God" comes, he will bring a salvation thematically consistent with Jude's:

With the righteous he will make peace, and over the chosen there will be protection (συντήρησις), and upon them will be mercy (ἔλεος). They will all be God's, and he will grant them his good pleasure. He will bless them all. Light will shine upon them, and he will make peace with them.[243]

In the "Lord Jesus Christ" believers already enjoy protection (τετηρημένοις) while they wait for the parousia when the redeemer will bestow his consummate mercy (ἔλεος) that leads to eternal life (Jude 1, 21).[244] Jesus is in Jude 25 the very means through which God accomplishes his work of salvation (διὰ Ἰησοῦ Χριστοῦ τοῦ κυρίου, "through our Lord Jesus Christ").[245] Just as κύριος ("the Lord"), God the Father proper, executed judgment against faithless Israel, disobedient angels, and immoral Sodom, Jesus will assume the role of κύριος and wield divine judgmental authority over all creation

---

241 L. Joseph Kreitzer, *Jesus and God in Paul's Eschatology*, JSNTSup 19 (JSOT Press, 1987), 113.

242 Cf. Isa 2:10, 19, 21 (2 Thess 1:9); Isa 45:23 (Phil 2:10–11); Isa 66:4–6, 15 (2 Thess 1:6–12); Joel 2:28–32 (Rom 10:13; 1 Cor 1:2); Zech 14:5 (Matt 16:27; 25:31; Mark 8:38; Luke 9:26; 1 Thess 3:13; 4:14; 2 Thess 1:7–10; Rev 19:14); Kreitzer, *Jesus and God*, 112–24.

243 Translated by Nickelsburg, *1 Enoch 1*, 142.

244 Cf. Isa 30:18; 49:23; 64:4 (LXX); Dan 12:12; Mic 7:7; Zeph 3:8–13; 2 Macc 2:7; 2 Bar. 78:7; 4 Ezra 14:34.

245 Grundmann, *Brief des Judas*, 50; Cantinat, *Jude*, 337; Bauckham, *Jude, 2 Peter*, 123–4.

(vv. 14–15).[246] The parousia will reveal Jesus as the "only Master and Lord" (v. 4) who divides humanity into the "ungodly" (v. 15) and the "beloved" (v. 1) and showers each with the appropriate expressions of his majesty.

CONCLUSION

Like the Jewish and Christian apocalyptic sources he employs, Jude responds to the crisis of invasive theological pluralism by asserting an apocalyptic eschatology that sets exclusionary boundaries around a besieged community. Insurgent antinomians openly redefining the faith according to their own anti-authoritarian biases endeavored to lead Jude's audience toward tolerance and acceptance. Jude's worldview, however, condemns their deviations from biblical authority, ostracizing such pluralists as faithless and reprobate. The elements of Jude's exclusivism follow the same general pattern found in apocalyptic Judaism and Christianity. His stand on the authoritative and revealed faith sets the precedent for a comprehensive and inflexible division between truth and error, faith and heresy. The elect are set against the reprobate, human depravity is exposed, and judgment is affirmed as the eternal separator. By exalting Jesus Christ as the unique divine mediator of the one true God's redemptive and judicial plans, Jude asserts the Son's authority to command universal submission. As the next chapter will attempt to demonstrate, Jude's apocalyptic eschatology results in a resloute theological exclusivism.

---

246 Cf. Deut 33:2; Isa 40:10; 59:15–19; 64:1; 66:15–16; Mic 1:3–4; Zech 14:5; Bauckham, "Jude's Christology," 307–12.

CHAPTER 4

JUDE'S APOCALYPTIC ESCHATOLOGY
AS THEOLOGICAL EXCLUSIVISM

T HE FIRST-CENTURY JUDEO-CHRISTIAN MISSION flourished in a Helle-nized pagan world awash with theological options. Pantheistic and ra-tional Stoic philosophy had subsumed the ever expanding pantheon under one universal governing principle. The gods of the nations, with all of their various names and characteristics, were interpreted as symbolic repre-sentations of a single divine ideal. This construct, rather than leading to the rejection of traditional polytheism, provided a universalizing "philosophical rationale" for theological pluralism.[1] Any and every god could be worshiped as a potential manifestation of divine reason. By necessity of its expansion, Hellenism evolved into a "culture of pragmatic pluralism"[2] that readily en-couraged ideological experimentation and syncretism.[3] The interaction be-tween indigenous religions and the Greek obsession with novelty produced an unlimited catalogue of philosophies, theologies, deities, magical arts, and mystery religions.[4]

Hellenistic egocentrism and skepticism[5] seeped into the religious con-sciousness and generated a climate of theological relativism. For exam-ple, the cult of Mithras, the "most important, most influential, and best

---

1 Koester, *History, Culture, and Religion*, 144; David Sedley, "Stoicism," *Routledge Encyclope-dia of Philosophy* 9:146; A. A. Long, "Epicureans and Stoics," in *Classical Mediterranean Spiritu-ality: Egyptian, Greek, Roman*, ed. A. H. Armstrong (Crossroad, 1989), 146–8.

2 Cf. Thiselton, *First Corinthians*, 1.

3 Grant, *Hellenistic Religions*, xiii–ix; Martin, *Hellenistic Religions*, 10–1; MacMullen, *Pa-ganism in the Roman Empire*, 2, 90–4; Ferguson, *Backgrounds of Early Christianity*, 161–5.

4 Cf. Hans-Josef Klauck, *The Religious Context of Early Christianity: A Guide to Graeco-Ro-man Religions*, trans. Brian McNeil (T&T Clark, 2000), 81–247; Jack Finegan, *Myth and Mystery: An Introduction to the Pagan Religions of the Biblical World* (Baker, 1989), 155–215.

5 Cf. W. T. Jones, *The Classical Mind: A History of Western Philosophy*, 2nd ed. (Harcourt Brace Jovanovich College Publishers, 1970), 316–53; Klauck, *Religious Context*, 365–85; Arthur H. Armstrong, *An Introduction to Ancient Philosophy*, 3rd ed. (Methuen, 1957), 114, 315; P. Mer-

organized mystery cult"[6] of the first century A.D., carefully guarded its rites and zealously regulated its patriarchal admission policies (i.e., men only).[7] Despite stringent community controls, the cult readily embraced those who continued to worship other gods.[8] In such contexts religious "authority" was particularly relative and individualistic. Ancient traditions and oracular ecstasies were readily adaptable, serving Hellenism's syncretistic ethos by catering to "people seeking the aid of supernatural powers for their personal endeavors."[9]

The Platonic dualism that pitted the illusory and transitory non-reality of matter against the "real" universal form of ideas[10] provided a convenient impetus for ethical and theological compartmentalization. Individuals could freely entertain the passions of the irrelevant material body while pursuing spiritual enlightenment through the real realm of the mind.[11] Religion in its highest and most sophisticated form could be libertine and virtuous simultaneously. Certain elements of Judaism that assimilated this anthropology could maintain a ritually strict monotheism while cultivating mystical "gnosticizing-libertine" tendencies.[12]

---

lan, "Greek Philosophy from Plato to Plotinus," in *The Cambridge History of Later Greek and Early Medieval Philosophy*, ed. A. H. Armstrong (Cambridge University Press, 1970), 125.

6 Koester, *History, Culture, and Religion*, 357.

7 Walter Burkert, *Ancient Mystery Cults* (Harvard University Press, 1987), 41–3; David Ulansey, *The Origins of the Mithraic Mysteries: Cosmology and Salvation in the Ancient World* (Oxford University Press, 1989), 6.

8 Manfred Clauss, *The Roman Cult of Mithras: The God and His Mysteries*, trans. Richard Gordon (Routledge, 2001), 155–67; Martin, *Hellenistic Religions*, 118.

9 Koester, *History, Culture, and Religion*, 356–8; Walter Burkert, *Greek Religion*, trans. John Raffan (Harvard University Press, 1985), 109–18; John Pollard, "Divination and Oracles: Greece," in *Civilization of the Ancient Mediterranean: Greece and Rome* 2, ed. Michael Grant and Rachel Kitzinger (Charles Scribner's Sons, 1988), 941–50; John Ferguson, "Divination and Oracles: Rome," Ibid., 951–8.

10 John Dillon, "Platonism, Early and Middle," *Routledge Encyclopedia of Philosophy* 7:424–5; Armstrong, *Introduction to Ancient Philosophy*, 37–43.

11 Christopher Stead, "Gnosticism," *Routledge Encyclopedia of Philosophy* 4:83; Walter Schmithals, *Gnosticism in Corinth: An Investigation of the Letters to the Corinthians*, trans. John E. Steely (Abingdon Press, 1971), 26, 31, 218–24, 230–7. Cf. the implications of 1 Cor 5:2 and "boasting" in immorality; Thiselton, *First Corinthians*, 388–9; F. F. Bruce, *1 and 2 Corinthians*, NCBC (Eerdmans, 1971), 54; Barrett, *First Epistle to the Corinthians*, 122.

12 E. Earle Ellis, "The Circumcision Party and the Early Christian Mission," in *Prophecy and Hermeneutic in Early Christianity* (Eerdmans, 1978; repr., Baker, 1993), 122, 125–6; Schmithals, *Gnosticism in Corinth*, 49–51; Edwin M. Yamauchi, *Pre-Christian Gnosticism: A Survey of Proposed Evidences* (Eerdmans, 1973), 162; Erwin R. Goodenough, *By Light, Light: The Mystic Gospel of Hellenistic Judaism* (Yale University Press, 1935), 6–10; idem, *The Archaeological Evidence from Palestine*, vol. 1 of *Jewish Symbols in the Greco-Roman Period* (Pantheon Books, 1953), 264–7; Jean Daniélou, *The Theology of Jewish Christianity*, trans. and ed. John A. Baker, The Development of Christian Doctrine Before the Council of Nicaea 1 (Darton, Longman and Todd, 1964), 69–72; Kurt Rudolph, *Gnosis: The Nature and History of Gnosticism*, trans. and ed. Robert Mc-

This pervasive first-century pluralism "provides an embarrassingly close model of a postmodern context" for the contemporary church, "even given the huge historical differences and distances in so many other respects."[13] Western culture's once stalwart Christian veneer has dissolved into a morass of profound religious diversity. Cross-fertilization throughout the new global community[14] has spawned the proliferation of Islam, Hinduism, Buddhism, neo-paganism, eastern mysticism, and the innumerable matrixes of "New Age" monistic and pantheistic philosophies, theosophies, and theologies.[15] Eerily reminiscent of the Hellenistic milieu, contemporary western culture at one level vaunts this religious diversity as a virtue. Theological multiplicity is celebrated, even prioritized.[16] At another level, however, the postmodern deconstruction of objectivity[17] has provided philosophical foundations for a totalitarian relativism that demonizes any truth claim.[18] The resulting philo-

---

Lachlan Wilson (Harper and Row, 1983), 52, 276–82. Cf. Nils A. Dahl, "The Arrogant Archon and the Lewd Sophia: Jewish Traditions in Gnostic Revolt," in *Gnosticism in the Early Church*, ed. David M. Scholer, Studies in Early Christianity 5 (Garland, 1993), 691, 698–701.

13 Thiselton, *First Corinthians*, 17; Robert L. Wilken, "Religious Pluralism and Early Christian Theology," *Int* 40, no. 4 (1986): 379–91; "We today are far closer in religious temper to apostolic times than any period since the Reformation" (David F. Wells, *No Place for Truth, or, Whatever Happened to Evangelical Theology?* [Eerdmans, 1993], 104). Cf. John J. Carey, "Apocalypticism as a Bridge Between the Testaments," in *The Old and New Testaments: Their Relationship and the "Intertestamental" Literature*, ed. James H. Charlesworth and Walter P. Weaver (Trinity Press International, 1993), 96.

14 Cf. Peter Beyer, *Religion and Globalization*, Theory, Culture and Society (Sage, 1994), 1–12; Mike Featherstone, *Undoing Culture: Globalization, Postmodernism and Identity*, Theory, Culture and Society (Sage, 1995), 1–14.

15 Timothy Miller, ed. *America's Alternative Religions*, SUNY Series in Religious Studies (State University of New York Press, 1995); Jacob Neusner, ed. *World Religions in America: An Introduction*, rev. ed. (Westminster John Knox, 2000); Wouter J. Hanegraaff, *New Age Religion and Western Culture: Esotericism in the Mirror of Secular Thought*, Studies in the History of Religions 72 (E. J. Brill, 1996); George Gallup Jr. and Jim Castelli, *The People's Religion: American Faith in the 90s* (Macmillan, 1989) 23–5, 44; George Barna and Mark Hatch, *Boiling Point: Monitoring Cultural Shifts in the 21st Century* (Regal, 2001), 183–202; George Barna, *What Americans Believe: An Annual Survey of Values and Religious Views in the United States* (Regal, 1991), 174–5; Catherine L. Albanese, *America: Religions and Religion*, 2nd ed. (Wadsworth, 1992), 350–92.

16 Lesslie Newbigin, *The Gospel in a Pluralist Society* (Eerdmans, 1989), 1; cf. Carson, *Gagging God*, 18.

17 See e.g. Mark C. Taylor, *Deconstructing Theology*, SR 28 (Crossroad, 1982), 45–59; Jacques Derrida, *Of Grammatology*, corrected ed., trans. Gayatri Chakravorty Spivak (John Hopkins University Press, 1997), 50; Jean-François Lyotard, *The Postmodern Condition: A Report on Knowledge*, trans. Geoff Bennington and Brian Massumi, Theory and History of Literature 10 (University of Minnesota Press, 1984), 81–2; cf. Stanley J. Grenz, *A Primer on Postmodernism* (Eerdmans, 1996), 6–7; David Ray Griffin, "Postmodern Theology and A/theology," in *Varieties of Postmodern Theology*, ed. David Ray Griffin (State University of New York Press, 1989), 33–4.

18 Bloom, *Closing of the American Mind*, 25–6; McGrath, *Passion for Truth*, 206, 219–20; S. D. Gaede, *When Tolerance is No Virtue: Political Correctness, Multiculturalism and the Future of Truth and Justice* (InterVarsity Press, 1993), 23–8, 44–7.

sophical and hermeneutical pluralism mandates a bizarre and self-contradic-
tory theological syncretism summarized succinctly by D. A. Carson:

> Any notion that a particular ideological or religious claim is intrinsically
> superior to another is *necessarily* wrong. The only absolute creed is the
> creed of pluralism. No religion has the right to pronounce itself right or
> true, and the others false, or even (in the majority view) relatively inferior.[19]

In the name of tolerance the possibility of religious authority and theological
error is rejected a priori, and efforts to assert otherwise are demonized as the
coercive systematization by the "'régime' of truth."[20] Theological truth and authority are the enemies "against which postmodernism defines its freedom:
the freedom to create one's own values set against submission to an absolute
truth, the autonomy of human beings set against obedience to a transcendent God, and the free play of interpretation set against belief in any final,
authoritative meaning."[21]

JUDE'S PLURALISTIC OPPONENTS

Jude's polemic was not of course directed against a pluralistic culture at large
but against the church's importation of certain worldview incompatibilities.
Jude's opponents were committed to a synthetic sampling of Christian grace
and pagan antinomianism (v. 4). Though they entered the church and took up
leadership positions (vv. 4, 12), they were unwilling to conform to the church's
objective transcendent standard for Christian belief and practice, "the faith
once for all delivered to the saints" (v. 3). Instead, they chose to base their
worldview and its outworking on the subjectivities of personal preference
and ecstatic experience.[22] As a result, their Christian confession was diluted

---

19 Carson, *Gagging God*, 19; cf. Millard J. Erickson, *The Promise and Perils of Postmodernism: Truth or Consequences* (InterVarsity Press, 2001), 208–10; C. Ben Mitchell, "Is That All There
Is? Moral Ambiguity in a Postmodern Pluralistic Culture," in *The Challenge of Postmodernism*,
2nd ed., ed. David S. Dockery (Baker, 2001), 148–51. See especially McGrath's discussion of the
"fatal intra-paradigmatic and extra-paradigmatic inconsistencies" inherent to this contemporary "prescriptive pluralism" (*Passion for Truth*, 206–20).

20 Michel Foucault, "Truth and Power," in *Power/Knowledge: Selected Interviews and Other Writings, 1972–1977*, ed. Colin Gordon (Pantheon Books, 1980), 133; Lyotard, *The Postmodern
Condition*, 82. Cf. Erickson, *Promise and Perils of Postmodernism*, 231–51; Terry Eagleton, "Awakening from Modernity," *TimesLitSupp*, 20 February 1987, 194; Gary Phillips, "Religious Pluralism in a Postmodern World," in *The Challenge of Postmodernism*, 2nd ed., ed. David S. Dockery
(Baker, 2001), 135–6.

21 Ingraffia, *Postmodern Theory and Biblical Theology*, 6; Thomas Finger, "Modernity, Postmodernity—What in the World Are They?" *Transformation* 10, no. 4 (1993): 24–5.

22 Cf. vv. 8, 10, 16, 18.

by anti-authoritarian bias, a narcissistic passion for freedom, and sexual in-dulgence.[23] In the spirit of Hellenistic theological relativism, their position demanded a kind of tolerance and inclusiveness that evacuates accountabil-ity to an immutable good and discourages worldview specificity. The success of their efforts is apparent from the letter's general purpose: Jude's audience had to be reminded and commanded not to tolerate distortions of the re-vealed faith.

Contemporary experimental syntheses of Christianity and postmodern pluralism, intentional or otherwise, suggest disturbing parallels with the first-century occasion confronted by Jude.[24] The church's vitality is threat-ened "because of its unwitting entanglement with a culture that, in its post-modern configuration, has the power to eviscerate the doctrinal substance" of genuine Christianity.[25] An "anti-theological" mood grips various elements of twenty-first century Christendom, separating the church from its moor-ings in historical orthodoxy and "emancipating contemporary evangelicals to form casual alliances at will with a multitude of substitutes."[26] Western cul-ture's consuming anthropocentrism[27] has been Christianized in the forms of "an accentuation of subjectivity and the virtual veneration of the self, exhibit-ed in deliberate efforts to achieve self-understanding, self-improvement, and self-fulfillment."[28] The sovereignty and omniscience of God are implicitly displaced by "old Arminian or non-Augustinian thinking"[29] that hints at a capitulation to the postmodern ethos of unqualified human freedom and

---

23 Cf. vv. 4, 8, 10, 16, 18–19.

24 Cf. Wendland, "Comparative Study of 'Rhetorical Criticism,'" 216; Douglas Groothuis, *Truth Decay: Defending Christianity Against the Challenge of Postmodernism* (InterVarsity Press, 2000), 21–2; Wells, *No Place for Truth*, 279–82; Timothy R. Phillips and Dennis L. Okholm, "The Nature of Confession: Evangelicals and Postliberals," in *The Nature of Confession: Evangelicals and Postliberals in Conversation*, ed. idem (InterVarsity Press, 1996), 8–9.

25 David F. Wells, "Introduction: The Word in the World," in *The Compromised Church: The Present Evangelical Crisis*, ed. John H. Armstrong (Crossway, 1998), 24.

26 Wells, *No Place for Truth*, 96.

27 Thomas Oden, "The Death of Modernity and Postmodern Evangelical Spirituality," in *The Challenge of Postmodernism*, 2nd ed., ed. David S. Dockery (Baker, 2001), 27–30.

28 James Davison Hunter, *Evangelicalism: The Coming Generation* (University of Chicago Press, 1987), 65–7; Walter C. Hobbs, "Faith Twisted by Culture: Syncretism in North American Christianity," in *Confident Witness – Changing World: Rediscovering the Gospel in North Ameri-ca*, ed. Craig Van Gelder (Eerdmans, 1999), 102–5.

29 Clark H. Pinnock, "The Arminian Option," *ChrT* 34, no. 3 (19, 1990): 15; idem, "System-atic Theology," in *The Openness of God: A Biblical Challenge to the Traditional Understanding of God*, ed. Clark Pinnock et al. (InterVarsity Press, 1994), 121–4. Cf. Nathan MacDonald, "From Augustine to Arminius, and Beyond," in *Reconstructing Theology: A Critical Assessment of the Theology of Clark Pinnock*, ed. Tony Gray and Christopher Sinkinson (Paternoster, 2000), 21–48; Tony Gray, "Beyond Arminius: Pinnock's Doctrine of God and the Evangelical Tradition," Ibid., 135–8.

tolerance.[30] Christianity is therefore increasingly defined in terms of pragmatic subjective experience rather than objective biblical truth.[31] Stanley Grenz betrays an awareness of these dangers inherent to his own "postmodern evangelicalism":"

> The focus on the practical nature of theology does not automatically lead to a new subjectivity; it does not aim to replace the subjectivity of the knowing subject with a subjectivity of the isolated believing community.[32]

Despite such a caveat, revisions of evangelical theology threaten to concede postmodernity's theological relativism by downplaying the propositional qualities of revelation and subtly shifting the locus of authority from Scripture to cultural or communal context.[33] Grenz's call for an evangelical "dialectical relationship to the wider society"[34] insinuates the need for synthesis: an evangelical thesis welded to the postmodern cultural antithesis. J. Richard Middleton and Brian J. Walsh embrace the postmodern deconstruction of truth[35] and opt for a genuinely subjective hermeneutic, an "internal prophetic critique" of biblical texts they reject as "downright offensive." In order to

---

30 R. Albert Mohler Jr., "'Evangelical': What's in a Name?" in *The Coming Evangelical Crisis: Current Challenges to the Authority of Scripture and the Gospel*, ed. John H. Armstrong (Moody, 1996), 35–6; D. A. Carson, "Is Sacrifice Passé?" *ChrT* 19 (1990): 15.

31 David F. Wells, "Assaulted by Modernity," *ChrT* 34, no. 3 (1990): 16; cf. Bill Hopkinson, "Changes in the Emphasis of Evangelical Belief, 1970–80: Evidence from New Hymnody," *Chm* 95, no. 2 (1981): 123–38.

32 Stanley J. Grenz, *Revisioning Evangelical Theology: A Fresh Agenda for the 21st Century* (InterVarsity Press, 1993), 78.

33 E.g. Stanley J. Grenz, *Theology for the Community of God* (Broadman and Holman, 1994), 21, 25–6; idem, *Revisioning Evangelical Theology*, 56–7, 72–80, 88, 93, 97–101. For Robert Brow, "new-model" evangelicalism deals with the problem of sin "primarily in the community of faith" rather than in the biblical model of Christ's substitutionary atonement ("Evangelical Megashift: Why You May Not Have Heard about Wrath, Sin, and Hell Recently," *ChrT* 34, no. 3 [1990]: 13). Cf. Millard J. Erickson, *The Evangelical Left: Encountering Postconservative Evangelical Theology* (Baker, 1997), 59; idem, *Postmodernizing the Faith: Evangelical Responses to the Challenge of Postmodernism* (Baker, 1998), 100–2; Carson, "Is Sacrifice Passé?" 14–5; R. Albert Mohler Jr., "The Integrity of the Evangelical Tradition and the Challenge of the Postmodern Paradigm," in *The Challenge of Postmodernism*, 2nd ed., ed. David S. Dockery (Baker, 2001), 64–7.

34 Stanley J. Grenz, *Renewing the Center: Evangelical Theology in a Post-Theological Era* (Baker, 2000), 335–6.

35 J. Richard Middleton and Brian J. Walsh, *Truth Is Stranger Than It Used to Be: Biblical Faith in a Postmodern Age* (InterVarsity Press, 1995), 4–5: "Since all worldviews in a postmodern reading are merely human inventions, decisively conditioned by the social context in which they occur, and certainly not given to us by either nature or revelation, any 'truth' we claim for our cherished positions must be kept strictly in quotation marks."

correlate their Christianity with postmodern sensibilities, they "must go not only beyond the biblical text but sometimes even *against* the text."[36]

These latent tendencies within evangelicalism are freely and openly embraced on more radical Christian fronts. The emergent postmodern theological enterprise abandons the doctrines of divine omniscience and omnipotence and "emphatically rejects any return to premodern authoritarianism" that "allows for supernatural, infallible inspiration or revelation."[37] Truth is an automatic casualty:

> If you think that truth has to be consistent, or universally valid, or objectively true or some other nonbiblical definition of true, then you ought to go worship that definition of truth and not bother with trying truthfully to serve the trinity.[38]

The result is a hermeneutical "liberation" that raises "doubts about the capacity to achieve ultimate clarity about the meaning of a text"[39] and supplants any hope of doctrinal truth with theological antinomianism.[40]

Soteriological inclusivists and pluralists entertain the postmodern moral imperative of "tolerance" by embracing all religions as at least cooperatively revelatory and redemptive.[41] The sociological fact of religious pluralism is allowed to completely negate the Christian claim to uniqueness and exclusivity. The church is encouraged to "move away from insistence on the superiority or finality of Christ and Christianity toward a recognition of the

---

36 Ibid., 176, 184.

37 Griffin, "Postmodern Theology and A/theology," 50.

38 William H. Willimon, "Postmodern Preaching: Learning to Love the Thickness of the Text," *Journal for Preachers* 19, no. 3 (Easter 1996): 35; Philip Kenneson, "There is No Such Thing as Objective Truth, and It's a Good Thing Too," in *Christian Apologetics in the Postmodern World*, ed. Timothy R. Phillips and Dennis L. Okholm (InterVarsity Press, 1995), 155–70.

39 George Aichele et al., eds., "Introduction," in *The Postmodern Bible* (Yale University Press, 1995), 2.

40 E.g. George Aichele et al., eds., "Ideological Criticism," in *The Postmodern Bible* (Yale University Press, 1995), 301–7; Robert P. Carroll, "Poststructuralist Approaches," 62. Cf. Robert E. Webber's declaration, "God accepts those who trust him, regardless of the interpretation they give to that trust" ("Out with the Old," *ChrT* 34, no. 3 [1990]: 17).

41 Clark H. Pinnock, "An Inclusivist View," in *More Than One Way? Four Views on Salvation in a Pluralistic World*, ed. Dennis L. Okholm and Timothy R. Phillips (Zondervan, 1995), 95–123; idem, *A Wideness in God's Mercy: The Finality of Jesus Christ in a World of Religions* (Zondervan, 1992), 94; Clark H. Pinnock and Robert C. Brow, *Unbounded Love: A Good News Theology for the 21st Century* (InterVarsity Press, 1994), 22–3, 33–4; John Patrick Brennan, *Christian Mission in a Pluralistic World* (St. Paul Publications, 1990), 10–4. Cf. Ronald H. Nash, "Restrictivism," in *What about Those Who Have Never Heard: Three View on the Destiny of the Unevangelized*, ed. John Sanders (InterVarsity, 1995), 107–39.

independent validity of other ways."[42] Christians must "construct a canopy that will embrace all of our complex life-world ... affirming all of modern life's many enclaves, both religious and secular."[43] Sharp distinctions between religious truth and error are therefore interpreted as barriers to the ultimate religious virtues of pluralism and tolerance.[44] Viewpoints in conflict with the historic gospel are not deemed erroneous because the "issue for God is not the content of theology but the reality of faith."[45] According to Carl Braaten, contradictions of the gospel are merely "realities in quest of the absolute future announced by the gospel." Braaten continues:

> The Christian attitude is neither one of intolerance nor one of laissez faire indifference. It is one of engaged interest in how God providentially has been preparing other religions to encounter the finality of the eschatological kingdom announced by Jesus.[46]

Belief in the relativity of religious conviction,[47] despite efforts to breach the impasse,[48] cripples any attempt to pass moral judgments. If every belief is valid, then no belief, regardless of its (im)moral quality, can be invalidated. The logical implications of such developments readily arm ethical libertines with pseudo-justifications for "integrating" sexual immorality with Christianity and aggressively promoting the results.[49] As one "gay Christian" reveals,

---

42 Paul F. Knitter, "Preface," in *The Myth of Christian Uniqueness: Toward a Pluralistic Theology of Religions*, ed. John Hick and Paul F. Knitter, Faith Meets Faith Series (Orbis, 1987), viii.

43 Christopher B. Kaiser, "Wearing Different Hats: Christian Living in a Fragmented World," in *Confident Witness – Changing World: Rediscovering the Gospel in North America*, ed. Graig Van Gelder (Eerdmans, 1999), 25.

44 Carson, *Gagging God*, 255, 350.

45 Pinnock, *Wideness in God's Mercy*, 105.

46 Carl E. Braaten, "The Problem of the Absoluteness of Christianity," *Int* 40, no. 4 (1986): 353.

47 Gordon D. Kaufmann, "Religious Diversity, Historical Consciousness, and Christian Theology," in *The Myth of Christian Uniqueness: Toward a Pluralistic Theology of Religions*, ed. John Hick and Paul F. Knitter, Faith Meets Faith Series (Orbis, 1987), 13.

48 Cf. Langdon Gilkey who recognizes the need to "assert some sort of ultimate values" only to grasp for a disjointed and incoherent "relative absoluteness" ("Plurality and Its Theological Implications," in *The Myth of Christian Uniqueness: Toward a Pluralistic Theology of Religions*, ed. John Hick and Paul F. Knitter, Faith Meets Faith Series [Orbis, 1987], 45–7).

49 Cf. Eric M. Rodriguez and Suzanne C. Ouellette, "Gay and Lesbian Christians: Homosexual and Religious Identity Integration in the Members and Participants of a Gay-Positive Church," *JSSR* 39, no. 3 (2000): 334–5; Kimberly A. Mahaffy, "Cognitive Dissonance and Its Resolution: A Study of Lesbian Christians," *JSSR* 35, no. 4 (1996): 397, 400–1; Laurel C. Schneider, "Homosexuality, Queer Theory, and Christian Theology," *RelSRev* 26, no. 1 (2000): 6–11; Darlene Fozard Weaver, "Sexuality, Ethics, and Christian Communities," *RelSRev* 26, no. 2 (2000): 166–9; Deirdre Good, "The New Testament and Homosexuality: Are We Getting Anywhere?" *RelSRev* 26, no. 4 (2000): 310.

"The religious right forced me to come up with a way to justify my life [as a gay Christian] in a real way, not a cosmetic way but in a way that's unified, that both go together and equal the whole that is me."[50]

JUDE'S THEOLOGICAL EXCLUSIVISM

Jude's apocalyptic eschatology does not synchronize well with the spirit of pre-modern or postmodern theological pluralism. Jude advances a worldview that is aggressively hostile to doctrinal oscillation, positing a belief system that is not open for negotiation. Jude's goals do not include dialogue or the dissolution of differences within a multi-layered Christianity. Jude seeks to clarify boundaries more precisely, to expose and refute deviation more thoroughly, to encourage conformity more forcefully, and to preserve and control the community more carefully. The assumptions and motifs on display throughout the letter and discussed in detail below are pointedly antithetical to any compromising inclination.

Authority

In order to foster non-exclusive theological diversity, pluralists blunt the force of intrusive authority claims.[51] Acclamations of theological authority agitate against the inclusion and tolerance of forms that do not conform.[52] Religious authority is therefore dismissed as an oppressive ideological weapon brandished by the narrow minded. Rather than accommodate and capitulate, Jude confronts theological pluralism with very specific and inflexible convictions about authority. Jude's worldview is authority dependent, founded on explicit claims to truth and revelation. The very nature of the letter, containing commandments and condemnations in the name of God,[53] assumes an authoritative posture. Jude's message derives from the fundamental assumptions that God has an authoritative and revealed will for humanity, that Jude knows what that will is, and that he has the authority to interpret that will for his audience. These overarching presuppositions dictate the tenor of Jude's entire work, resulting in an outlook that is necessarily particular and

---

50 Rodriguez and Ouellette, "Gay and Lesbian Christians," 341.

51 Ingraffia, *Postmodern Theory and Biblical Theology*, 6.

52 Collins, *Apocalyptic Imagination*, 215.

53 Cf. in particular the authority implied by the "woe-oracle" in v. 11; Wendland, "Comparative Study of 'Rhetorical Criticism,'" 213; Gerstenberger, "The Woe-Oracles of the Prophets," 249–63; Nickelsburg, "The Apocalyptic Message of 1 Enoch 92–105," 317; Robert A. Coughenour, "The Woe-Oracles in Ethiopic Enoch," *JSJ* 9, no. 2 (1978): 194–7.

exclusionary, an outlook that commands the church to actively distinguish between truth and error.

As a brother of the Lord commissioned with apostolic authority (v. 1), Jude guides the church with normative and now canonical exhortations. Jude appeals most explicitly however, not to his own authority, but to the objective authority of the apostolic faith which has been delivered to Christendom once and for all (v. 3). This faith is the divine standard that defines genuine Christianity and separates saint from reprobate. By substantiating his argument for the faith with an exposition of biblical texts,[54] Jude exalts Scripture as the source for theological authority. In the clash of ideas, the teachings of Scripture are the teachings of universal truth. As canonical Scripture of the new covenant, Jude's message is itself a timeless authoritative word for a church assailed by "every wind of doctrine" (Eph 4:14).

Dualism

Theological pluralism dissolves barriers[55] between conflicting doctrines and beliefs with the "facile self-deception of universal relativism."[56] Jude's apocalyptic dualism, however, demands unyielding commitment to antithesis: "Truth is exclusive, specific, and antithetical. For every theological yes, there are a million no's. What is true excludes all that opposes it."[57] Jude's specifically Christian God has established a clear boundary between himself and finite evil (vv. 6, 14–15) and he will not be equated with or assimilated to contradictions of his revealed character (v. 4). God has ordained a universal order that has been violated on physical and metaphysical planes (vv. 6–8). The omnipotent and omniscient Christian God therefore divides the universe between good and evil, the righteous and the wicked, acceptable and unacceptable, the included and excluded (vv. 4–5, 11, 13). Humanity is divided into the objects of his love (vv. 1–2, 24) and the objects of his wrath (vv. 4, 11, 13). The essentials of these dualities, including their exclusionary implications, will only be resolved at the parousia when the Lord returns to permanently destroy every form of opposition that operates from the wrong side of the divide (v. 15).

---

54 Ellis, "Prophecy and Hermeneutic in Jude," 224.

55 Cf. Stanley J. Grenz's critique of "'two-party' taxonomy" within contemporary Protestantism (*Renewing the Center*, 326–31).

56 Ernest Gellner, *Postmodernism, Reason, and Religion* (Routledge, 1992), 95.

57 Groothuis, *Truth Decay*, 75.

Determinism

The pluralist idolization of individual autonomy seeks to champion and preserve inviolate Everyman's power, perspective, and opinion. The ultra-tolerant have no tolerance for Jude's omnipotent God who rules the past, present, and future according to his own will. Jude does not, of course, deny the reality of human responsibility. His polemic is a demand for correct theological and ethical decision making in the face of ideological competition. Nevertheless, Jude does not shrink from asserting God's sovereignty over cosmic and human destiny. Fallen angels are reserved for eternal doom (v. 6), and the future consummation of this age is a fixed event described proleptically (v. 14). God's preservation of a righteous community destined for life (vv. 1, 21, 24) and a wicked contingent destined for judgment (vv. 11, 13, 14–16) signifies his active role in distinguishing clearly between those he will accept and those he will reject. By declaring God's sovereignty, Jude ultimately excludes any in the church who would insist on the preeminence of personal preference. Regardless of individual preference, God defines legitimate belief and practice by the faith he has delivered to the church. By insisting on the sovereignty of the Christian God, Jude alienates every other form of theism. Glory, majesty, dominion, and authority belong to the "only God," the "savior" who accomplishes his perfect will "through Jesus Christ" the "Lord" (v. 25).

Pessimism

Theological pluralism that embraces deviation from "the faith" derives in part from a basic confidence in humanity's innate spiritual competence. The assumption is that individuals have the capacity to judge for themselves, apart from an objective authority source, what is theologically and ethically acceptable. The existence and nature of Jude's document, however, excludes this option with a very direct apocalyptic pessimism. Jude's decision to write is motivated by the presupposition that his readers are at least partially deficient and ill-prepared to face their current circumstances. Though they are called and beloved recipients of divine eschatological promises (vv. 1, 24), eternal life has yet to be revealed in its fullness (v. 21). They are in this sense vulnerable and subject to failure. Otherwise, Jude could have simply aborted his effort, relying instead on his audience's spiritual independence and self-sufficiency. If from the outset Jude assumed his addressees were incorruptible and immune to the wiles of deception, there would have been no need to pen this type of letter. The impending crisis, however, compelled Jude to redirect his epistolary intentions. What might have been a complimentary discourse on their shared experience of God's benevolence (v. 3a) is replaced by penetrating exhortation (vv. 3b, 20–23), scathing condemnation (vv. 4–19), and fiery warning (v. 23). The force of Jude's message necessarily depends on the possibility that his readers could falter. At the most basic conceptual level, Jude's letter therefore impugns human nature and excludes those who trust it.

On a more overt theological level, Jude's pessimism opens an irreparable breach between his worldview and the influx of pluralistic sympathies. Jude could have approached his opponents optimistically, affirming their antinomianism as the product of humanity's inherent virtue, nobility, and creativity. Instead, Jude found in his opponents the fulfillment of a prophetic tradition anticipating a gross outpouring of wickedness at the end of the age (vv. 4, 14–19). According to Jude, they are in fact hopelessly excluded from the kingdom, doomed to face eschatological judgment (vv. 7, 11, 13). These heretics belong to a fatally corrupt age which Jude and the faithful look to abandon for a new age, a new life (v. 21). The flesh, that unregenerate natural state bound to this age, is excoriated as an unredeemable object of hate (v. 23).

Judgment

Jude's exclusivism comes sharply to light through his doctrine of judgment. Rather than affirm the premodern and postmodern exaltation of worldview accommodation and compromise, Jude issues a command for "laying charges and producing a guilty verdict" against those in the church who tamper with the truth.[58] Charges and verdicts depend on a standard that accurately differentiates between guilt and innocence. According to Jude, the received faith functions as that standard and commands the rejection of contrary views (v. 3). There is no provision for flexibility. The unorthodox beliefs and practices exposed by Jude are deadly errors, the grounds for God's supreme displeasure. The faith as interpreted by Jude defines unbelief, transgression of the ordained order, sexual immorality, and rebellion against authority. In response, judgment is the great separation event when those who have combined such errors into apostasy are eternally excluded from the community of grace (vv. 5–7, 11, 13). Theology that does approach the issues with openness and flexibility is completely contradicted by Jude's demand for theological and behavioral modifications under threat of judgment (vv. 3–4, 23). The universal scope of Jude's judgment theme (v. 15) further alienates any pluralistic tendencies that might favor a multiplicity of "true" religious options.

---

58 Webb, "Eschatology," 147.

Paraenesis

The pluralist's commitment to universal freedom and tolerance opposes any tendencies that seek to dictate universal obedience to specific religious forms. By advocating polyvalence and the veracity of all religious experience, pluralists discourage the propagation of theological or moral imperatives: No one has the right to critique the beliefs or behaviors of others. The postmodern contempt for objectivity cannot allow for a transcendent standard that articulates the truth for everyone. In the names of compassion and mutual respect for differences of opinion, the paraenetic voice is silenced. Jude, however, demands wholesale personal change, expressing an extreme intolerance for those perspectives that do not faithfully represent his interpretation of normative Christianity. Antinomianism is not a legitimate option within a sphere of diverse and equally valid theological opinions. Theological and ethical pluralism is a complete rejection of divine authority (v. 4). Jude therefore commands the faithful to guard the truth, repudiating error with militaristic fervor (v. 3). Believer's must reflect on the deposit of faithful teaching and conform their thoughts and actions completely (vv. 5, 17, 20–21). Those who drift into compromise must be confronted and rescued from their deviations, not affirmed for their openness and independence (vv. 22–23).

Redeemer/Jude

Theological pluralists seeking to broaden their religious possibilities inevitably endeavor to circumvent Jesus' unique authority to command universal allegiance. Like Jude's opponents, they deny aspects of orthodox Christology that conflict with their theological or philosophical preferences. The supreme redeemer who judges is reinterpreted as one who merely forgives and licenses (v. 4). The way is then opened for a general theological relativism that can accommodate various errors and distortions of true religion. Jude, however, insists on a theology and Christology that excludes all competing theisms. Jesus Christ is the "only master and Lord" (v. 4). As κύριος ("Lord"), Jesus exercises the "exclusive lordship of the one God"[59] on display throughout the history of redemption and judgment (vv. 5–7).[60] As the unique agent of the one true God (μόνῳ θεῷ, v. 25), Jesus performs a dual function of liberating a people for God and judging those who have opposed God.[61] The redemption

---

59 Bauckham, "Jude's Christology," 307.

60 Cf. 1 Pet 3:22. See also 1 Enoch 69:26–29 where the "son of man" judges imprisoned angels; Osburn, "Discourse Analysis," 295.

61 Martin, *Theology of Jude*, 77.

he provides is particular, predicated on a faith commitment informed by a definitive body of truths (v. 3, 20). The judgment he will execute at his parousia is comprehensive, encompassing "every soul" (πᾶσαν ψυχὴν, v. 15). As Jude's apocalyptic redeemer/judge, Jesus Christ's essence and advent are preeminently exclusionary, driving a wedge between the redeemed and the doomed, cosmic good and evil, and this fallen age and the life to come.

Conclusion

The premodern and postmodern cultural contexts, though profoundly different in most respects, are intriguingly similar at points relevant to theological discourse. In both the NT and postmodern eras, the church confronts a cultural ethos that favors theological tolerance, compromise, and assimilation over doctrinal precision and inflexibility. In the first century and the twenty-first century, the church endures internal pressure to incorporate cultural values that radically augment the content and nature of the "once for all delivered" Christian faith. In the first century, Jude responded to the challenge with an apocalyptic eschatology that can only be described as theologically exclusive. If affirmed and obeyed, his doctrinal stances push the church toward a stricter theological conservatism, a more closed and guarded worldview that expressly contradicts the spirit of the age.

CONCLUSION

AFTER GENERATIONS OF INTERPRETIVE NEGLECT,[1] Jude is being reclaimed from the dungeon of scholarly skepticism that has slavishly denigrated its authenticity, composition, and theological value. Thanks primarily to the work of Richard Bauckham, twenty-first-century exegesis should reaffirm Jude as an eminently valuable witness to first-century, Jewish, Palestinian Christianity penned by Jesus Christ's half-brother. As E. Earle Ellis, J. D. Charles, and others have proven, Jude's depth, complexity, and artistry command the church's respect. Jude is the product, not of spontaneous ecclesiastical anger and ineptitude, but of careful theological reflection compelled by passion for the truth.

Jude's dependence on apocalyptic material follows the pattern typical of Judaism and early Christianity. Jews and Christians were consistently challenged by aggressive ideological trends and belief systems that threatened to rob their faith communities of their uniqueness and theological integrity. In response, Judeo-Christian theologians advanced an apocalyptic eschatology inspired by unapologetic trust in revelation. Revelation defined their worldview and the boundaries of their community. Revelation defined truth and dictated the correct responses to that truth. Their apocalyptic eschatology, borne out of God's self-disclosure, protected the community from ideological dilution by exposing error and excluding nonconformists. From the certainty of theological authority to the expectant hope for a redeemer/judge's advent, each element of apocalyptic exclusivism maintained an irreconcilable division between truth and error and identified men with one or the other.

---

1 Richard Bauckham, "The Letter of Jude: A Survey of Research," in *Jude and the Relatives of Jesus in the Early Church* (T&T Clark, 1990), 135.

From within this socio-religious context, Jude observed a church whose ideological boundaries had been breached by apostates intent on synthesizing Christianity and antinomianism. These heretics were not, however, content with tolerance for their syncretistic theological pluralism. By assuming positions of church leadership, they aimed to normalize error by redefining authentic Christianity according to imported standards. Rather than embrace the clamor for freedom and innovation, Jude sought to further purge and restrict membership by reinforcing the church's apocalyptic eschatology. Jude's collage of motifs boldly condemned his opposition by contrasting their beliefs and behaviors with the objective immutable "faith." According to Jude, revealed truth could never be compromised to accommodate distorting variations. Fidelity to the truth demanded the ostracism of insurgent theological revisionists and their ideas.

The divisiveness inherent to apocalyptic eschatology provokes a predictable contemporary rebuttal. Apocalyptic eschatology includes, according to Carey, a "negative, dark, or problematic side." It's rigid distinction "between good and evil, purity and impurity ... fosters mentalities of exclusivism ... a nation of exclusivity.... Most of the exclusive Christian theological claims to truth, most of the Christian postures that look down on other religions, and most of the claims that Christianity is qualitatively different from all other religious faiths are rooted in this model of dualistic thinking." In Carey's opinion, "That kind of thinking has a hard time with religious and cultural pluralism, and in that regard may be leading us backward rather than forward as we approach the third millennium."[2]

The similarities between first-century and third-millennium postmodern pluralism, however, provide a unique juxtaposition of historical and theological contexts that make Jude's difficult message poignantly relevant. In both eras, tolerance of divergent ideas included a warped intolerance of religious truth claims, and the near deification of relativism stigmatized the confessional community that refused to compromise. In both eras, pluralistic values that conflict with the historic gospel seeped into the church and threatened to destroy its very identity. Jude's ancient defense of orthodoxy pronounces a severe canonical ruling against compromises the church is willing to entertain today. His stark and disturbing rebuke is a necessary canonical challenge to error in every age. Jude's apocalyptic eschatology, his exclusionary response to theological pluralism in his own age, dictates the proper Christian

---

2 John J. Carey, "Apocalypticism as a Bridge Between the Testaments," in *The Old and New Testaments: Their Relationship and the "Intertestamental" Literature*, ed. James H. Charlesworth and Walter P. Weaver (Trinity Press International, 1993), 97–8.

response to theological pluralism in the postmodern age.

When professing Christians exchange the love that "rejoices with the truth" (1 Cor 13:6) for an indiscriminate license that glosses over error, Jude calls the faithful to draw lines, even when drawing lines is rude.[3] The church must advance Jude's apocalyptic eschatology and its interdependent theological exclusivism by refusing to abdicate revelation as the foundation for its worldview. The faith has been delivered by God to the saints, once and for all time, in the Scriptures. Regardless of the cultural climate, Christian theology defers to Scripture as the locus of authority and judges all of life by the light of its testimony. Appeals for less biblicism and more freedom from Scriptural authority are automatically suspect when filtered through Jude's apocalyptic worldview. Believers must "constantly guard against the dilution of biblical truth"[4] and the postmodern (ir)rationality that seeks autonomy at all costs. Fidelity to the biblical worldview demands tenacious submission to the Word, allowing the Word to "provide the framework" out of which Christian thought is developed.[5] On this basis the "well-formed Christian world view" will exclude and reject contradictory structures.[6]

As Scripture, Jude calls the church to guard the antithesis, the duality, that differentiates theological fact from fiction. At the expense of political correctness and sentimentality, Jude's biblical distinctions between the righteous and the wicked, this evil age and the age to come, and beliefs that are right and beliefs that are wrong must be maintained. The truth of Scripture must be allowed to divide the cosmos according to the will of God until he returns to judge humanity (vv. 14–15) and sum up "all things in Christ, things in the heavens and things upon the earth" (Eph 1:10).

Jude's determinism declares the absolute preeminence of the Christian God and only the Christian God. Other competing religious historical systems and notions of god, impersonal fate, or non-specific fortune are categorically rejected. According to Jude, one true God rules the created order, determining the course of history and the destinies of men. He executes his rule according to his own immutable standards apart from the fluctuating whims of human desire or ingenuity. Jude's willingness to publicly expose his opponents and equate them with the objects of God's predetermined

---

3 D. A. Carson, *The Gagging of God: Christianity Confronts Pluralism* (Zondervan, 1996), 347–67.

4 John P. Newport, *Life's Ultimate Questions: A Contemporary Philosophy of Religion* (Scripta, 1989), 12.

5 Ibid., 12.

6 Ronald H. Nash, *Faith and Reason: Searching for a Rational Faith* (Zondervan, 1988), 37, 40–3.

displeasure forces the church to acknowledge the unpleasant possibility of reprobation. The God who determines to include "the beloved," "those kept for Jesus Christ" (v. 1), may also exclude those who exhibit the marks of those "appointed for condemnation long ago" (v. 4).

Jude's apocalyptic pessimism boldly contradicts pluralistic confidence in an inherently virtuous human nature. Rather than affirm human nature and its theological creativity, Jude castigates humanity and its basic depravity. The cosmic realm itself has been tainted by evil (v. 6), and the world is populated by sinners bent on defying their Creator (v. 15). The saints themselves must carefully avoid the sinful flesh's magnetic drag (vv. 5, 20–23). By adopting the biblical standard and censuring humanity by its strictures, Jude's pessimism counters the pluralistic push to validate Everyman and his theologies.

Theological pluralists who defend the validity of polyvalent and incongruous beliefs must habitually resist the doctrine of judgment because it assumes that God will accept some and reject others on the basis of authoritative criteria. Jude's apocalyptic eschatology contends that because his opponents have "chosen to oppose the will of God, and to reject his influence from their hearts, they can have no place in a world in which his will alone is done."[7] As the church strives to reach and disciple the nations, it cannot ignore or circumvent the certainty of judgment, regardless of the negative cultural connotations. The church must declare humanity's accountability to the holy and righteous Judge. As Jude has illustrated, the church must actively judge the beliefs and behaviors of its own in order to ensure the body's purity and vitality.[8]

Postmodern relativism invading the church militates against the paraenetic act. No one, it is assumed, has the authority to prescribe universal theological or ethical standards. According to Jude, however, believers cling to the standards defined by Scripture and call the wayward to repentance and obedience. Error and immorality within the brotherhood must be confronted and purged, and the recalcitrant, if necessary, must be ostracized (vv. 22–23).[9] The faithful church informed by Scripture will boldly command, "Thus says the Lord."

---

7 H. H. Rowley, *The Relevance of Apocalyptic: A Study of Jewish and Christian Apocalypses from Daniel to the Revelation*, rev. ed. (Lutterworth Press, 1963), 191.

8 Cf. Matt 18:15–20; 1 Cor 5:9–13; Gal 1:6–9; 1 Thess 5:21; 1 Tim 1:18–19; 2 Tim 2:24–26; 3:1–9; 4:1–5; Titus 1:10–16; R. Albert Mohler Jr., "Church Discipline: The Missing Mark," in *The Compromised Church: The Present Evangelical Crisis*, ed. John H. Armstrong (Crossway, 1998), 171–87.

9 Cf. Paul's admonition to the Corinthians "not to associate with any so-called brother if he should be an immoral person, or covetous, or an idolater, or a reviler, or a drunkard, or a swindler – not even to eat with such a one" (1 Cor 5:11).

Theological pluralists who defend the legitimacy of various redemptive paths also defend the individual's autonomous right to serve as his own
judge. In direct contrast, Jude's apocalyptic eschatology declares that Jesus
Christ alone is humanity's redeemer and judge (vv. 21, 25). There is no room in
Jude's thinking for compromise or power sharing. At his second advent, Jesus
the Messiah will concretize the singularity and finality of his authority, bringing to an end the possibility of rebellion and assuming the locus of all authority in himself (v. 14–15). In an era deluged by alternatives, Jude would have the
church confess Jesus' unique identity and universal authority. Christ alone
is the Savior, and Christ alone will judge mankind, separating the righteous
and wicked from one another "as the shepherd separates the sheep from the
goats" (Matt 25:32). To Christ alone belongs "glory, majesty, power, and authority before all time, now, and forever, amen" (Jude 25).

BIBLIOGRAPHY

Abraham, W. P. "Epistemology, Religious." Pages 156-61 in *BEMCT,* ed. Alister E. Mc-Grath. Basil Blackwell, 1993.

Abraham, William J. *An Introduction to the Philosophy of Religion.* Prentice-Hall, 1985.

Achtemeier, Paul J., Joel B. Green, and Marianne Meyer Thompson. *Introducing the New Testament: Its Literature and Theology.* Eerdmans, 2001.

Adler, William. "Introduction." Pages 1-31 in *The Jewish Apocalyptic Heritage in Early Christianity,* ed. James C. VanderKam and William Adler. Fortress Press, 1996.

Aharoni, Yohanan. *The Land of the Bible: A Historical Geography.* Westminster Press, 1979.

Aichele, George et al., eds. "Ideological Criticism." In *The Postmodern Bible.* Yale University Press, 1995.

Aichele, George et al., eds. "Introduction." In *The Postmodern Bible.* Yale University Press, 1995.

Aland, Kurt. *The Problem of the New Testament Canon.* A. R. Mowbray, 1962.

Aland, Kurt, Annette Benduhn-Mertz, and Gerd Mink, eds. *Die katholischen Briefe* 2/1. Text und Textwert der griechischen Handschriften des Neuen Testaments 1. Walter de Gruyter, 1987.

_____. *Die katholischen Briefe* 2/2. Text und Textwert der griechischen Handschriften des Neuen Testaments 1. Walter de Gruyter, 1987.

_____. *Die katholischen Briefe* 3. Text und Textwert der griechischen Handschriften des Neuen Testaments 1. Walter de Gruyter, 1987.

_____. *Die katholischen Briefe* 1. Text und Textwert der griechischen Handschriften des Neuen Testaments 1. Walter de Gruyter, 1987.

Albanese, Catherine L. *America: Religions and Religion.* 2nd ed. Wadsworth, 1992.

Albertz, Rainer. *From the Beginnings to the End of the Monarchy.* Vol. 1 of *A History of Israelite Religion in the Old Testament Period.* Translated by John Bowden. OTL. Westminster John Knox Press, 1994.

_____. *From the Exile to the Maccabees.* Vol. 2 of *A History of Israelite Religion in the Old Testament Period.* Translated by John Bowden. OTL. Westminster John Knox Press, 1994.

Albin, C. A. *Judasbrevet: Traditionen Texten Tolkningen.* Natur och Kultur, 1962.

Albright, W. F. *Yahweh and the Gods of Canaan: A Historical Analysis of Two Contrasting Faiths.* The Athlone Press, 1968.

Alexander, Philip S. "The Targumim and Early Exegesis of 'Sons of God' in Genesis 6." *JJS* 23, no. 1 (1972): 60-71.

_____. "Jewish Aramaic Translations of Hebrew Scriptures." Pages 217-53 in *Mikra: Text, Translation, Reading and Interpretation of the Hebrew Bible in Ancient Judaism and Early Christianity,* ed. Martin Jan Mulder. Fortress Press, 1988.

Allen, Joel S. "A New Possibility for the Three-Clause Format of Jude 22-3." *NTS* 44, no. 1 (1998): 133-43.

Allison, Dale C., Jr. "Apocalyptic." Pages 17-20 in *DJG,* ed. Joel B. Green and Scot McKnight. InterVarsity Press, 1992.

_____. "Apocalyptic Ethics and Behavior." Pages 295-311 in *The Oxford Handbook of Apocalyptic Literature,* ed. John J. Collins. Oxford University Press, 2014.

_____. "Eschatology." Pages 206-9 in *DJG,* ed. Joel B. Green and Scot McKnight. InterVarsity Press, 1992.

Altizer, Thomas J. "Modern Thought and Apocalypticism." Pages 325-359 in *Apocalypticism in the Modern Period and the Contemporary Age.* Vol. 3 of *The Encyclopedia of Apocalypticism,* ed. Stephen J. Stein. The Continuum Publishing Company, 1999.

Anderson, Hugh. "A Future for Apocalyptic?" Pages 56-71 in *Biblical Studies: Essays in Honor of William Barclay,* ed. Johnston R. McKay and James F. Miller. Westminster, 1976.

Archer, Gleason L., Jr. *Daniel.* EBC 7. Zondervan, 1985.

Arichea, Daniel C. and Howard A. Hatton. *A Handbook on the Letter from Jude and the Second Letter from Peter.* UBS Handbook Series. United Bible Societies, 1993.

Armstrong, Arthur H. *An Introduction to Ancient Philosophy.* 3rd ed. Methuen, 1957.

Ashley, Timothy R. *The Book of Numbers.* NICOT. Eerdmans, 1993.

Aune, David E. "The Apocalypse of John and the Problem of Genre." Pages 65-96 in *Early Christian Apocalypticism: Genre and Social Setting,* ed. Adela Yarbro Collins. Semeia 36. Scholars Press, 1986.

_____. "Apocalypticism." Pages 25-35 in *DPL,* ed. Gerald F. Hawthorne and Ralph P. Martin. InterVarsity Press, 1993.

_____. *The New Testament in Its Literary Environment.* Westminster Press, 1987.

_____. *Prophecy in Early Christianity and the Ancient Mediterranean World.* Eerdmans, 1983.

_____. *Revelation 1-5.* WBC 52. Word, 1997.

Avi-Yonah, Michael. "The Foundation of Tiberias." *IEJ* 1, no. 3 (1950-1951): 160-69.

Bailey, James L. and Lyle D. Vander Broek. *Literary Forms in the New Testament: A Handbook.* Westminster John Knox Press, 1992.

Baldwin, Joyce G. *Daniel: An Introduction and Commentary.* TOTC. InterVarsity Press, 1978.

Balz, Horst. "προγράφω." *EDNT* 3:154.

Balz, Horst and Gerhard Schneider. "παρεισδύω." *EDNT* 3:37.

Balz, Horst and Gerhard Schneider, eds. *EDNT*. 3 vols. Eerdmans, 1990-1993.

Bandstra, Andrew J. "Onward Christian Soldiers – Praying in Love, with Mercy: Preaching on the Epistle of Jude." *CTJ* 32, no. 1 (1997): 136-39.

Barker, Margaret. "Slippery Words, III. Apocalyptic." *ExpTim* 89, no. 11 (1978): 324-29.

Barna, George. *What Americans Believe: An Annual Survey of Values and Religious Views in the United States.* Regal, 1991.

Barna, George and Mark Hatch. *Boiling Point: Monitoring Cultural Shifts in the 21ˢᵗ Century.* Regal, 2001.

Barns, Thomas. "The Epistle of St Jude: A Study in the Marcosian Heresy." *JTS* 6, no. 23 (1905): 391-411.

Barr, George K. "Literary Dependence in the New Testament Epistles." *IBS* 19 (1997): 148-60.

_____. "Scale and the Pauline Epistles." *IBS* 17 (1995): 22-41.

_____. "Scaleometry and the Dating of the New Testament Epistles." *IBS* 22 (2000): 71-90.

_____. "The Structure of Hebrews and of 1ˢᵗ and 2ⁿᵈ Peter." *IBS* 19 (1997): 17-31.

Barr, James. "Jewish Apocalyptic in Recent Scholarly Study." *BJRL* 58, no. 1 (1975): 9-35.

Barrett, C. K. *A Commentary on the First Epistle to the Corinthians.* HNTC. Harper and Row, 1968.

Barth, Gerhard. "πίστις, εως, ή." *EDNT* 3:91-7.

Bartlet, James Vernon. *The Apostolic Age: Its Life, Doctrine, Worship and Polity.* Charles Scribner's Sons, 1899.

Barton, John. "Historical-critical Approaches." Pages 9-20 in *The Cambridge Companion to Biblical Interpretation,* ed. John Barton. Cambridge University Press, 1998.

_____. *Oracles of God: Perceptions of Ancient Prophecy in Israel after the Exile.* Darton, Longman, and Todd, 1986.

_____. "Prophecy (Postexilic Hebrew)." *ABD* 5:489-95.

Bassler, Jouette M. "Cain and Abel in the Palestinian Targums: A Brief Note on an Old Controversy." *JSJ* 17, no. 1 (1986): 56-64.

Bateman, Herbert W., IV. *Jude*: EEC. Lexham Press, 2015.

Batey, Richard A. *Jesus and the Forgotten City: New Light on Sepphoris and the Urban World of Jesus.* Baker, 1991.

Bauckham, Richard J. "Conclusion." In *Jude and the Relatives of Jesus in the Early Church.* T&T Clark, 1990.

_____. "Introduction." In *Jude and the Relatives of Jesus in the Early Church.* T&T Clark, 1990.

_____. "James, 1 and 2 Peter, Jude." Pages 303-17 in *It is Written: Scripture Citing Scripture,* ed. D. A. Carson and H. G. Williamson. Cambridge University Press, 1988.

_____. *Jude and the Relatives of Jesus in the Early Church.* T&T Clark, 1990.

_____. "Jude and the Testament of Moses." In *Jude and the Relatives of Jesus in the Early Church.* T&T Clark, 1990.

_____. "Jude's Christology." In *Jude and the Relatives of Jesus in the Early Church.* T&T Clark, 1990.

_____. "Jude's Exegesis." In *Jude and the Relatives of Jesus in the Early Church.* T&T Clark, 1990.

_____. "The Letter of Jude: A Survey of Research." In *Jude and the Relatives of Jesus in the Early Church.* T&T Clark, 1990.

_____. "The Letter of Jude: An Account of Research." Pages 3791-826 in *ANRW* 25.5. Part 2, *Principat,* 25.5. Edited by W. Haase. de Gruyter, 1988.

_____. "The Lukan Genealogy of Jesus." In *Jude and the Relatives of Jesus in the Early Church.* T&T Clark, 1990.

_____. *Jude, 2 Peter.* WBC 50. Word Books, 1983.

_____. "2 Peter: An Account of Research." Pages 3713-52 in *ANRW* 25.5. Part 2, *Principat,* 25.5. Edited by W. Haase. de Gruyter, 1988.

_____. "Pseudo-Apostolic Letters." *JBL* 107, no. 3 (1988): 469-94.

_____. "The Relatives of Jesus in the Early Church." In *Jude and the Relatives of Jesus in the Early Church.* T&T Clark, 1990.

_____. "The Rise of Apocalyptic." *Them* 3, no. 2 (1978): 10-23.

Bauer, Walter, William F. Arndt, F. Wilbur Gingrich, and Frederick W. Danker. *Greek-English Lexicon of the New Testament and Other Early Christian Literature.* 3rd ed. Rev. and ed. Frederick W. Danker. University of Chicago Press, 2000.

Baumgarten, Albert I. *The Flourishing of Jewish Sects in the Maccabean Era: An Interpretation.* SJSJ 55. E. J. Brill, 1997.

Beardslee, William A. "New Testament Apocalyptic in Recent Interpretation." *Int* 25, no. 4 (1971): 419-35.

Beasley-Murray, G. R. "Revelation, Book of." Pages 1025-38 in *DLNT,* ed. Ralph P. Martin and Peter H. Davids. InterVarsity Press, 1997.

Bebbington, David W. *Patterns in History: A Christian View.* InterVarsity Press, 1979.

Beker, J. Christian. *Paul's Apocalyptic Gospel: The Coming Triumph of God.* Fortress Press, 1982.

_____. *Paul the Apostle: The Triumph of God in Life and Thought.* Fortress Press, 1980.

_____. *The Triumph of God: The Essence of Paul's Thought.* Fortress Press, 1990.

Berkhof, Hendrikus. *Christian Faith: An Introduction to the Study of the Faith.* Translated by Sierd Woudstra. Eerdmans, 1979.

Benetreau, Samuel. *La deuxième épître de Pierre et l'*épître de Jude. CEB 16. Édifac, 1994.

Berger, Klaus. "Hartherzigkeit und Gottes Gesetz, die Vorgeschichte des antijüdischen Vorwurfs in Mc 10:5." *ZNW* 61, nos. 1/2 (1970): 1-47.

Bertram, Georg. "παίζω, ἐμπαίζω, κτλ." *TDNT* 5:625-36.

_____. "φυλάσσω, φυλακή." *TDNT* 9:236-44.

Best, Ernest. *A Commentary on the First and Second Epistles to the Thessalonians.* Hendrickson, 1986.

Betz, Hans Dieter. *Galatians: A Commentary on Paul's Letter to the Churches in Galatia.* Hermeneia. Fortress Press, 1979.

_____. "On the Problem of the Religio-Historical Understanding of Apocalypticism," Pages 134-56 in *Apocalypticism*, ed. Robert W. Funk. Herder and Herder, 1969.

_____. "The Problem of Apocalyptic Genre in Greek and Hellenistic Literature: The Case of the Oracle of Trophonius." Pages 577-97 in *AMWNE*, ed. David Hellholm. J. C. B Mohr (Paul Siebeck) 1983.

Beyer, Peter. *Religion and Globalization*. Sage, 1994.

Bickerman, Elias. *From Ezra to the Last of the Maccabees: Foundations of Post-biblical Judaism*. Schocken Books, 1972.

Bieder, Werner. "Judas 22f.: Οὓς δὲ ἐᾶτε ἐν φόβῳ." *TZ* 6, no. 1 (1950): 75-7.

Bietenhard, Hans. "Fire: πῦρ." *NIDNTT* 1:653-8.

Bigg, Charles. *A Critical and Exegetical Commentary on the Epistles of St. Peter and St. Jude*. ICC. T&T Clark, 1978.

Birdsall, J. Neville. "The Text of Jude in P⁷²" *JTS* 14, no. 2 (1963): 394-9.

Bitzer, Lloyd F. "The Rhetorical Situation." Pages 247-60 in *Rhetoric: A Tradition in Transition*, ed. Walter R. Fisher. Michigan State University Press, 1974.

Black, Matthew. *The Book of Enoch or 1 Enoch: A New English Edition with Commentary and Notes*. SVTP 7. E. J. Brill, 1985.

_____. "The Christological Use of the Old Testament in the New Testament." *New Testament Studies* 18, no. 1 (1971): 1-14.

_____. "Critical and Exegetical Notes on Three New Testament Texts: Heb. 11:11, Jude 5, James 1:27." Pages 39-45 in *Apophoreta: Festschrift Für Ernst Haenchen*, ed. W. Eltester and F. H. Kettler. Verlag Alfred Töpelmann, 1964.

_____. "The Maranatha Invocation and Jude 14, 15 (1 Enoch 1:9)." Pages 189-96 in *Christ and Spirit in the New Testament*, ed. Barnabas Lindars and Stephen S. Smalley. Cambridge University Press, 1973.

Black, Matthew, ed. *Apocalypsis Henochi Graece*. PVTG. E. J. Brill, 1970.

Blass, F. and A. Debrunner. *A Greek Grammar of the New Testament and other Early Christian Literature*. Translated by Robert W. Funk. University of Chicago Press, 1961.

Bloch, Joshua. *On the Apocalyptic in Judaism*. Jewish Quarterly Review 11. Dropsie College, 1952.

Bloom, Allan David. *The Closing of the American Mind*. Simon and Schuster, 1987.

Blum, Edwin A. *Jude*. EBC 12. Zondervan, 1981.

Boccaccini, Gabriele. *Middle Judaism: Jewish Thought, 300 B.C.E to 200 C.E.* Fortress Press, 1991.

de Boer, Martinus C. *The Defeat of Death: Apocalyptic Eschatology in 1 Corinthians 15 and Romans 5*. JSNTSup 22. JSOT Press, 1988.

_____. "Paul and Jewish Apocalyptic Eschatology." Pages 169-90 in *Apocalyptic and the New Testament*, JSNTSup 24, ed. Joel Marcus and Marion L. Soards. Sheffield Academic Press, 1989.

Boobyer, G. H. "The Verbs in Jude 11." *NTS* 5, no. 1 (1958): 45-7.

Borg, Marcus J. and N. T. Wright. *The Meaning of Jesus: Two Visions*. Harper San Francisco, 1999.

Bornkamm, Günther. *The New Testament: A Guide to Its Writings.* Translated by Reginald H. Fuller and Ilse Fuller. Fortress Press, 1973.

Braaten, Carl E. "The Problem of the Absoluteness of Christianity." *Int* 40, no. 4 (1986): 341-53.

Braaten, Carl E. "The Significance of Apocalypticism for Systematic Theology." *Int* 25, no. 4 (1971): 480-99.

Braumann, Georg. "Present: ἡμέρα." *NIDNTT* 2:886-95.

Brennan, John Patrick. *Christian Mission in a Pluralistic World.* St. Paul Publications, 1990.

Brenton, Lancelot C. L., ed. *The Septuagint Version of the Old Testament and Apocrypha with an English Translation, and with Various Readings and Critical Notes.* Zondervan, 1972.

Bright, John. *A History of Israel,* 4th ed. Westminster John Knox Press, 2000.

Broneer, Oscar. "Paul and the Pagan Cults at Isthmia." *HTR* 64, nos. 2/3 (1971): 169-87.

Brooke, George J. "The Scrolls and the Study of the New Testament." Pages 61-76 in *The Dead Sea Scrolls at Fifty: Proceedings of the 1997 Society of Biblical Literature Qumran Section Meetings,* ed. Robert A. Kugler and Eileen M. Schuller. Scholars Press, 1999.

Brooks, James A. "Clement of Alexandria as a Witness to the Development of the New Testament Canon." *SecCent* 9, no. 1 (1992): 41-55.

Brooks, James A. and Carlton L. Winbery. *Syntax of New Testament Greek.* University Press of America, 1979.

Brow, Robert. "Evangelical Megashift: Why You May Not Have Heard about Wrath, Sin, and Hell Recently." *ChrT* 34, no. 3 (1990): 12-14.

Brown, Colin, ed. *NIDNTT.* 4 vols. Zondervan, 1975-1985.

Brown, Raymond E. *An Introduction to the New Testament.* ABRL. Doubleday, 1997.

Bruce, F. F. *The Canon of Scripture.* InterVarsity Press, 1988.

_____. *1 and 2 Corinthians.* NCBC. Eerdmans, 1971.

_____. *1 and 2 Thessalonians.* WBC 45. Word Books, 1982.

_____. "Jesus is Lord." Pages 23-36 in *Soli Deo Gloria: New Testament Studies in Honor of William Childs Robinson,* ed. J. McDowell Richards. John Knox Press, 1968.

_____. *The New Testament Development of Old Testament Themes.* Eerdmans, 1968.

Büchsel, Friedrich. " ἐλέγχω, κτλ." *TDNT* 2:473-6.

Bultmann, Rudolf. "ἔλεος, κτλ." *TDNT* 2:477-87.

_____. *The History of the Synoptic Tradition.* Translated by John Marsh. Harper and Row, 1963.

_____. "New Testament and Mythology." Pages 1-44 in *Kerygma and Myth: A Theological Debate,* ed. Hans Werner Bartsch. Translated by Reginald H. Fuller. SPCK, 1960.

_____. "πιστεύω, κτλ." *TDNT* 6:174-228.

_____. *Primitive Christianity in Its Contemporary Setting.* Translated by R. H. Fuller. Thames and Hudson, 1956.

_____. *Theology of the New Testament,* vol. 1. Translated by Kendrick Grobel. Charles Scribner's Sons, 1951.

Burkert, Walter. *Ancient Mystery Cults.* Harvard University Press, 1987.

_____. *Greek Religion.* Translated by John Raffan. Harvard University Press, 1985.

Calvin, John. *The Epistles of James and Jude.* Translated by A. W. Morrison. Eerdmans, 1972.

Cantinat, Jean. "The Catholic Epistles." Pages 549-600 in *Introduction to the New Testament,* ed. A. Robert and A. Feuillet. Translated by Patrick W. Skehan et al.. Desclee, 1965.

_____. "L'épître de Jude." Pages 275-86 in *Les épîtres apostoliques.* Introduction critique au Nouveau Testament 3. Desclée, 1977.

_____. *Les épîtres de Saint Jacques et de Saint Jude.* SB. J. Gabalda, 1973.

Carey, John J. "Apocalypticism as a Bridge Between the Testaments." Pages 89-105 in *The Old and New Testaments: Their Relationship and the "Intertestamental" Literature,* ed. James H. Charlesworth and Walter P. Weaver. Trinity Press International, 1993.

Carr, Wesley. *Angels and Principalities: The Background, Meaning, and Development of the Pauline Phrase hai archai kai hai exousiai.* Cambridge University Press, 1981.

Carroll, Robert P. "Poststructuralist Approaches: New Historicism and Postmodernism." Pages 50-66 in *The Cambridge Companion to Biblical Interpretation,* ed. John Barton. Cambridge University Press, 1998.

Carson, D. A. *The Gagging of God: Christianity Confronts Pluralism.* Zondervan, 1996.

_____. "Is Sacrifice Passé?" *ChrT* 34, no. 3 (1990): 14-15.

Castel, Francois. *The History of Israel and Judah in Old Testament Times.* Translated by Matthew J. O'Connell. Paulist Press, 1985.

Charles, J. D. "Jude's Use of Pseudepigraphal Source-Material as Part of a Literary Strategy." *NTS* 37, no. 1 (1991): 130-45.

_____. "Literary Artifice in the Epistle of Jude." *ZNW* 82 (1991): 106-24.

_____. "'Those' and 'These:' The Use of the Old Testament in the Epistle of Jude." *JSNT* 38 (1990): 109-24.

_____. "The Use of Tradition-Material in the Epistle of Jude." *BBR* 4 (1994): 1-14.

Charles, R. H. *The Assumption of Moses.* Adam and Charles Black, 1897.

_____. *Eschatology: The Doctrine of a Future Life in Israel, Judaism and Christianity.* 1899. Repr., Schocken Books, 1963.

Charlesworth, James H. "Ancient Apocalyptic Thought and the New Testament." Pages 222-32 in *Biblical Theology: Problems and Perspectives,* ed. Steven J. Kraftchick, Charles D. Myers Jr., and Ben C. Ollenburger. Abingdon Press, 1995.

_____. "A Critical Comparison of the Dualism in 1QS 3:13-4:26 and the 'Dualism' Contained in the Fourth Gospel." *NTS* 15, no. 4 (1969): 389-418.

_____. *The New Testament Apocrypha and Pseudepigrapha: A Guide to Publications, with Excursuses on Apocalypses.* The Scarecrow Press, 1987.

_____. *The Old Testament Pseudepigrapha and the New Testament: Prolegomena for the Study of Christian Origins.* Cambridge University Press, 1985.

_____. *The Pseudepigrapha and Modern Research, with a Supplement.* Scholars Press, 1981.

Charlesworth, James H., ed. *The Old Testament Pseudepigrapha,* 2 vols. Doubleday, 1983.

Chase, F. H. "Jude, Epistle of." *A Dictionary of the Bible,* ed. James Hastings, 2:799-806. Charles Scribner's Sons, 1900.

Childs, Brevard S. *Memory and Tradition in Israel.* SBT 37. SCM Press, 1962.

Cladder, H. J. "Strophical Structure in St Jude's Epistle." *JTS* 5 (1904): 589-601.

Clark, Andrew C. "Apostleship: Evidence from the New Testament and Early Christian Literature." Pages 49-82 in *Vox Evangelica* 19, ed. Harold H. Rowdon. The London Bible College, 1989.

Clark, Gordon H. *Religion, Reason and Revelation.* 2nd ed. Trinity Foundation, 1986.

Clauss, Manfred. *The Roman Cult of Mithras: The God and His Mysteries.* Translated by Richard Gordon. Routledge, 2001.

Clement. *Le Pédagogue.* Sources Chrétiennes, ed. Claude Mondésert, Chantal Matray, and Henri-Irénéne Marrou, no. 158, Livre 3. Les Éditions du Cerf, 1970.

Clements, Ronald E. *Isaiah 1-39.* NCBC. Eerdmans, 1980.

Coenen, Lothar. "Call: καλέω." *NIDNTT* 1:271-6.

Collins, Adela Yarbro. "Apocalypses and Apocalypticism: Early Christianity." *ABD* 1:288-92.

_____. *Cosmology and Eschatology in Jewish and Christian Apocalypticism.* SJSJ 50. E. J. Brill, 1996.

_____. *Crisis and Catharsis: The Power of the Apocalypse.* Westminster Press, 1984.

_____. "The Early Christian Apocalypses." Pages 61-121 in *Apocalypse: The Morphology of a Genre,* ed. John J. Collins. Semeia 14. Society of Biblical Literature, 1979.

_____. "Introduction: Early Christian Apocalypticism." Pages 1-11 in *Early Christian Apocalypticism: Genre and Social Setting,* ed. Adela Yarbro Collins. Semeia 36. Scholars Press, 1986.

_____. "Vilification and Self-Definition in the Book of Revelation." *HTR* 79, nos. 1-3 (1986): 308-20.

Collins, Adela Yarbro, ed. *Early Christian Apocalypticism: Genre and Social Setting.* Semeia 36. Scholars Press, 1986.

Collins, John J., ed. *Apocalypse: The Morphology of a Genre.* Semeia 14. Society of Biblical Literature, 1979.

_____. "Apocalypses and Apocalypticism: Early Jewish Apocalypticism." *ABD* 1:282-8.

_____. "The Apocalyptic Context of Christian Origins." In *The Bible and Its Traditions,* ed. Michael P. O'Connor and David N. Freedman. *MQR* 22, no. 3 (1983): 250-64.

_____. *The Apocalyptic Imagination: An Introduction to Jewish Apocalyptic Literature.* 2nd ed. Eerdmans, 1998.

_____. "Apocalyptic Literature." Pages 345-70 in *Early Judaism and Its Modern Interpreters,* ed. Robert A. Kraft and George W. E. Nickelsburg. Scholars Press, 1986.

_____. *Between Athens and Jerusalem: Jewish Identity in the Hellenistic Diaspora.* Crossroad, 1982.

_____. "Cult and Culture: The Limits of Hellenization in Judea." Pages 38-61 in *Hellenism in the Land of Israel,* ed. John Collins and Gregory E. Sterling. University of Notre Dame Press, 2001.

_____. *Daniel: A Commentary on the Book of Daniel.* Hermeneia. Fortress Press, 1993.

_____. "Genre, Ideology and Social Movements in Jewish Apocalypticism." Pages 11-32 in *Mysteries and Revelations: Apocalyptic Studies since the Uppsala Colloquium,* ed. John J. Collins and James H. Charlesworth. Sheffield Academic Press, 1991.

_____. "Introduction: Towards the Morphology of a Genre." Pages 1-20 in *Apocalypse: The Morphology of a Genre,* ed. John J. Collins. Semeia 14. Society of Biblical Literature, 1979.

_____. "The Jewish Apocalypses." Pages 21-59 in *Apocalypse: The Morphology of a Genre,* ed. John J. Collins. Semeia 14. Society of Biblical Literature, 1979.

_____. "The Origin of the Qumran Community: A Review of the Evidence." Pages 239-60 in *Seers, Sybils, and Sages in Hellenistic-Roman Judaism.* SJSJ 54. E. J. Brill, 1997.

_____, ed. *The Origins of Apocalypticism in Judaism and Christianity.* The Encyclopedia of Apocalypticism, vol. 1. The Continuum Publishing Company, 1998.

_____. "The Place of Apocalypticism in the Religion of Israel." Pages 539-58 in *Ancient Israelite Religion: Essays in Honor of Frank Moore Cross,* ed. Patrick D. Miller Jr., Paul D. Hanson, and S. Dean McBride. Fortress Press, 1987.

_____. "From Prophecy to Apocalypticism: The Expectation of the End." Pages 129-61 in *The Origins of Apocalypticism in Judaism and Christianity.* Vol. 1 of *The Encyclopedia of Apocalypticism.* The Continuum Publishing Company, 1998.

_____. "Was the Dead Sea Sect an Apocalyptic Movement?" Pages 261-85 in *Seers, Sybils, and Sages in Hellenistic-Roman Judaism.* SJSJ 54. E. J. Brill, 1997.

Conzelmann, Hans. *1 Corinthians: A Commentary on the First Epistle to the Corinthians.* Translated by James W. Leitch. Hermeneia. Fortress Press, 1975.

_____. *Interpreting the New Testament: An Introduction to the Principles and Methods of N. T. Exegesis.* Translated by Siegfried S. Schatzmann. Hendrickson, 1988.

Cothenet, Édouard. "La Tradition selon Jude et 2 Pièrre." *NTS* 35, no 3 (1989): 407-20.

Coughenour, Robert A. "The Woe-Oracles in Ethiopic Enoch." *JSJ* 9, no. 2 (1978): 192-7.

Craigie, Peter C. and Gerald H. Wilson. "Religions of the Biblical World: Canaanite (Syria and Palestine)." *ISBE* 4:95-101.

Cranfield, C. E. B. *A Critical and Exegetical Commentary on the Epistle to the Romans,* vol 1. ICC. T&T Clark, 1987.

Cross, Frank M. *The Ancient Library of Qumran.* 3rd ed. Fortress Press, 1995.

_____. "New Directions in the Study of Apocalyptic." Pages 157-65 in *Apocalypticism,* ed. Robert W. Funk. Herder and Herder, 1969.

Cullmann, Oscar. *The Christology of the New Testament.* Rev. ed. Translated by Shirley C. Guthrie and Charles A. M. Hall. Westminster Press, 1963.

_____. "The Tradition." In *The Early Church: Studies in Early Christian History and Theology,* ed. A. J. B. Higgins. Westminster Press, 1956.

Dahl, Nils A. "The Arrogant Archon and the Lewd Sophia: Jewish Traditions in Gnostic Revolt." Pages 71-94 in *Gnosticism in the Early Church,* ed. David M. Scholer. Studies in Early Christianity 5. Garland, 1993.

_____. *Jesus the Christ: The Historical Origins of Christological Doctrine.* Edited by Donald H. Juel. Fortress Press, 1991.

Dana, H. E. and Julius R. Mantey. *A Manual Grammar of the Greek New Testament.* Macmillan, 1955.

Daniel, Constantin. "La mention des Esséniens dans le texte grec de l'épître de S. Jude." *Mus* 81 (1968): 503-21.

Daniélou, Jean. *The Theology of Jewish Christianity.* Translated and edited by John A. Baker. The Development of Christian Doctrine Before the Council of Nicaea 1. Darton, Longman and Todd, 1964.

Daube, David. "Participle and Imperative in 1 Peter." Appendix to *The First Epistle of St. Peter: The Greek Text with Introduction, Notes, and Essays,* 2nd ed., by Edward G. Selwyn. Baker, 1981.

Dautzenberg, Gerhard. "ἀγών." *EDNT* 1:25-7.

Davids, Peter. *The Epistle of James: A Commentary on the Greek Text.* NIGTC. Eerdmans, 1982.

_____. "The Pseudepigrapha in the Catholic Epistles." Pages 228-45 in *The Pseudepigrapha and Early Biblical Interpretation,* ed. James H. Charlesworth and Craig Evans. JSPSup 14. Sheffield Academic Press, 1993.

Davies, G. I. "Apocalyptic and Historiography." *JSOT* 5 (1978): 15-28.

Davies, Philip R. "The Social World of Apocalyptic Writings." Pages 251-71 in *The World of Ancient Israel: Sociological, Anthropological and Political Perspectives,* ed. R. E. Clements. Cambridge University Press, 1989.

Davies, W. D. *Paul and Rabbinic Judaism: Some Rabbinic Elements in Pauline Theology.* Fortress Press, 1980.

_____. *Torah in the Messianic Age and/or the Age to Come.* Journal of Biblical Literature Monograph Series 7. Society of Biblical Literature, 1952.

Day, John. *Yahweh and the Gods and Goddesses of Canaan.* JSOTSup 265. Sheffield Academic Press, 2000.

Deichgräber, Reinhard. *Gotteshymnus und Christushymnus in der frühen Christenheit: Untersuchungen zu Form, Sprache und Stil der frühchristlichen Hymen.* SUNT 5. Vanderhoeck and Ruprecht, 1967.

Delling, Gerhard. *Bibliographie zur jüdisch-hellenistischen und intertestamentarischen Literatur, 1900-1970.* Akademie-Verlag, 1975.

Derrida, Jacques. *Of Grammatology,* corrected ed. Translated by Gayatri Chakravorty Spivak. John Hopkins University Press, 1997.

Desjardins, Michel. "The Portrayal of the Dissidents in 2 Peter and Jude: Does It Tell Us More about the 'Godly' Than the 'Ungodly?'" *JSNT* 30 (1987): 89-102.

Dibelius, Martin. *James: A Commentary on the Epistle of James.* Revised by Heinrich Greeven. Translated by Michael A. Williams. Hermeneia. Fortress Press, 1976.

Dillon, John. "Platonism, Early and Middle." *Routledge Encyclopedia of Philosophy*, 7:421-29.

Doty, William G. *Letters in Primitive Christianity.* Fortress Press, 1973.

Dunn, James D. G. *The Epistles to the Colossians and to Philemon: A Commentary on the Greek Text.* NIGTC. Eerdmans, 1996.

_____. *Romans 1-8.* WBC 38a. Word Books, 1988.

_____. *Unity and Diversity in the New Testament: An Inquiry into the Character of Earliest Christianity.* 2nd ed. Trinity Press International, 1990.

Dunnett, Walter M. "The Hermeneutics of Jude and 2 Peter: The Use of Ancient Jewish Traditions." *JETS* 31, no. 3 (1988): 287-92.

Eagleton, Terry. "Awakening from Modernity," *TimesLitSupp*, 20 February 1987, 194.

Ebeling, Gerhard. "The Ground of Christian Theology." Pages 47-68 in *Apocalypticism*, ed. Robert W. Funk. Herder and Herder, 1969.

Eckert, Jost. "καλέω, κτλ." *EDNT* 2:240-4.

Ehrman, Bart D. *Jesus: Apocalyptic Prophet of the New Millennium.* Oxford University Press, 1999.

_____. *The New Testament: A Historical Introduction to the Early Christian Writings.* 2nd. ed. Oxford University Press, 2000.

Elliott, Mark Adam. *The Survivors of Israel: A Reconsideration of the Theology of Pre-Christian Judaism.* Eerdmans, 2000.

Ellis, E. Earle. "Biblical Interpretation in the New Testament Church." Pages 77-121 in *The Old Testament in Early Christianity: Canon and Interpretation in the Light of Modern Research.* Baker, 1991.

_____. *Christ and the Future in New Testament History.* NovTSup 97. E. J. Brill, 2000.

_____. "The Circumcision Party and the Early Christian Mission." Pages 116-28 in *Prophecy and Hermeneutic in Early Christianity.* Eerdmans, 1978. Repr., Baker, 1993.

_____. *Eschatology in Luke.* FBBS 30. Fortress Press, 1972.

_____. "How the New Testament Uses the Old." Pages 147-72 in *Prophecy and Hermeneutic in Early Christianity.* Eerdmans, 1978. Repr., Baker, 1993.

_____. *The Making of the New Testament Documents.* BibInt 39. E. J. Brill, 1999.

_____. "New Directions in the History of Early Christianity." Pages 71-92 in *Early Christianity, Late Antiquity and Beyond.* Vol. 2 of *Ancient History in a Modern University,* ed. T. W. Hillard et al. Eerdmans, 1998.

_____. "The Old Testament Canon in the Early Church." Pages 3-50 in *The Old Testament in Early Christianity: Canon and Interpretation in the Light of Modern Research.* Baker, 1991.

_____. *The Old Testament in Early Christianity: Canon and Interpretation in the Light of Modern Research.* Baker, 1991.

_____. "Paul and His Co-Workers." Pages 3-22 in *Prophecy and Hermeneutic in Early Christianity.* Eerdmans, 1978. Repr., Baker, 1993.

_____. "Paul and His Opponents." Pages 80-115 in *Prophecy and Hermeneutic in Early Christianity.* Eerdmans, 1978. Repr., Baker, 1993.

_____. "Present and Future Eschatology in Luke." *NTS* 12 (1965): 27-41.

_____. "Prophecy and Hermeneutic in Jude." Pages 221-36 in *Prophecy and Hermeneutic in Early Christianity*. Eerdmans, 1978. Repr., Baker, 1993.

_____. "The Role of the Christian Prophet in Acts." Pagse 129-44 in *Prophecy and Hermeneutic in Early Christianity*. Eerdmans, 1978. Repr., Baker, 1993.

Elwell, Walter A. and Robert W. Yarbrough. *Encountering the New Testament: A Historical and Theological Survey*. Baker, 1998.

Erickson, Millard J. *The Evangelical Left: Encountering Postconservative Evangelical Theology*. Baker, 1997.

_____. *Postmodernizing the Faith: Evangelical Responses to the Challenge of Postmodernism*. Baker, 1998.

_____. *The Promise and Perils of Postmodernism: Truth or Consequences*. InterVarsity Press, 2001.

_____. *Where is Theology Going? Issues and Perspectives on the Future of Theology*. Baker, 1994.

Eusebius. *The Ecclesiastical History*, vol. 1. Translated by Kirsopp Lake. LCL. William Heinemann, 1926.

_____. *The Ecclesiastical History*, vol 2. Translated by J. E. L. Oulton and H. J. Lawlor. LCL. William Heinemann, 1932.

Fanning, Buist M. *Verbal Aspect in New Testament Greek*. Oxford Theological Monographs. Clarendon Press, 1990.

Farmer, Herbert H. *Revelation and Religion: Studies in the Theological Interpretation of Religious Types*. Texts and Studies in Religion 80. Nisbet, 1954. Repr., Edwin Mellen, 1999.

Farnell, Lewis Richard. *The Cults of the Greek States*, vol. 2. Caratzas Brothers, 1977.

Farrar, Frederic W. *The Early Days of Christianity*, 3rd ed., vol. 1. Cassell, Petter, Galpin, 1882.

Featherstone, Mike. *Undoing Culture: Globalization, Postmodernism and Identity*. Theory, Culture and Society. Sage, 1995.

Fee, Gordon D. *The First Epistle to Corinthians*. NICNT. Eerdmans, 1987.

Ferch, Arthur J. "The Book of Daniel and the 'Maccabean Thesis." *AUSS* 21, no. 2 (1983): 129-41.

Ferguson, Everett. *Backgrounds of Early Christianity*. 2nd ed. Eerdmans, 1993.

Ferguson, John. "Divination and Oracles: Rome." Pages 951-58 in *Civilization of the Ancient Mediterranean: Greece and Rome*, vol 2, ed. Michael Grant and Rachel Kitzinger. Charles Scribner's Sons, 1988.

Feuillet, André. "Le péché évoqué aux chapitres 3 et 6,1-3 de la Genèse. Le péché des anges de l'Epître de Jude et de la seconde Epître de Pierre." *Divinitas* 35 (1991): 207-29.

Fiedler, Peter. "ἀσεβέω." *EDNT* 1:168-9.

Finegan, Jack. *Myth and Mystery: An Introduction to the Pagan Religions of the Biblical World*. Baker, 1989.

Finger, Thomas. "Modernity, Postmodernity – What in the World Are They?" *Transformation* 10, no. 4 (1993): 20-6.

Fiorenza, Elisabeth Schüssler. "The Phenomenon of Early Christian Apocalyptic: Some Reflections on Method." Pages 295-316 in *AMWNE*, ed. David Hellholm. J. C. B Mohr (Paul Siebeck) 1983.

Fitzmyer, Joseph A. "κύριος." *EDNT* 2:328-31.

Foerster, Werner. "εἰρήνη, κτλ." *TDNT* 1:406-20.

Fohrer, Georg. *History of Israelite Religion.* Translated by David. E. Green. Abingdon Press, 1972.

Ford, David F., ed. *The Modern Theologians: An Introduction to Christian Theology in the Twentieth Century.* 2nd ed. Blackwell Publishers, 1997.

Fornberg, Tord. *An Early Church in a Pluralistic Society: A Study of 2 Peter.* Doctoral Dissertation, Uppsala University. Carl Bloms Boktryckeri, 1977.

Fossum, Jarl. "Kyrios Jesus as the Angel of the Lord in Jude 5-7." *NTS* 33, no. 2 (1987): 226-43.

Foucault, Michel. "Truth and Power." Pages 109-33 in *Power/Knowledge: Selected Interviews and Other Writings, 1972-1977,* ed. Colin Gordon. Pantheon Books, 1980.

Frankemölle, Hubert. *1. und 2. Petrusbrief, Judasbrief.* NEchtB 18/20. Echter Verlag, 1987.

Freedman, David Noel, et al., eds. *ABD.* 6 vols. Doubleday, 1992.

Frey, Jörg. "Apocalyptic Dualism." Pages 271-94 in *The Oxford Handbook of Apocalyptic Literature*, ed. John J. Collins. Oxford University Press, 2014.

Freyne, Seán. "The Geography, Politics, and Economics of Galilee and the Quest for the Historical Jesus." Pages 75-121 in *Studying the Historical Jesus: Evaluations of the State of Current Research,* ed. Bruce Chilton and Craig A. Evans. E. J. Brill, 1994.

Frost, Stanley Brice. *Old Testament Apocalyptic: Its Origin and Growth.* Epworth Press, 1952.

Fuchs, Eric and Pierre Reymond. *La Deuxième Épitre de Saint Pierre l'*Épitre de Saint Jude. CNT, 13b. Delachaux and Niestlé, 1980.

Fuller, R. H. *A Critical Introduction to the New Testament.* Duckworth, 1966.

Funk, Robert W., ed. *Apocalypticism.* Herder and Herder, 1969.

Gaede, S. D. *When Tolerance Is No Virtue: Political Correctness, Multiculturalism, and the Future of Truth and Justice.* InterVarsity Press, 1993.

Gallup, George, Jr. and Jim Castelli. *The People's Religion: American Faith in the 90s.* Macmillan, 1989.

Gammie, John G. "The Classification, Stages of Growth, and Changing Intentions in the Book of Daniel." *JBL* 95, no. 2 (1976): 192-204.

Garland, David E. *The Intention of Matthew 23.* NovTSup 52. E. J. Brill, 1979.

Garrett, James Leo. *Systematic Theology: Biblical, Historical, Evangelical,* 2nd ed., vol. 1. Bibal Press, 2000.

Geddert, T. J. "Apocalyptic Teaching." Pages 20-7 in *DJG,* ed. Joel B. Green and Scot McKnight. InterVarsity Press, 1992.

Gellner, Ernest. *Postmodernism, Reason, and Religion.* Routledge, 1992.

Gerhardsson, Birger. *Memory and Manuscript: Oral Tradition and Written Transmis-*

sion in Rabbinic Judaism and Early Christianity. Translated by Eric J. Sharpe. C. W. K. Gleerup, 1961.

Gerstenberger, Erhard. "The Woe-Oracles of the Prophets." *JBL* 81, no. 3 (1962): 249-63.

Gesenius, Wilhelm. *Gesenius' Hebrew Grammar.* Edited by E. Kautzsch. Translated by A. E. Cowley. Clarendon Press, 1910.

Gibson, J. C. L. *Davidson's Introductory Hebrew Grammar: Syntax.* 4th ed. T&T Clark, 1994.

Gilkey, Langdon. "Plurality and Its Theological Implications." Pages 37-50 in *The Myth of Christian Uniqueness: Toward a Pluralistic Theology of Religions,* ed. John Hick and Paul F. Knitter. Faith Meets Faith Series. Orbis, 1987.

Ginzberg, Louis. *Bible Times and Characters from the Exodus to the Death of Moses.* Vol. 3 of *The Legends of the Jews.* Translated by Paul Radin. The Jewish Publication Society of America, 1911.

Glasson, T. Francis. "What is Apocalyptic?" *NTS* 27, no. 1 (1980): 98-105.

Goldingay, John E. *Daniel.* WBC 30. Word, 1987.

Goldstein, Horst. "ἀσέλγεια." *EDNT* 1:169-70.

Good, Deirdre. "The New Testament and Homosexuality: Are We Getting Anywhere?" *RelSRev* 26, no. 4 (2000): 307-12.

Goodenough, Erwin R. *By Light, Light: The Mystic Gospel of Hellenistic Judaism.* Yale University Press, 1935.

_____. *The Archaeological Evidence from Palestine.* Vol. 1 of *Jewish Symbols in the Greco-Roman Period.* Pantheon Books, 1953.

Grabbe, Lester L. "Chronography in Hellenistic Jewish Historiography." Pages 43-68 in *Society of Biblical Literature 1979 Seminar Papers,* vol. 2, ed. Paul J. Achtemeier. Scholars, 1979.

_____. *The Persian and Greek Periods.* Vol. 1 of *Judaism from Cyrus to Hadrian.* Fortress Press, 1992.

_____. *The Roman Period.* Vol. 2 of *Judaism from Cyrus to Hadrian.* Fortress Press, 1992.

Grant, Frederick C. *Hellenistic Religions: The Age of Syncretism.* Liberal Arts Press, 1953.

Gray, John. *The Canaanites.* Ancient Peoples and Places 38. Frederick A. Praeger, 1964.

Gray, Tony. "Beyond Arminius: Pinnock's Doctrine of God and the Evangelical Tradition." Pages 120-46 in *Reconstructing Theology: A Critical Assessment of the Theology of Clark Pinnock,* ed. Tony Gray and Christopher Sinkinson. Paternoster, 2000.

Green, Gene L. *Jude and 2 Peter.* BECNT. Baker Academic, 2008.

Green, Michael. *The Second Epistle General of Peter and the General Epistle of Jude: An Introduction and Commentary.* TNTC. Eerdmans, 1987.

Grenz, Stanley J. *A Primer on Postmodernism.* Eerdmans, 1996.

_____. *Renewing the Center: Evangelical Theology in a Post-Theological Era.* Baker, 2000.

_____. *Revisioning Evangelical Theology: A Fresh Agenda for the 21st Century.* InterVarsity Press, 1993.

_____. *Theology for the Community of God.* Broadman and Holman, 1994.

Grenz, Stanley J. and Roger E. Olson. *Twentieth-Century Theology: God and the World in a Transitional Age.* InterVarsity Press, 1992.

Griffin, David Ray. "Postmodern Theology and A/theology." Pages 29-61 in *Varieties of Postmodern Theology.* State University of New York Press, 1989.

Groothuis, Douglas. *Truth Decay: Defending Christianity Against the Challenge of Postmodernism.* InterVarsity Press, 2000.

Gruen, Erich S. *The Hellenistic World and the Coming of Rome,* vol. 1. University of California Press, 1984.

Grundmann, Walter. *Der Brief des Judas und der zweite Brief des Petrus,* 3. Auflage. THKNT 15. Evangelische Verlagsanstalt, 1986.

Grunewald, Winfried and K. Junack. *Die katholischen Briefe.* Das Neue Testament auf Papyrus 1. Walter de Gruyter, 1986.

Gundry Volf, Judith M. *Paul and Perseverance: Staying in and Falling Away.* WUNT 2/37. J. C. B. Mohr (Paul Siebeck), 1990.

Gunkel, Hermann. *Schöpfung und Chaos in Urzeit und Endzeit: Eine religionsgeschichtliche Untersuchung über Gen 1 und Ap Joh 12.* Vandenhoeck und Ruprecht, 1895.

Gunther, John J. "The Alexandrian Epistle of Jude." *NTS* 30, no 4 (1984): 549-62.

Guthrie, Donald. *New Testament Introduction.* InterVarsity Press, 1970.

Hahn, Ferdinand. "Randbemerkungen zum Judasbrief." *TZ* 37, no. 4 (1981): 209-18.

_____. "Χριστός." *EDNT* 3:478-86.

Hahn, Hans-Christoph. "Time: χρόνος." *NIDNTT* 3:839-45.

Hanegraaff, Wouter J. *New Age Religion and Western Culture: Esotericism in the Mirror of Secular Thought.* Studies in the History of Religions 72. E. J. Brill, 1996.

Hanson, Paul D. "Apocalypse, genre." Pages 27-8 in *IDBSup,* ed. Keith Crim. Abingdon Press, 1984.

_____. "Apocalypses and Apocalypticism: The Genre." *ABD* 1:279-80.

_____. "Apocalypses and Apocalypticism: Introductory Overview." *ABD* 1:280-2.

_____. "Apocalyptic Literature." Pages 465-88 in *The Hebrew Bible and Its Modern Interpreters,* ed. Douglas A. Knight and Gene M. Tucker. Fortress Press, 1985.

_____. "Apocalypticism." Pages 28-34 in *IDBSup,* ed. Keith Crim. Abingdon Press, 1984.

_____. *The Dawn of Apocalyptic: The Historical and Sociological Roots of Jewish Apocalyptic Eschatology.* Rev. ed. Fortress Press, 1979.

_____. "Introduction." Pages 1-15 in *Visionaries and Their Apocalypses.* Fortress Press, 1983.

_____. "Israelite Religion in the Early Postexilic Period." Pages 485-508 in *Ancient Israelite Religion: Essays in Honor of Frank Moore Cross,* ed. Patrick D. Miller Jr., Paul D. Hanson, and S. Dean McBride. Fortress Press, 1987.

_____. *Old Testament Apocalyptic.* Interpreting Biblical Texts, ed. Lloyd R. Bailey Sr. and Victor P. Furnish. Abingdon Press, 1987.

_____. "Old Testament Apocalyptic Reexamined." Pages 37-60 in *Visionaries and Their Apocalypses,* ed. Paul D. Hanson. IRT 4. Fortress Press, 1983.

_____. "Prolegomena to the Study of Jewish Apocalyptic." Pages 387-413 in *Magnalia*

Dei: The Mighty Acts of God, ed. Frank Moore Cross, Werner E. Lemke, and Patrick D. Miller Jr.. Doubleday and Company, 1976.

Harder, Günther. " φθείρω, κτλ." *TDNT* 9:93-106.

Harm, Harry. "Logic Line in Jude: The Search for Syllogisms in a Hortatory Text." *Occasional Papers in Translation and Textlinguistics* 1, nos. 3-4 (1987):147-72.

Harnack, Adolf. *Geschichte der altchristlichen Litteratur bis Eusebius II: Die Chronologie der altchristlichen Litteratur bis Eusebius* 1. J. C. Hinrichs, 1897.

Harrington, Daniel J. "The 'Early Catholic' Writings of the New Testament: The Church Adjusting to World-History." Pages 97-113 in *The Word in the World: Essays in Honor of Frederick L. Moriarty,* ed. Richard J. Clifford and George W. MacRae. Weston College Press, 1973.

Harris, Stephen L. *The New Testament: A Student's Introductio.* 2nd. ed. Mayfield Publishing Company, 1995.

Harrison, R. K. *Introduction to the Old Testament.* Eerdmans, 1969.

Hartman, Lars. *Prophecy Interpreted: The Formation of Some Jewish Apocalyptic Texts and of the Eschatological Discourse Mark 13 Par.* Translated by Neil Tomkinson and Jean Gray. ConBNT 1. Boktryckeri Aktiebolag, 1966.

_____. "Survey of the Problem of Apocalyptic Genre." Pages 329-44 in *AMWNE,* ed. David Hellholm. J. C. B Mohr (Paul Siebeck) 1983.

Hasel, Gerhard F. "The Book of Daniel and Matters of Language: Evidences Relating to Names, Words, and the Aramaic Language," *AUSS* 19, no. 3 (1981): 211-25.

_____. "The Book of Daniel: Evidence Relating to Persons and Chronology." *AUSS* 19, no. 1 (1981): 37-49.

_____. "Resurrection in the Theology of Old Testament Apocalyptic." *ZAW* 92, no. 2 (1980): 267-84.

Haufe, Günter. "δεσπότης." *EDNT* 1:290-1.

Hayes, John H. and Sara R. Mandell. *The Jewish People in Classical Antiquity: From Alexander to Bar Kochba.* Westminster John Knox Press, 1998.

Hays, Richard B. "'The Righteous One' as Eschatological Deliverer: A Case Study in Paul's Apocalyptic Hermeneutics." Pages 191-215 in *Apocalyptic and the New Testament,* ed. Joel Marcus and Marion L. Soards. JSNTSup 24. Sheffield Academic Press, 1989.

Heiligenthal, Roman. "Der Judasbrief: Aspekte der Forschung in den letzten Jahrzehnten." *TRu* 51, no. 2 (1986): 117-29.

_____. "Die Weisheitsschrift aus der Kairoer Geniza und der Judasbrief." *ZRGG* 44, no. 4 (1992): 356-61.

_____. *Zwischen Henoch und Paulus: Studien zum theologiegeschichtlichen Ort des Judasbriefes.* Texte und Arbeiten zum neutestamentlichen Zeitalter 6. Francke Verlag, 1992.

Hellholm, David, ed. *AMWNE.* J. C. B Mohr (Paul Siebeck) 1983.

_____. "The Problem of Apocalyptic Genre and the Apocalypse of John." Pages 13-64 in *Early Christian Apocalypticism: Genre and Social Setting,* ed. Adela Yarbro Collins. Semeia 36. Scholars Press, 1986.

Hengel, Martin. *Acts and the History of Earliest Christianity.* Translated by John Bowden. SCM Press, 1979.

_____. *The Johannine Question.* SCM Press, 1989.

_____. *Judaism and Hellenism.* Translated by John Bowden. Fortress Press, 1974.

Herford, R. Travers. *Talmud and Apocrypha: A Comparative Study of the Jewish Ethical Teaching in the Rabbinical and Non-rabbinical Sources in the Early Centuries.* Soncino Press, 1933.

Herr, Moshe David. "*Aggadah.*" *EncJud* 2:354-56.

Hick, John. "Revelation." Pages 189-91 in *The Encyclopedia of Philosophy,* vol. 7, ed. Paul Edwards. MacMillan and the Free Press, 1967.

Hiebert, D. Edmond. "Selected Studies from Jude, Part 1: An Exposition of Jude 3-4." *BSac* 142, no. 566 (1985): 142-51.

Hilgenfeld, A. *Die jüdische Apokalyptik in ihrer geschichtlichen Entwicklung.* Jena, 1857. Repr., Rodopi, 1966.

Hobbs, Walter C. "Faith Twisted by Culture: Syncretism in North American Christianity." Pages 94-109 in *Confident Witness – Changing World: Rediscovering the Gospel in North America,* ed. Craig Van Gelder. Eerdmans, 1999.

Hopkinson, Bill. "Changes in the Emphasis of Evangelical Belief, 1970-80: Evidence from New Hymnody." *Chm* 95, no. 2 (1981): 123-38.

Horsley, Richard A. *Archaeology, History, and Society in Galilee: The Social Context of Jesus and the Rabbis.* Valley Forge: Trinity Press International, 1996.

Horstmann, Axel. "αἰσχύνομαι." *EDNT* 1:42-3.

Humphries-Brooks, Stephenson. "Apocalyptic Paraenesis in Matthew 6:19-34." Pages 95-112 in *Apocalyptic and the New Testament,* ed. Joel Marcus and Marion L. Soards. JSNTSup 24. Sheffield Academic Press, 1989.

Hunter, James Davison. *Evangelicalism: The Coming Generation.* University of Chicago Press, 1987.

Ingraffia, Brian D. *Postmodern Theory and Biblical Theology: Vanquishing God's Shadow.* Cambridge University Press, 1995.

Jagersma, H. *A History of Israel from Alexander the Great to Bar Kochba.* Fortress Press, 1986.

_____. *A History of Israel in the Old Testament Period.* Translated by John Bowden. Fortress Press, 1983.

James, Montague Rhodes. *The Lost Apocrypha of the Old Testament: Their Titles and Fragments.* MacMillan, 1920.

Jasper, David. "Literary Readings of the Bible." Pages 21-34 in *The Cambridge Companion to Biblical Interpretation,* ed. John Barton. Cambridge University Press, 1998.

Jensen, Robert. *The Triune Identity.* Fortress Press, 1982.

Jeremias, Joachim. *Jerusalem in the Time of Jesus: An Investigation into Economic and Social Conditions during the New Testament Period.* Translated by F. H. Cave and C. H. Cave. Fortress Press, 1969.

Jeremias, Jörg. *Theophanie: Die Geschichte einer alttestamentlichen Gattung.* WMANT 10. Neukirchener Verlag des Erziehungsvereins, 1965.

Jerome. *Lives of Illustrious Men.* In vol. 1 of *NPNF,* Series 2. Edited by Philip Schaff. 1886-1889. 14 vols. Repr., Eerdmans, 1979.

Jewett, Robert. *Paul's Anthropological Terms: A Study of Their Use in Conflict Settings.* AGJU 10. E. J. Brill, 1971.

Jones, Peter R. "1 Corinthians 15:8: Paul the Last Apostle." *TynBul* 36 (1985): 3-34.

Jones, W. T. *The Classical Mind: A History of Western Philosophy.* 2nd ed. Harcourt Brace Jovanovich College Publishers, 1970.

Josephus. Translated by Henry St. J. Thackeray et al. 10 vols. LCL. Harvard University Press, 1926-1965.

Joubert, Stephan J. "Facing the Past: Transtextual Relationships and Historical Understanding in the Letter of Jude." *BZ* 42, no. 1 (1998): 56-70.

_____. "Language, Ideology and the Social Context of the Letter of Jude." *Neot* 24, no. 2 (1990): 335-49.

_____. "Persuasion in the Letter of Jude." *JSNT* 58 (1995): 75-87.

Jülicher, Adolf. *An Introduction to the New Testament.* Translated by Janet Penrose Ward. Smith, Elder, 1904.

Kaiser, Christopher B. "Wearing Different Hats: Christian Living in a Fragmented World." Pages 16-25 in *Confident Witness – Changing World: Rediscovering the Gospel in North America,* ed. Craig Van Gelder. Eerdmans, 1999.

Kallas, James. "The Apocalypse – an Apocalyptic Book?" *JBL* 86, no. 1 (1967): 69-80.

Käsemann, Ernst. "Eine Apologie der urchristlichen Eschatologie." *ZTK* 49 (1952): 272-96.

_____. "The Beginnings of Christian Theology." In *New Testament Questions of Today.* Translated by W. J. Montague. Fortress Press, 1969.

_____. "The New Testament Canon and the Unity of the Church." In *Essays on New Testament Themes.* Translated by W. J. Montague. SCM Press, 1964.

_____. *New Testament Questions of Today.* Translated by W. J. Montague. Fortress Press, 1969.

_____. "Paul and Early Catholicism." In *New Testament Questions of Today.* Translated by W. J. Montague. Fortress Press, 1969.

_____. "On the Subject of Primitive Christian Apocalyptic." In *New Testament Questions of Today.* Translated by W. J. Montague. Fortress Press, 1969.

Kaufmann, Gordon D. "Religious Diversity, Historical Consciousness, and Christian Theology." Pages 3-15 in *The Myth of Christian Uniqueness: Toward a Pluralistic Theology of Religions,* ed. John Hick and Paul F. Knitter. Faith Meets Faith Series. Orbis, 1987.

Keck, Leander E. "Paul and Apocalyptic Theology." *Int* 38, no. 3 (1984): 229-41.

Kelly, J. N. D. *A Commentary on the Epistles of Peter and Jude.* HNTC. Hendrickson, 1969.

Kennedy, George A. *New Testament Interpretation through Rhetorical Criticism.* The University of North Carolina Press, 1984.

Kenneson, Philip. "There is No Such Thing as Objective Truth, and It's a Good Thing Too." Pages 155-70 in *Christian Apologetics in the Postmodern World,* ed. Timothy R. Phillips and Dennis L. Okholm. InterVarsity Press, 1995.

Kistemaker, Simon J. *Exposition of the Epistles of Peter and the Epistle of Jude.* Baker Book House, 1987.

Kittel, Gerhard, and Gerhard Friedrich, eds. *TDNT.* Translated by Geoffrey W. Bromiley. 10 vols. Eerdmans, 1964-1976.

Klauck, Hans-Josef. *The Religious Context of Early Christianity: A Guide to Graeco-Roman Religions.* Translated by Brian McNeil. T&T Clark, 2000.

Klijn, Albertus F. J. "Jude 5 to 7." Pages 237-44 in *The New Testament Age: Essays in Honor of Bo Reicke,* vol. 1, ed. William C. Weinrich. Mercer University Press, 1984.

Knibb, Michael A. "Prophecy and the Emergence of the Jewish Apocalypses." Pages 155-80 in *Israel's Prophetic Tradition: Essays in Honour of Peter R. Ackroyd,* ed. Richard Coggins, Anthony Phillips, and Michael Knibb. Cambridge University Press, 1982.

Knitter, Paul F. "Preface." Pages vii-xii in *The Myth of Christian Uniqueness: Toward a Pluralistic Theology of Religions,* ed. John Hick and Paul F. Knitter. Faith Meets Faith Series, ed. Paul F. Knitter. Orbis, 1987.

Knoch, Otto. *Der Erste und Zweite Petrusbrief, Der Judasbrief.* RNT. Verlag Friedrich Pustet, 1990.

Koch, Klaus. *The Rediscovery of Apocalyptic.* Translated by Margaret Kohl. SBT 2:22. Alec R. Allenson, 1970.

Koester, Helmut. "ΓΝΩΜΑΙ ΔΙΑΦΟΡΟΙ: The Origin and Nature of Diversification in the History of Early Christianity." *HTR* 58, no. 3 (1965): 279-318.

———. *History and Literature of Early Christianity.* Vol. 2 of *Introduction to the New Testament.* Walter de Gruyter, 1982.

———. *History, Culture, and Religion of the Hellenistic Age,* 2nd ed. Vol. 1 of *Introduction to the New Testament.* Walter de Gruyter, 1995.

Kraus, Thomas. "Der Artikel im griechischen: Nutzen einer systematischen Beschäftigung anhand von ausgewählten Syntagmata (Hab 1:12; Jud 17; Joh 6:32." *RB* 107, no. 2 (2000): 260-72.

Kreitzer, Larry J. "Apocalyptic, Apocalypticism." Pages 55-68 in *DLNT,* ed. Ralph P. Martin and Peter H. Davids. InterVarsity Press, 1997.

———. "Eschatology." Pages 253-69 in *DPL,* ed. Gerald F. Hawthorne and Ralph P. Martin. InterVarsity Press, 1993.

———. *Jesus and God in Paul's Eschatology.* JSNTSup 19. JSOT Press, 1987.

Kruger, M. A. "ΤΟΥΤΟΙΣ in Jude 7." *Neot* 27, no. 1 (1993): 119-32.

Kubo, Sakae. "Jude 22-23: Two-division Form or Three?" Pages 239-53 in *New Testament Textual Criticism: Its Significance for Exegesis,* ed. Eldon Jay Epp and Gordon D. Fee. Clarendon Press, 1981.

———. *P⁷² and the Codex Vaticanus.* Studies and Documents 27. University of Utah Press, 1965.

Kümmel, Werner Georg. *Introduction to the New Testament.* Rev. ed. Translated by Howard Clark Kee. Abingdon Press, 1975.

———. *The New Testament: The History of the Investigation of Its Problems.* Translated by S. McLean Gilmour and Howard C. Kee. Abingdon Press, 1972.

_____. *Promise and Fulfillment: The Eschatological Message of Jesus.* Translated by Dorothea M. Barton. SCM Press, 1961.

_____. *The Theology of the New Testament according to Its Major Witnesses: Jesus – Paul – John.* Translated by John E. Steely. Abindgon Press, 1973.

Ladd, George E. "Apocalyptic." Pages 62-4 in *Evangelical Dictionary of Theology,* ed. Walter A. Elwell. Baker, 1984.

_____. *The Presence of the Future: The Eschatology of Biblical Realism.* Eerdmans, 1974.

Lancellotti, Angelo. *Uso delle forme verbali.* Vol. 1 of *Sintassi ebraica nel greco dell'Apocalisse.* Collectio Assisiensis 1. Studio Teologico "Porziuncola," 1964.

Landon, Charles. "The Text of Jude 4." *HvTSt* 49, no. 4 (1993): 823-43.

_____. *A Text-Critical Study of the Epistle of Jude.* JSNTSup 135. Sheffield Academic Press, 1996.

Lang, Friedrich. "πῦρ, κτλ." *TDNT* 6:928-52.

LaSor, William, David Hubbard, and Frederic Bush. *Old Testament Survey: The Message, Form, and Background of the Old Testament.* Eerdmans, 1982.

Laws, Sophie. "Can Apocalyptic Be Relevant?" Pages 89-102 in *What About the New Testament: Essays in Honour of Christopher Evans,* ed. Morna Hooker and Colin Hickling. SCM, 1975.

Leaney, A. R. C. *The Letters of Peter and Jude.* CBC. Cambridge University Press, 1967.

Lebram, Jürgen C. H. "The Piety of the Jewish Apocalyptists." Pages 171-207 in *AMWNE,* ed. David Hellholm. J. C. B Mohr (Paul Siebeck) 1983.

Lee, E. Kenneth. "Words Denoting 'Pattern' in the New Testament." *NTS* 8, no. 2 (1962): 166-73.

Levine, Baruch A. *Numbers 1-20: A New Translation with Introduction and Commentary.* AB 4a. Doubleday, 1993.

Licht, Jacob. "An Analysis of the Treatise of the Two Spirits in DSD." Pages 88-100 in *Aspects of the Dead Sea Scrolls.* ScrHier 4. Magnes Press, 1958.

Lichtenberger, Hermann. "πῦρ." *EDNT* 3:197-200.

Liddell, Henry George, Robert Scott, Henry Stuart Jones. *A Greek-English Lexicon.* 9th ed. with revised supplement. Clarendon, 1996.

Lietzmann, Hans. *An die Korinther, I-II.* Revised by Werner Georg Kümmel. HNT 9. J. C. B. Mohr (Paul Siebeck), 1949.

Link, Hans-Georg. "Guilt: ἐλέγχω." *NIDNTT* 2:140-2.

Loewenstamm, Samuel E. "The Death of Moses." Pages 185-217 in *Studies on the Testament of Abraham,* ed. George W. E. Nickelsburg Jr. Society of Biblical Literature Septuagint and Cognate Studies 6. Scholars Press, 1976.

Loisy, Alfred. *The Origins of the New Testament.* Translated by L. P. Jacks. George Allen and Unwin, 1950.

Long, A. A. "Epicureans and Stoics." Pages 135-53 in *Classical Mediterranean Spirituality: Egyptian, Greek, Roman,* ed. A. H. Armstrong. Crossroad, 1989.

Long, Thomas G. "Preaching Apocalyptic Literature." *RevExp* 90, no. 3 (1993): 371-81.

Louw, Johannes P. and Eugene A. Nida, eds. *Greek-English Lexicon of the New Testament Based on Semantic Domains.* 2nd ed. 2 vols. United Bible Societies, 1989.

Lövestam, Evald. "Eschatologie und Tradition im 2. Petrusbrief." Pages 287-300 in *The New Testament Age: Essays in Honor of Bo Reicke,* vol. 2, ed. William C. Weinrich. Mercer University Press, 1984.

Lücke, Friedrich. *Versuch einer vollständigen Einleitung in die Offenbarung des Johannes oder allgemeine Untersuchungen über die apokalyptische Literatur überhaupt und die Apokalypse des Johannes insbesondere.* Eduard Weber, 1852.

Lunström, Gösta. *The Kingdom of God in the Teaching of Jesus: A History of Interpretation from the Last Decades of the Nineteenth Century to the Present Day.* Translated by Joan Bulman. John Knox Press, 1963.

Luther, Martin. *The Catholic Epistles.* Luther's Works, ed. Jaroslav Pelikan and Walter A. Hansen, vol. 30. Concordia Publishing House, 1967.

Lyotard, Jean-François. *The Postmodern Condition: A Report on Knowledge.* Translated by Geoff Bennington and Brian Massumi. Theory and History of Literature 10. University of Minnesota Press, 1984.

MacDonald, Nathan. "From Augustine to Arminius, and Beyond." Pages 21-48 in *Reconstructing Theology: A Critical Assessment of the Theology of Clark Pinnock,* ed. Tony Gray and Christopher Sinkinson. Paternoster, 2000.

MacMullen, Ramsay. *Paganism in the Roman Empire.* Yale University Press, 1981.

Magaß, Walter. "Semiotik einer Ketzerpolemik am Beispiel von Judas 12f." *LB* 19 (1972): 36-47.

Mahaffy, Kimberly A. "Cognitive Dissonance and Its Resolution: A Study of Lesbian Christians." *JSSR* 35, no. 4 (1996): 392-402.

Maher, Michael. *Targum Pseudo-Jonathan: Genesis, Translated, with Introduction and Notes.* The Aramaic Bible 1b. Liturgical Press, 1992.

Maier, Friedrich. *Der Judasbrief: Seine Echtheit, Abfassungszeit und Leser: Ein Beitrag zur Einleitung in die katholischen Briefe.* BibS(F) 11/1-2. Herdersche Verlagshandlung, 1906.

Malina, Bruce J. and Jerome H. Neyrey, *Calling Jesus Names: The Social Value of Labels in Matthew.* FF. Polebridge Press, 1988.

Marsden, George. *Fundamentalism and American Culture.* Oxford University Press, 1980.

_____, ed. *Evangelicalism and Modern America.* Eerdmans, 1984.

Marshall, I. Howard. "Is Apocalyptic the Mother of Christian Theology?" Pages 33-42 in *Tradition and Interpretation in the New Testament: Essays in Honor of E. Earle Ellis,* ed. Gerald F. Hawthorne and Otto Betz. Eerdmans, 1988.

_____. *Kept by the Power of God: A Study of Perseverance and Falling Away.* Bethany Fellowship, 1969.

_____. "Pauline Theology in the Thessalonian Correspondence." Pages 173-83 in *Paul and Paulinism: Essays in Honour of C. K. Barrett,* ed. M. D. Hooker and S. G. Wilson. SPCK, 1982.

_____. "Slippery Words, I. Eschatology." *ExpTim* 89, no. 9 (1978): 264-9.

Martin, Luther H. *Hellenistic Religions: An Introduction.* Oxford University Press, 1987.

Martin, Ralph P. *The Acts, the Letters, The Apocalypse.* Vol. 2 of *New Testament Foundations: A Guide for Christian Students.* Rev. ed. Eerdmans, 1986.

_____. *The Theology of the Letters of James, Peter, and Jude.* Cambridge University Press, 1994.

Martínez, Florentino García. *The Dead Sea Scrolls Translated: The Qumran Texts in English.* Translated by Wilfred G. E. Watson. E. J. Brill, 1994.

_____. *Qumran and Apocalyptic: Studies on the Aramaic Texts from Qumran.* STDJ 9. E. J. Brill, 1992.

Martyn, J. Louis. "Apocalyptic Antinomies in Paul's Letter to the Galatians." *NTS* 31, no. 3 (1985): 410-24.

Mayer, Reinhold. "Scripture, Writing: γραφή." *NIDNTT* 3:482-97.

Mayor, Joseph B. *The Epistle of St. Jude and the Second Epistle of St. Peter.* Macmillan, 1907.

McDonald, James I. H. *Kerygma and Didache: The Articulation and Structure of the Earliest Christian Message.* SNTSMS 37. Cambridge University Press, 1980.

McKay, K. L. "Time and Aspect in New Testament Greek," *NovT* 34, no. 3 (1992): 209-28.

McDonald, Lee Martin and Stanley E. Porter. *Early Christianity and Its Sacred Literature.* Hendrickson, 2000.

McGrath, Alister. *Historical Theology: An Introduction to the History of Christian Thought.* Blackwell Publishers, 1998.

_____. *Evangelicalism and the Future of Christianity.* InterVarsity Press, 1995.

_____. *A Passion for Truth: The Intellectual Coherence of Evangelicalism.* InterVarsity Press, 1996.

_____. *Understanding Doctrine: What It Is, and Why It Matters.* Zondervan, 1990.

Meeker, Kevin and Philip L. Quinn. "Introduction: The Philosophical Challenge of Religious Diversity." Pages 1-28 in *The Philosophical Challenge of Religious Diversity,* ed. Philip L. Quinn and Kevin Meeker. Oxford University Press, 2000.

Meeks, Wayne A. *The First Urban Christians: The Social World of the Apostle Paul.* Yale University Press, 1983.

_____. "Social Functions of Apocalyptic Language in Pauline Christianity." Pages 687-705 in *AMWNE,* ed. David Hellholm. J. C. B Mohr (Paul Siebeck) 1983.

Mees, M. "Papyrus Bodmer VII (P⁷²) und die Zitate aus dem Judasbrief bei Clemens von Alexandrien." *La Ciudad de Dios* 181 (1968): 551-9.

Merlan, P. "Greek Philosophy from Plato to Plotinus." Pages 14-132 in *The Cambridge History of Later Greek and Early Medieval Philosophy,* ed. A. H. Armstrong. Cambridge University Press, 1970.

Metzger, Bruce M. *The Canon of the New Testament: Its Origin, Development, and Significance.* Clarendon Press, 1987.

_____. *A Textual Commentary on the Greek New Testament.* 3rd ed. United Bible Societies, 1971.

Meyers, Carol and Eric M. Meyers. "Sepphoris." *OEANE* 4:527-36.

Meyers, Eric M. "Galilean Regionalism as a Factor in Historical Reconstruction." *BASOR* 221 (1976): 93-101.

_____, ed. *OEANE*. 5 vols. Oxford University Press, 1997.

Meyers, Eric M. and James F. Strange. *Archaeology, the Rabbis, and Early Christianity.* Abingdon Press, 1981.

Michel, Otto. *Der Brief an die Römer.* KEK. Vandenhoeck and Ruprecht, 1978.

_____. "Faith: πίστις." *NIDNTT* 1:593-606.

Mickelsen, A. Berkeley. *Interpreting the Bible.* Eerdmans, 1963.

Middleton, J. Richard and Brian J. Walsh. *Truth Is Stranger Than It Used to Be: Biblical Faith in a Postmodern Age.* InterVarsity Press, 1995.

Milgrom, Jacob. *Numbers.* The JPS Torah Commentary. The Jewish Publication Society, 1990.

Milik, J. T. *The Books of Enoch: Aramaic Fragments of Qumrân Cave 4.* Clarendon Press, 1976.

_____. *Ten Years of Discovery in the Wilderness of Judaea.* Translated by J. Strugnell. SCM Press, 1959.

Miller, M. P. "Targum, Midrash and the Use of the Old Testament in the New Testament." *JSJ* 2 (1970): 29-82.

Miller, Timothy, ed. *America's Alternative Religions.* SUNY Series in Religious Studies. State University of New York Press, 1995.

Mitchell, C. Ben. "Is That All There Is? Moral Ambiguity in a Postmodern Pluralistic Culture." Pages 144-57 in *The Challenge of Postmodernism,* 2nd ed., ed. David S. Dockery. Baker, 2001.

Moffatt, James. *An Introduction to the Literature of the New Testament.* 2nd rev. ed. International Theological Library. T&T Clark, 1912.

Mohler, R. Albert, Jr. "Church Discipline: The Missing Mark." Pages 171-87 in *The Compromised Church: The Present Evangelical Crisis,* ed. John H. Armstrong. Crossway, 1998.

_____. "'Evangelical': What's in a Name?" Pages 29-44 in *The Coming Evangelical Crisis: Current Challenges to the Authority of Scripture and the Gospel,* ed. John H. Armstrong. Moody, 1996.

_____. "The Integrity of the Evangelical Tradition and the Challenge of the Postmodern Paradigm." Pages 53-74 in *The Challenge of Postmodernism,* 2nd ed., ed. David S. Dockery. Baker, 2001.

Moltmann, Jürgen. *Theology of Hope: On the Ground and Implications of a Christian Eschatology.* Translated by James W. Leitch. Fortress Press, 1993.

Moo, Douglas J. *2 Peter and Jude: From Biblical Text to Contemporary Life.* The NIV Application Commentary. Zondervan, 1996.

Moore, George Foot. *Judaism in the First Centuries of the Christian Era: The Age of the Tannaim,* vol. 1. Harvard University Press, 1927.

Moore, Stephen D. *Poststructuralism and the New Testament: Derrida and Foucault at the Foot of the Cross.* Fortress Press, 1994.

Morris, Leon. *Apocalyptic.* Eerdmans, 1972.

_____. "Faith." Pages 285-91 in *DPL,* ed. Gerald F. Hawthorne and Ralph P. Martin. InterVarsity Press, 1993.

Motyer, J. Alec. *The Prophecy of Isaiah: An Introduction and Commentary.* InterVarsity Press, 1993.

Moule, C. F. D. *The Birth of the New Testament.* HNTC. Harper and Row, 1962.

_____. *An Idiom Book of New Testament Greek.* 2nd ed. Cambridge University Press, 1968.

_____. "A Reconsideration of the Context of *Maranatha.*" *NTS* 8, no. 4 (1960): 307-10.

Moulton, James Hope. *Prolegomena.* Vol 1. of *A Grammar of New Testament Greek.* T&T Clark, 1906.

Moulton, James Hope and Nigel Turner. *Syntax.* Vol. 3 of *A Grammar of New Testament Greek.* T&T Clark, 1963.

_____. *Style.* Vol. 4 of *A Grammar of New Testament Greek.* T&T Clark, 1976.

Mowinckel, S. *He that Cometh.* Translated by G. W. Anderson. Abingdon Press, 1954.

Müller, Peter. "Der Judasbrief." *TRu* 63, no. 3 (1998): 267-89.

Müller, Ulrich B. *Zur frühchristlichen Theologiegeschichte.* Gütersloher Verlagshaus Mohn, 1976.

Mullins, Terence Y. "Petition as a Literary Form." *NovT* 5, no. 1 (1962): 46-54.

Murdock, William R. "History and Revelation in Jewish Apocalypticism." *Int* 21, no. 2 (1967): 167-87.

Murphy, Frederick J. "Apocalypses and Apocalypticism: The State of the Question." *CurBS* 2 (1994): 147-179.

_____. *The Religious World of Jesus: An Introduction to Second Temple Judaism.* Abingdon Press, 1991.

Murphy-O'Connor, Jerome. "The Corinth that Saint Paul Saw." *BA* 47, no. 3 (1984): 147-59.

Mußner, Franz. *Der Jakobsbrief.* HThKNT 13/1. Herder, 1975.

Myers, Charles D., Jr. "The Persistence of Apocalyptic Thought in New Testament Theology." Pages 209-21 in *Biblical Theology: Problems and Perspectives,* ed. Steven J. Kraftchick, Charles D. Myers Jr., and Ben. C. Ollenburger. Abingdon Press, 1995.

Nash, Ronald H. *Faith and Reason: Searching for a Rational Faith.* Zondervan, 1988.

_____. *The Meaning of History.* Broadman and Holman, 1998.

_____. "Restrictivism." Pages 107-39 in *What about Those Who Have Never Heard: Three View on the Destiny of the Unevangelized,* ed. John Sanders. InterVarsity, 1995.

Neill, Stephen. *The Interpretation of the New Testament: 1861-1961.* Oxford University Press, 1964.

Nemet-Nejat, Karen Rhea. *Daily Life in Ancient Mesopotamia.* Greenwood Press, 1998.

Neusner, Jacob. *Judaism in the Beginning of Christianity.* Fortress Press, 1984.

_____. *The Mishnah: A New Translation.* Yale University Press, 1988.

_____, ed. *World Religions in America: An Introduction.* Rev. ed. Westminster John Knox, 2000.

Newbigin, Lesslie. *The Gospel in a Pluralistic Society.* Eerdmans, 1989.

Newport, John P. *Life's Ultimate Questions: A Contemporary Philosophy of Religion.* Scripta, 1989.

Neyrey, Jerome H. *2 Peter, Jude: A New Translation with Introduction and Commentary.* AB 37c. Doubleday, 1993.

Nicholson, E. W. "Apocalyptic." Pages 189-213 in *Tradition and Interpretation: Essays by Members of the Society for Old Testament Study,* ed. G. W. Anderson. Clarendon Press,1979.

Nickelsburg, George W. E. "The Apocalyptic Message of 1 Enoch 92-105," *CBQ* 39, no. 3 (1977): 309-28.

_____. *1 Enoch 1: A Commentary on the Book of 1 Enoch, Chapters 1-36; 81-108.* Hermeneia. Fortress Press, 2001.

_____. "Social Aspects of Palestinian Jewish Apocalypticism." Pages 641-54 in *AMWNE,* ed. David Hellholm. J. C. B Mohr (Paul Siebeck) 1983.

Noll, Stephen. *The Intertestamental Period: A Study Guide.* InterVarsity Press, 1985.

North, Robert. "Prophecy to Apocalyptic via Zechariah." Pages 47-71 in *VTSup* 22, ed. G. W. Anderson et al.. E. J. Brill, 1972.

Noth, Martin. *Numbers: A Commentary.* Translated by James D. Martin. OTL. Westminster, 1968.

Oden, Thomas C. *After Modernity ... What? Agenda for Theology.* Zondervan, 1990.

_____. *Agenda for Theology.* Harper and Row, 1979.

_____. "The Death of Modernity and Postmodern Evangelical Spirituality." Pages 19-33 in *The Challenge of Postmodernism,* 2nd ed., ed. David S. Dockery. Baker, 2001.

_____. *Requiem: A Lament in Three Movements.* Abingdon Press, 1995.

_____. *Two Worlds: Notes on the Death of Modernity in America and Russia.* InterVarsity Press, 1992.

Oesterley, W. O. E. *The Jews and Judaism during the Greek Period: The Background of Christianity.* Macmillan, 1941.

Olyan, Saul M. *Asherah and the Cult of Yahweh in Israel.* SBLMS 34. Scholars Press, 1988.

Oppenheim, A. Leo. *Ancient Mesopotamia: Portrait of a Dead Civilization.* University of Chicago Press, 1964.

Osborne, Grant R. *The Hermeneutical Spiral: A Comprehensive Introduction to Biblical Interpretation.* InterVarsity Press, 1991.

Osburn, Carroll D. "The Christological Use of 1 Enoch 1:9 in Jude 14, 15." *NTS* 23, no. 3 (1977): 334-41.

_____. "Discourse Analysis and Jewish Apocalyptic in the Epistle of Jude." Pages 287-319 in *Linguistics and New Testament Interpretation: Essays on Discourse Analysis,* ed. David Alan Black. Broadman Press, 1992.

_____. "1 Enoch 80:2-8 (67:5-7) and Jude 12-13." *CBQ* 47, no. 2 (1985): 296-303.

_____. "The Text of Jude 5." *Bib* 62, no. 1 (1981): 107-15.

_____. "The Text of Jude 22-23." *ZNW* 63 (1972): 139-44.

Oswalt, John N. "Recent Studies in Old Testament Eschatology and Apocalyptic." *JETS* 24, no. 4 (1981): 289-301.

Paulsen, Henning. "Judasbrief." Page 307-10 in *TRE* 17, ed. Horst Robert Balz et al. Walter de Gruyter, 1988.

_____. *Der Zweite Petrusbrief und der Judasbrief.* KEK 12/1. Vandenhoeck and Ruprecht, 1992.

Pausanias. *Description of Greece.* Translated by W. H. S. Jones. 5 vols. LCL. Harvard University Press, 1918-1935.

Pearson, Birger A. "James, 1-2 Peter, Jude." Pages 371-406 in *The New Testament and Its Modern Interpreters,* ed. Eldon Jay Epp and George W. MacRae. Fortress Press, 1989.

Perkins, Pheme. *First and Second Peter, James, and Jude.* IBC. John Knox Press, 1995.

Perrin, Norman and Dennis C. Duling. *The New Testament - An Introduction: Proclamation and Paraenesis, Myth and History.* 2nd ed. Harcourt Brace Jovanovich, 1982.

Pfitzner, Victor C. *Paul and the Agon Motif: Traditional Athletic Imagery in the Pauline Literature.* NovTSup 16. E. J. Brill, 1967.

Pfleiderer, Otto. *Primitive Christianity: Its Writings and Teachings in Their Historical Connections,* vol. 4. Translated by W. Montgomery. G. P. Putman, 1911.

Phillips, Gary. "Religious Pluralism in a Postmodern World." Pages 131-43 in *The Challenge of Postmodernism,* 2nd ed., ed. David S. Dockery. Baker, 2001.

Phillips, Timothy R. and Dennis L. Okholm. "The Nature of Confession: Evangelicals and Postliberals." Pages 7-20 in *The Nature of Confession: Evangelicals and Postliberals in Conversation.* InterVarsity Press, 1996.

Pinnock, Clark H. "The Arminian Option." *ChrT* 34, no. 3 (1990): 15.

_____. "An Inclusivist View." Pages 95-123 in *More Than One Way? Four Views on Salvation in a Pluralistic World,* ed. Dennis L. Okholm and Timothy R. Phillips. Zondervan, 1995.

_____. "Systematic Theology." Pages 101-25 in *The Openness of God: A Biblical Challenge to the Traditional Understanding of God,* ed. Clark Pinnock et al. InterVarsity Press, 1994.

_____. *A Wideness in God's Mercy: The Finality of Jesus Christ in a World of Religions.* Zondervan, 1992.

Pinnock, Clark H. and Robert C. Brow. *Unbounded Love: A Good News Theology for the 21st Century.* InterVarsity Press, 1994.

Plöger, Otto. *Theocracy and Eschatology.* Translated by S. Rudman. John Knox Press, 1968.

Pollard, John. "Divination and Oracles: Greece." Pages 941-50 in *Civilization of the Ancient Mediterranean: Greece and Rome,* vol. 4, ed. Michael Grant and Rachel Kitzinger. Charles Scribner's Sons, 1988.

Popovic, Mladen. "Apocalyptic Determinism." Pages 255-70 in *The Oxford Handbook of Apocalyptic Literature,* ed. John J. Collins. Oxford University Press, 2014.

Porsch, Felix. "ἔλεγχος." EDNT 1:427-8.

Porter, Stanley E. *Idioms of the Greek New Testament.* Sheffield Academic Press, 1992.

_____. "Jesus and the Use of Greek in Galilee." Pages 123-54 in *Studying the Historical Jesus: Evaluations of the State of Current Research,* ed. Bruce Chilton and Craig A. Evans. E. J. Brill, 1994.

_____. *Verbal Aspect in the Greek of the New Testament, with Reference to Tense and Mood.* Studies in Biblical Greek 1. Peter Lang, 1989.

Porton, Gary G. "Diversity in Postbiblical Judaism." Pages 57-80 in *Early Judaism and Its Modern Interpreters,* ed. Robert A. Kraft and George W. E. Nickelsburg. Scholars Press, 1986.

Postgate, J. N. *Early Mesopotamia: Society and Economy at the Dawn of History.* Routledge, 1994.

Pregeant, Russell. *Engaging the New Testament: An Interdisciplinary Introduction.* Fortress Press, 1995.

Reed, Jeffrey T. and Ruth A. Reese. "Verbal Aspect, Discourse Prominence, and the Letter of Jude." *FilNeot* 9, no. 18 (1996): 181-99.

Reicke, Bo. *The Epistles of James, Peter, and Jude.* AB 37. Doubleday and Company, 1964.

Renan, Ernest. *Saint Paul.* Translated by Ingersoll Lockwood. Michel Levy Freres, 1869.

Rengstorf, Karl Heinrich. "δεσπότης, κτλ." *TDNT* 2:44-49.

_____. "δοῦλος, κτλ." *TDNT* 2:261-80.

Ridderbos, Jan. *The Bible Student's Commentary: Isaiah.* Translated by John Vriend. Zondervan, 1985.

Riehl, Carolyn. "Pulpit Fiction: Lives and Perspectives of Gay and Lesbian Persons Serving in the ELCA's Ordained Ministry." *CurTM* 27, no. 1 (2000): 14-29.

Riesenfeld, Harald. "τηρέω, κτλ." *TDNT* 8:140-51.

Ringgren, Helmer. *The Faith of Qumran: Theology of the Dead Sea Scrolls.* Translated by Emilie T. Sander. Fortress Press, 1963.

Robertson, A. T. *A Grammar of the Greek New Testament in the Light of Historical Research.* Broadman Press, 1934.

Robertson, Archibald and Alfred Plummer. *A Critical and Exegetical Commentary on the First Epistle of St. Paul to the Corinthians.* ICC. T&T Clark, 1914.

Robinson, William Childs. "Apostle." *ISBE* 4:192-5.

Rodriguez, Eric M. and Suzanne C. Ouellette. "Gay and Lesbian Christians: Homosexual and Religious Identity Integration in the Members and Participants of a Gay-Positive Church." *JSSR* 39, no. 3 (2000): 333-47.

Rollins, Wayne G. "The New Testament and Apocalyptic." *NTS* 17, no. 4 (1971): 454-76.

Ross, J. M. "Church Discipline in Jude 22-23." *ExpTim* 100, no. 8 (1989): 297-8.

Rowland, Christopher. "Apocalyptic, God, and the World." Pages 238-49 in *Early Christian Thought in Its Jewish Context,* ed. John Barclay and John Sweet. Cambridge University Press, 1996.

_____. "Apocalyptic Literature." Pages 170-89 in *It is Written: Scripture Citing Scripture,* ed. D. A. Carson and H. G. Williamson. Cambridge University Press, 1988.

_____. *The Open Heaven: A Study of Apocalyptic in Judaism and Early Christianity.* Crossroad, 1982.

Rowley, H. H. *The Relevance of Apocalyptic: A Study of Jewish and Christian Apocalypses from Daniel to the Revelation.* Rev. ed. Lutterworth Press, 1963.

Rowston, Douglas J. "The Most Neglected Book in the New Testament." *NTS* 21, no. 4 (1975): 554-63.

_____. "The Setting of the Letter of Jude." Th.D. diss., Southern Baptist Theological Seminary, 1971.

Rudolph, Kurt. *Gnosis: The Nature and History of Gnosticism.* Translated and edited by Robert McLachlan Wilson. Harper and Row, 1983.

Russell, D. S. *Apocalyptic: Ancient and Modern.* Fortress Press, 1978.

_____. "Apokalyptik - Prophetie - Pseudonymität." Pages 311-26 in *Apokalyptik,* ed. Klaus Koch and Hohann Michael Schmidt. Wissenschaftliche Buchgesellschaft, 1982.

_____. *Divine Disclosure: An Introduction to Jewish Apocalyptic.* Fortress Press, 1992.

_____. *The Method and Message of Jewish Apocalyptic: 200 BC - AD 100.* OTL. Westminster Press, 1964.

_____. *Prophecy and the Apocalyptic Dream: Protest and Promise.* Hendrickson, 1994.

Saggs, H. W. F. *The Greatness That Was Babylon: A Survey of the Ancient Civilization of the Tigris-Euphrates Valley.* Sidgwick and Jackson, 1988.

Saldarini, Anthony J. *Pharisees, Scribes and Sadducees in Palestinian Society: A Sociological Approach.* Eerdmans, 1988.

Sanders, E. P. "The Genre of Palestinian Jewish Apocalypses." Pages 447-59 in *AMWNE,* ed. David Hellholm. J. C. B Mohr (Paul Siebeck) 1983.

Sass, Gerhard. "Zur Bedeutung von δοῦλος bei Paulus." *ZNW* 40 (1941): 25-32.

Schelkle, Karl Hermann. "Der Judasbrief bei den Kirchenvätern." Pages 405-16 in *Abraham unser Vater: Juden und Christen im Gespräch über die Bibel: Festschrift für Otto Michel,* ed. Otto Betz, Martin Hengel, and Peter Schmidt. E. J. Brill, 1963.

_____. *Die Petrusbriefe - Der Judasbrief.* HThKNT 13/2. Herder, 1964.

_____. "Spätapostolische Briefe als frühkatholisches Zeugnis." Pages 225-32 in *Neutestamentliche Aufsätze: Festschrift für Professor Josef Schmid,* ed. J. Blinzler, O. Kuss, and F. Mußner. Verlag Friedrich Pustet, 1963.

Schiffman, Lawrence H., ed. *Texts and Traditions: A Source Reader for the Study of Second Temple and Rabbinic Judaism.* KTAV Publishing House, 1998.

Schlatter, Adolf. *The Church in the New Testament Period.* Translated by Paul P. Levertoff. SPCK, 1955.

Schmidt, K. L. "καλέω, κτλ." *TDNT* 3:487-536.

Schmidt, Werner H. *The Faith of the Old Testament: A History.* Translated by John Sturdy. Westminster Press, 1983.

Schmithals, Walter. *The Apocalyptic Movement: Introduction and Interpretation.* Translated by John E. Steely. Abingdon Press, 1975.

_____. *Gnosticism in Corinth: An Investigation of the Letters to the Corinthians.* Translated by John E. Steely. Abingdon Press, 1971.

_____. *The Office of Apostle in the Early Church.* Translated by John E. Steely. Abingdon Press, 1969.

Schneider, Laurel C. "Homosexuality, Queer Theory, and Christian Theology." *RelSRev* 26, no. 1 (2000): 3-12.

Schnelle, Udo. *The History and Theology of the New Testament Writings.* Translated by M. Eugene Boring. Fortress Press, 1998.

Schnider, Franz. "προφητεύω, κτλ." *EDNT* 3:183-6.

Schrage, Wolfgang. *Der Judas Brief.* NTD 10, *Die "Katholischen" Briefe: Die Briefe des Jakobus, Petrus, Johannes und Judas.* Vandenhoeck and Ruprecht, 1980.

Schreiner, Thomas R. *1, 2 Peter, Jude.* NAC 37. B&H Publishing Group, 2003.

_____. *Romans.* BECNT 6. Baker, 1998.

Schrenk, Gottlob. "γράφω, κτλ." *TDNT* 1:742-73.

Schubert, Kurt. *The Dead Sea Community: Its Origins and Teachings.* Translated by John W. Doberstein. Adam and Charles Black, 1959.

Schunck, K. D. "Strukturlinien in der Entwicklung der Vorstellung vom 'Tag Jahwes.'" *VT* 14, no. 3 (1964): 319-30.

Schürer, Emil. *The History of the Jewish People in the Age of Jesus Christ (175 B.C. – A.D. 135)*, vol. 2. T&T Clark, 1979.

Schweitzer, Albert. *They Mystery of the Kingdom of God: The Secret of Jesus' Messiahship and Passion.* Translated by Walter Lowrie. A. and C. Black, 1925.

Schweizer, Eduard. *Church Order in the New Testament.* Translated by Frank Clarke. SBT. SCM, 1961.

Sedley, David. "Stoicism." *Routledge Encyclopedia of Philosophy* 9:141-61.

_____. *1. und 2. Petrusbrief, Judasbrief,* 2 Auflage. SKKNT 16. Verlag Katholisches Bibelwerk, 1986.

Seethaler, Paula-Angelika. "Kleine Bemerkungen zum Judasbrief." *BZ* 31, no. 2 (1987): 261-4.

Segal, Alan F. *Rebecca's Children: Judaism and Christianity in the Roman World.* Harvard University Press, 1986.

Sellin, Gerhard. "Die Häretiker des Judasbriefes." *ZNW* 77 (1986): 206-25.

Selwyn, Edward G. *The First Epistle of St. Peter: The Greek Text with Introduction, Notes and Essays.* 2nd ed. Baker, 1981.

Seow, C. L. *A Grammar for Biblical Hebrew.* Abingdon Press, 1987.

Shatz, David. "Prophecy." *Routledge Encyclopedia of Philosophy* 7:767-71.

Shea, William H. "Daniel 3: Extra-Biblical Texts and the Convocation on the Plain of Dura." *AUSS* 20, no. 1 (1982): 29-52.

_____. "Darius the Mede: An Update," *AUSS* 20, no. 3 (1982): 229-47.

Sidebottom, E. M. *James, Jude and 2 Peter.* The Century Bible: New Edition. Thomas Nelson and Sons, 1967.

Silberman, Neil Asher. "Searching for Jesus: The Politics of First-Century Judea." *Arch* 47, no. 6 (1994): 30-40.

Sim, David C. *Apocalyptic Eschatology in the Gospel of Matthew.* Cambridge University Press, 1996.

Simon, Marcel. *Jewish Sects at the Time of Jesus.* Translated by James H. Farley. Fortress Press, 1967.

Smith, Dennis Edwin. "The Egyptian Cults at Corinth." *HTR* 70, no. 3-4 (1977): 201-31.

Smith, Morton. "On the history of ΑΠΟΚΑΛΥΠΤΩ and ΑΠΟΚΑΛΥΨΙΣ." Pages 9-20 in *AMWNE,* ed. David Hellholm. J. C. B Mohr (Paul Siebeck) 1983.

Soards, Marion L. "1 Peter, 2 Peter, and Jude as Evidence for a Petrine School." Pages 3827-49 in *ANRW* 25.5. Part 2, *Principat,* 25.5. Edited by W. Haase. de Gruyter, 1988.

Spicq, Ceslas. "εἰρηνεύω, κτλ.." *TLNT* 1:434. Peabody, MA: Hendrickson, 1994.

_____. "μακάριος, οὐαί." *TLNT* 2:443-44. Peabody, MA: Hendrickson, 1994.

_____. *TLNT.* Translated and edited by James D. Ernest. 3 vols. Peabody, MA: Hendrickson, 1994.

Spitta, Friedrich. *Der zweite Brief des Petrus und der Brief des Judas.* Verlag der Buchhandlung des Waisenhauses, 1885.

Stauffer, Ethelbert. " ἀγών, κτλ." *TDNT* 1:134-40.

Stead, Christopher. "Gnosticism." *Routledge Encyclopedia of Philosophy* 4:83-5.

Stevens, Gerald L. *New Testament Greek.* University Press of America, 1994.

Stewart, James S. *A Faith to Proclaim.* Hodder and Stoughton, 1953.

Stone, Michael E. "Apocalyptic Literature." Pages 383-441 in *Jewish Writings of the Second Temple Period: Apocrypha, Pseudepigrapha, Qumran Sectarian Writings, Philo, Josephus,* ed. Michael E. Stone. Fortress Press, 1984.

_____. "Lists of Revealed Things in the Apocalyptic Literature." Pages 414-52 in *Magnalia Dei, the Mighty Acts of God: Essays on the Bible and Archaeology in Memory of G. Ernest Wright,* ed. Frank Moore Cross, Werner E. Lemke, and Patrick D. Miller Jr. Doubleday, 1976.

Strange, James F. "Nazareth." *OEANE* 4:113-4.

Strecker, Georg. *Literaturgeschichte des Neuen Testaments.* Vandenhoeck und Ruprecht, 1992.

Sturm, Richard E. "Defining the Word 'Apocalyptic:' A Problem in Biblical Criticism." Pages 17-48 in *Apocalyptic and the New Testament,* ed. Joel Marcus and Marion L. Soards. JSNTSup 24. Sheffield Academic Press, 1989.

Sweet, Leonard I. "The Modernization of Protestant Religion in America." Pages 19-41 in *Altered Landscapes: Christianity in America, 1935-1985,* ed. David W. Lotz. Eerdmans, 1989.

Swinburne, Richard. "Revelation." *Routledge Encyclopedia of Philosophy* 8:297-300.

Taylor, Mark C. *Deconstructing Theology.* SR 28. Crossroad, 1982.

Taylor, Vincent. "The Message of the Epistles: Second Peter and Jude." *ExpTim* 45, no. 10 (1934): 437-41.

Tcherikover, Victor. *Hellenistic Civilization and the Jews.* Translated by S. Applebaum. The Jewish Publication Society of America, 1959.

Testuz, Michel. *Papyrus Bodmer VII-IX.* Bibliothèque Bodmer, 1959.

Theissen, Gerd. *Sociology of Early Palestinian Christianity.* Translated by John Bowden. Fortress Press, 1978.

Thiselton, Anthony C. "Biblical Studies and Theoretical Hermeneutics." Pages 95-113 in *The Cambridge Companion to Biblical Interpretation,* ed. John Barton. Cambridge University Press, 1998.

_____. *The First Epistle to the Corinthians: A Commentary on the Greek Text.* NIGTC. Eerdmans, 2000.

Thompson, Leonard. "A Sociological Analysis of Tribulation in the Apocalypse of John." Pages 147-74 in *Early Christian Apocalypticism: Genre and Social Setting,* ed. Adela Yarbro Collins. Semeia 36. Scholars Press, 1986.

Thurén, Lauri. "Hey Jude! Asking for the Original Situation and Message of a Catholic Epistle." *NTS* 43, no. 3 (1997): 451-65.

Tigchelaar, Eibert J. C. *Prophets of Old and the Day of the End: Zechariah, the Book of Watchers and Apocalyptic.* E. J. Brill, 1996.

Trilling, Wolfgang. "ἡμέρα." *EDNT* 2:119-21.

Ulansey, David. *The Origins of the Mithraic Mysteries: Cosmology and Salvation in the Ancient World.* Oxford University Press, 1989.

van Unnik, W. C. "Jesus the Christ." *NTS* 8, no. 2 (1962): 101-16.

Van Voorst, Robert E. "The Relevance of Apocalyptic for Theology and Ministry." *RefR* 47, no. 3 (1994): 188-96.

VanderKam, James. "The Theophany of *Enoch* 1:3b-7, 9." *VT* 23, no. 2 (1973): 129-50.

VanderKam, James C. and William Adler, eds. *The Jewish Apocalyptic Heritage in Early Christianity.* Fortress Press, 1996.

Vermes, Geza. "The Story of Balaam – The Scriptural Origin of Haggadah." Pages 127-77 in *Scripture and Tradition in Judaism: Haggadic Studies,* ed. P. A. H. de Boer. Studia Post-Biblica 4. E. J. Brill, 1961.

_____. "The Targumic Versions of Genesis 4:3-16." Pages 92-126 in *Post Biblical Studies,* ed. Jacob Neusner. Studies in Judaism in Late Antiquity 8. E. J. Brill, 1975.

Vielhauer, Philipp. *Geschichte der urchristlichen Literatur: Einleitung in das Neue Testament, die Apokryphen und die Apostolischen Väter.* Walter de Gruyter, 1975.

_____. "Introduction." Pages 581-607 in *New Testament Apocrypha,* vol. 2, ed. R. McL. Wilson. Westminster Press, 1964.

Vögtle, Anton. *Der Judasbrief/Der 2. Petrusbrief.* EKKNT 22. Benziger Verlag, 1994.

Volz, Paul. *Die Eschatologie der jüdischen Gemeinde im neutestamentlichen Zeitalter: Nach den Quellen der rabbinischen, apokalyptischen und apokryphen Literatur.* Georg Olms Verlagsbuchhandlung, 1966.

Wallace, Daniel B. *Greek Grammar Beyond the Basics: An Exegetical Syntax of the New Testament.* Zondervan, 1996.

Wanamaker, Charles A. *The Epistles to the Thessalonians: A Commentary on the Greek Text.* NIGTC. Eerdmans, 1990.

Wand, J. W. C. *The General Epistles of St. Peter and St. Jude.* WC. Methuen, 1934.

Ward, Keith. "Truth and the Diversity of Religions." Pages 109-25 in *The Philosophical Challenge of Religious Diversity,* ed. Philip L. Quinn and Kevin Meeker. Oxford University Press, 2000.

Watson, Duane F. *Invention, Arrangement, and Style: Rhetorical Criticism of Jude and 2 Peter.* Scholars Press, 1988.

_____. *The Letter of Jude.* NIB 12. Abingdon Press, 1998.

Weaver, Darlene Fozard. "Sexuality, Ethics, and Christian Communities." *RelSRev* 26, no. 2 (2000): 165-70.

Webb, Robert L. "'Apocalyptic:' Observations on a Slippery Term." *JNES* 49, no. 2 (1990): 115-26.

_____. "The Eschatology of the Epistle of Jude and Its Rhetorical and Social Functions." *BBR* 6 (1996): 139-51.

_____. "Jude." Pages 611-21 in *DLNT,* ed. Ralph P. Martin and Peter H. Davids. InterVarsity Press, 1997.

Webber, Robert E. "Out with the Old." *ChrT* 34, no. 3 (1990): 16-7.

Webster, John B. "Revelation, Concept of." Pages 557-61 in *The Blackwell Encyclopedia of Modern Christian Thought,* ed. Alister E. McGrath. Basil Blackwell, 1993.

Weiss, Bernhard. *A Manual of Introduction to the New Testament,* vol. 2. Translated by A. J. K. Davidson. Funk and Wagnalls, 1889.

Weiss, Johannes. *Jesus' Proclamation of the Kingdom of God.* Translated by Richard Hyde Hiers and David Larrimore Holland. Fortress Press, 1971.

Welles, C. Bradford. *Alexander and the Hellenistic World.* Toronto: A. M. Hakkert, 1970.

Wellhausen, Julius. *Prolegomena to the History of Ancient Israel.* 1878. Repr., Meridian Books, 1957.

Wells, David. "Assaulted by Modernity." *ChrT* 34, no. 3 (1990): 16.

_____. "Introduction: The Word in the World." Pages 19-34 in *The Compromised Church: The Present Evangelical Crisis,* ed. John H. Armstrong. Crossway, 1998.

_____. *No Place for Truth, or, Whatever Happened to Evangelical Theology?* Eerdmans, 1993.

Wendland, E. R. "A Comparative Study of 'Rhetorical Criticism,' Ancient and Modern - with Special Reference to the Larger Structure and Function of the Epistle of Jude." *Neot* 28, no. 1 (1994): 193-228.

Wenham, Gordon J. *Genesis 1-15.* WBC 1. Word Books, 1987.

Werner, Martin. *The Formation of Christian Dogma: An Historical Study of Its Problem.* Translated by S. G. F. Brandon. Adam and Charles Black, 1957.

Whallon, William. "Should We Keep, Omit, or Alter the οἱ in Jude 12?" *NTS* 34, no. 1 (1988): 156-9.

White, John Lee. *The Form and Function of the Body of the Greek Letter: A Study of the Letter-Body in the Non-Literary Papyri and in Paul the Apostle.* 2nd ed. SBLDS 2. Scholars Press, 1972.

Wikgren, Allen. "Some Problems in Jude 5." Pages 147-52 in *Studies in the History and Text of the New Testament in Honor of Kenneth Willis Clark,* ed. Boyd L. Daniels and M. Jack Suggs. University of Utah Press, 1967.

Wilder, Amos N. *Eschatology and Ethics in the Teaching of Jesus.* Rev. ed. Harper and Brothers, 1950.

Wilken, Robert L. "Religious Pluralism and Early Christian Theology," *Int* 40, no. 4 (1986): 379-91.

Wilkens, Ulrich. "The Understanding of Revelation Within the History of Primitive Christianity." Pages 55-121 in *Revelation as History,* ed. Wolfhart Pannenberg. Translated by David Granskou. Macmillan, 1968.

Williams, Charles K., II. "The City of Corinth and Its Domestic Religion." *Hesperia* 50, no. 4 (1981): 408-21.

_____. "Corinth and the Cult of Aphrodite." Pages 12-24 in *Corinthiaca,* ed. Mario A. Del Chiaro. University of Missouri Press, 1986.

Willimon, William H. "Postmodern Preaching: Learning to Love the Thickness of the Text." *Journal for Preachers* 19, no. 3 (Easter 1996): 32-7.

Wilson, Robert Dick. *Studies in the Book of Daniel: A Discussion of the Historical Questions.* G. P. Putnam's Sons, 1917.

Windisch, Hans. *Die Katholischen Briefe.* HNT 15. J. C. B. Mohr (Paul Siebeck), 1951.

Winter, S. C. "Jude 22-23: A Note on the Text and Translation." *HTR* 87, no. 2 (1994): 215-22.

Wiseman, D. J. et al., eds. *Notes on Some Problems in the Book of Daniel.* Tyndale Press, 1965.

Wisse, Frederick. "The Epistle of Jude in the History of Heresiology." Pages 133-43 in *Essays on the Nag Hammadi Texts in Honour of Alexander Böhlig,* ed. Martin Krause. NHS 3. E. J. Brill, 1972.

Wohlenberg, D. G. *Der erste und zweite Petrusbrief und der Judasbrief.* KNT 15. A. Deichert'sche, 1915.

Wolff, Christian. *Der erste Brief des Paulus an die Korinther.* THKNT 7/2. Evangelische Verlangsanstalt, 1982.

Wolthuis, Thomas. "Jude and Jewish Traditions." *CTJ* 22, no. 1 (1987): 21-41.

_____. "Jude and the Rhetorician: A Dialogue on the Rhetorical Nature of the Epistle of Jude." *CTJ* 24, no. 1 (1989): 126-34.

Wright, N. T. *The Climax of the Covenant: Christ and the Law in Pauline Theology.* Fortress Press, 1991.

_____. "Jesus." Pages 43-58 in *Early Christian Thought in Its Jewish Context,* ed. John Barclay and John Sweet. Cambridge University Press, 1996.

_____. *Jesus and the Victory of God.* Vol. 2 of *Christian Origins and the Question of God.* Fortress Press, 1996.

_____. *The New Testament and the People of God.* Vol. 1 of *Christian Origins and the Question of God.* Fortress Press, 1992.

Yamauchi, Edwin M. *Pre-Christian Gnosticism: A Survey of Proposed Evidences.* Eerdmans, 1973.

Young, Edward J. *The Prophecy of Daniel: A Commentary.* Eerdmans, 1964.

Young, Richard A. *Intermediate New Testament Greek: A Linguistic and Exegetical Approach.* Broadman and Holman, 1994.

Zahn, Theodor. *Introduction to the New Testament,* vol 2. Translated by John Moore Trout et al., 1909. Repr., Klock and Klock, 1977.

Zerwick, Maximilian. *Biblical Greek: Illustrated by Examples.* Translated by Joseph Smith. Scripta Pontificii Instituti Biblici, 1963.

Zoepfl, Friedrich, ed. *Didymi Alexandrini in Epistolas Canonicas Brevis Enarratio.* NTAbh 4/1. Aschendorffsche Verlagsbuchhandlung, 1914.

Zuurdeeg, Willem F. *An Analytical Philosophy of Religion.* Abingdon, 1958.

INDEX

www.ingramcontent.com/pod-product-compliance
Lightning Source LLC
Chambersburg PA
CBHW060228030426
42335CB00014B/1370